PENGUIN CLASSICS

MEISTER ECKHART: SELECTED WRITINGS

JOHANNES ECKHART, more commonly known as Meister Eckhart, was born near Gotha in eastern Germany in around 1260. He had an illustrious career in the Dominican Order, holding senior ecclesiastical and teaching posts all over Europe including Saxony, Bohemia, Paris, Strasburg and Cologne. Eckhart is one of the great speculative mystics of Western Europe, who sought to reconcile traditional Christian belief with the transcendental metaphysics of Neoplatonism. Although accused of heretical teaching during his own lifetime, Eckhart is widely regarded today not only as fundamentally orthodox but also as a foremost exponent of Christian mysticism and Christian philosophical theology. He died in the winter of 1327/8 in Avignon.

OLIVER DAVIES studied modern languages at Oxford where he completed his doctorate on modern German literature. Since then he has researched and published mainly in the area of theology, specializing in medieval mysticism and Celtic Christianity. He lectured for a number of years at the University of Cologne, and is now senior lecturer in theology at the University of Wales, Lampeter.

Meister Eckhart

SELECTED WRITINGS

Selected and Translated by OLIVER DAVIES

PENGUIN BOOKS

PENGUIN BOOKS

Published by the Penguin Group
Penguin Books Ltd, 27 Wrights Lane, London w8 5tz, England
Penguin Putnam Inc., 375 Hudson Street, New York, New York 10014, USA
Penguin Books Australia Ltd, Ringwood, Victoria, Australia
Penguin Books Canada Ltd, 10 Alcorn Avenue, Toronto, Ontario, Canada m4v 3b2
Penguin Books (NZ) Ltd, 182–190 Wairau Road, Auckland 10, New Zealand

Penguin Books Ltd, Registered Offices: Harmondsworth, Middlesex, England

This translation first published 1994
5 7 9 10 8 6 4

Filmset in 10.5/13.5 pt Monotype Janson
Typeset by Datix International Limited, Bungay, Suffolk
Printed in England by Clays Ltd, St Ives plc

For Cyprian Smith, osb

CONTENTS

ACKNOWLEDGEMENTS

My personal thanks are due to the many scholars who in conversation and the printed word have contributed to my understanding of Meister Eckhart, as they are also to the many members of the Eckhart Society, living and dead, who have, on more than one occasion, given me the opportunity to expound these ideas at their annual conference.

MEISTER ECKHART: AN INTRODUCTION
TO HIS LIFE AND THOUGHT

Meister Eckhart fascinates us today, as he did many of his contemporaries, and yet there are few medieval thinkers whose thought is so complex and challenging – and so easily misunderstood. There is in Eckhart's system a complexity first of all of depth in that he explores many of the great technical themes of medieval theology, such as theory of analogy, metaphysics of the image, constitution of the human soul, epistemology (theory of knowledge) and ontology (theory of being). But there is in Eckhart's work no less a complexity of surface which results from his brilliant use of imagery and virtuosic ability to manipulate the forms and structures of language in order to communicate a metaphysical vision. It is primarily in these rhetorical skills that we see Eckhart's great originality and we experience the metaphysical passion which makes Meister Eckhart stand out as one of the most exciting and radical thinkers of his own, or indeed of any age.

MEISTER ECKHART: THE DOMINICAN

Life

Eckhart was born in around 1260 and joined the Dominican priory in nearby Erfurt probably at fifteen years of age.[1] In joining the Friars Preacher, he was following a well-trodden path which would guarantee him an education commensurate with his ability: the opportunity to study, to teach and to travel. Eckhart appears to have followed the Dominican route typical of the best students of his time. He may have undertaken his early studies of the Arts (grammar, logic and rhetoric) either in his native Germany or possibly in Paris, which was the principal centre of medieval academic excellence, but he was certainly in Paris, as a Reader of the Sentences, in 1294. As the title suggests, he was engaged at this time in studying Peter Lombard's *Sentences*, which was the main textbook of the Middle Ages that formed the basis of intermediate theological studies. He left Paris soon after to serve as Prior of the Dominican house in Erfurt, where he wrote his early *Talks of Instruction* and, perhaps, a number of early sermons (including Sermons 1 and 2 of the present selection).[2] The *Talks of Instruction*, which are included here, are an important testimony to the relative maturity of Eckhart even at this stage. It is indeed striking how little change there is in the principal structures of his thought between this exciting early work and the later, more sophisticated, sermons of his maturity. In 1302 Eckhart left Erfurt to return to Paris, this time in order to take up the Dominican chair in theology, and it is possible that during this period he wrote some of the extensive scriptural commentaries (composed exclusively in Latin) that survive from his hand.

Eckhart's success as an academic theologian was matched by his popularity as an administrator. In 1303 he was named the first Provincial of the new Dominican province of Saxonia, a post which he seems to have held with great ability and energy. In 1311, despite an attempt to lure him to the province of Teutonia, Eckhart was sent back to Paris to the same Dominican chair he had occupied a decade previously. Thus, in addition to receiving high administrative honours, Eckhart twice held a chair in theology at the University of Paris, an achievement which he has in common only with the greatest of Dominican theologians, Thomas Aquinas.

Eckhart's next move was to Strasburg, in the year 1313, where he served as Vicar-General with oversight of the many women's convents in south-west Germany. This move was out of the ordinary in that a Parisian professor would generally return to his native province. Eckhart's arrival in Strasburg was probably the result of decrees formulated at the Council of Vienne (1311–12) which had accused a number of religious women known as Beguines of holding heretical views. The many Beguine communities of continental Europe had for some time represented a challenge to the Bishops in that these devout women, with temporary vows and sometimes practising mendicancy (begging), did not fall easily into any of the existing categories for women's religious life. During the thirteenth century they were increasingly seen as a threat, culminating in two decrees which accused Beguines of harbouring the so-called heresy of the Free Spirit (which supposedly taught that a soul in union with God was freed from conventional moral constraints), although there was also an attempt to distinguish between 'good' and 'bad' Beguines. One of these decrees specifically refers to the problem of the Beguines in 'the German lands', and both probably reflect the influence of the two prominent German prelates at the Council: John of Zürich (Bishop of Strasburg) and Henry II of Virneburg (Archbishop of Cologne). The political connotations of the Vienne decrees were immense in that it was the Franciscans and Dominicans who were responsible for many of the Beguine communities, which were often loosely affiliated to one or other of the mendicant orders. Eckhart's move to Strasburg in 1313, then, can easily be viewed as an attempt by the Dominican Order to protect its own interests in the face of an imminent conflict with the Bishops. This would centre on the condemnation of 'certain' women for whom they, the Dominicans, bore a close pastoral responsibility.

It was probably during this period in Strasburg that Eckhart's own troubles began. It was here that he wrote the *Liber Benedictus* ('The Book of Divine Consolation' and 'On the Noble Man', both included in the present selection), and we begin to hear references to 'those who do not understand', suggesting that Eckhart was himself becoming subject to criticism. Also, much of the material which was used in the first trial of his work during the subsequent period in Cologne was taken from the *Liber Benedictus*. But when Meister Eckhart arrived in Cologne, in around 1323, he came as a leading Christian scholar and senior figure within the Dominican Order.

And yet in 1325 Nicholas of Strasburg, who was both the papal Visitor to the Dominican Province of Teutonia and Eckhart's academic subordinate, conducted an investigation into his work, pronouncing it to be orthodox. It is impossible not to see this as an attempt to pre-empt a more serious threat from the Archbishop of Cologne, who did however initiate inquisitorial proceedings against Eckhart in 1326. The charge against him was the grave one of heresy, and it was in certain respects an extraordinary accusation. Eckhart was both the first (and only) Dominican to be charged with heresy under the Inquisition and he was also the first theologian of major rank to face this particular charge. Controversial theologians were otherwise subjected to an examination of faith, since heresy was a matter of the will and not merely the propagation of theological error. It is notable that the charge against him was immediately reduced when his case was finally referred to the Holy See. Eckhart responded to the lists of suspect propositions, drawn up by his accusers, with a written defence, which has survived. It is significant that the attitude adopted by Eckhart in this and at other points in his defence is not that he was introducing new teachings which were either different or superior to the doctrines of the Catholic Church, but rather that he was within the orthodox tradition and was being misunderstood. If his accusers charged Eckhart with heresy, then he charged them with stupidity.

When his case moved to Avignon, where Pope John XXII was currently in exile, he was flanked by Henricus de Cigno, the Dominican Provincial of Teutonia, and three lectors. Despite such strong local support, there is some evidence to suggest that the Dominican Order at large had already distanced itself from Eckhart during its General Chapter at Venice in 1325, and again in Toulouse in 1328, which prepared the way for his condemnation. This duly followed on 27 March 1329, shortly after Eckhart's death, with the publication of the Bull *In agro dominico*. This identified twenty-eight articles, seventeen of which were judged to 'contain error or the mark of heresy' and eleven of which were 'evil-sounding, rash and suspect of heresy'. We have already indicated the extraordinary character of the accusations against Eckhart, and his condemnation is no less strange. In the first place, it was published only in Cologne, although Eckhart had also lived and taught (in German) in Erfurt and Strasburg. Secondly, the Bull was published after his death, when any threat from Eckhart's preaching, if threat there was, could reasonably be considered to have passed. To this extent *In agro dominico* stands out as a condemnatory text without parallel in the history of Catholic medieval Europe.

But there is, in fact, a single perfectly consistent explanation for all the unusual factors that surround the accusations against Eckhart and his condemnation.[3] It was the Archbishop of Cologne who instigated inquisitorial proceedings against Eckhart and who opposed Eckhart's appeal to the Holy See. It was Henry too who wrote to John XXII evoking the assurance that the condemnation would be pronounced despite Eckhart's death. The fact that the Bull was promulgated only in Cologne well illustrates Henry's key influence in the affair, and we need only inquire why it was that the Pope felt himself unable to oppose Henry or, as we might have expected, simply to allow the case to sit on the shelf. The condemnation of a prominent Dominican can only have embarrassed the Pope and his close ally, the Dominican Order.

A clear answer to this question emerges from a consideration of the political situation in which the papacy found itself in the first decades of the fourteenth century. Since the exile of the papacy to Avignon in 1309, Clement V and his successor John XXII entertained the ambition to return to Italy. In particular, the latter viewed the Italian ambitions of Lewis of Bavaria, the German Emperor, with great foreboding, fearing that the incursions into Italy by Lewis would destroy his hope of returning to Rome with a benign Habsburg buffer to the north. Accordingly the Pope engaged in a fierce controversy with Lewis which culminated in his excommunication in 1324. Henry of Virneburg's role in this complex political situation was that of chief supporter of Lewis's challenger to the throne, the Habsburg Frederick of Austria, and he was thus one of John XXII's principal allies. The extent of the Pope's obligation to the Archbishop can be judged by a letter which John wrote to Henry on 3 June 1324 in which he urged him to publish the process against Lewis (which he had so far failed to do on account of local opposition). As an enticement, the Pope offered to force the return of whatever toll-rights King Albrecht had removed from him during the toll-war in the Rhineland area; all the Archbishop had to do was inform him who the present owners of such rights were. This letter clearly shows that shortly before the trial against Eckhart began, the Pope believed himself to be so indebted to the Archbishop of Cologne as to explicitly offer him favours.

Finally, the question must be asked why Henry of Virneburg should have felt himself provoked by Meister Eckhart, to the extent of pursuing him mercilessly by all the means at his disposal. The answer probably lies in Henry's campaign against the Beguines. Not only did Eckhart become involved in that controversy on behalf of the Dominican Order and thus, indirectly, on behalf of the Beguines themselves who were their pastoral charges, but also he himself seemed, to an unsympathetic mind, to be teaching the very heresy of which the Beguines stood accused. In sermons attributed to Eckhart it is not difficult to read certain statements, removed from their context, as advocating a mystical religion which is potentially free of ethical content. Indeed, it is very likely that his sermons were read in this way in certain quarters. Eckhart himself was aware that there was much that was subtly put, with a rhetorical *élan*, but in his defence he also disclaimed a number of statements attributed to his name. Also, of course, he frequently warned against just such an antinomian misinterpretation of his thought, stressing the place of morality and of the practices of the Church.

With hindsight we know today that Meister Eckhart emphatically taught the Christian faith, albeit in a highly original manner and with certain philosophical presuppositions which lent his thought a wholly distinctive edge. But the distasteful events surrounding his trial point not only to the political machinations of the age, they also remind us how easy it is to misread Meister Eckhart and to misappropriate his teachings for purposes remote from his own. To some extent this was the consequence of his own occasional predilection for quite extravagant rhetoric, but it was also the result of the discrepancy between the deep structures of his thought and the brilliant surface of his imagery and language. Moreover, the failure to see any single part of Eckhart's work within the context of the whole, and the whole in the context of his intellectual and social world, remains as much a danger now as it was then.

Intellectual Formation

Once again it is Meister Eckhart's status as a Dominican which is of importance as we assess the intellectual influences upon him. Since his entrance into the Dominican Order guaranteed him an immensely privileged education and access to the finest libraries, there is little philosophical or theological material extant in the medieval West which we can assume Meister Eckhart *did not* read. This is in marked contrast to the great majority of medieval writers for whom access to texts was severely restricted on practical grounds. But, most importantly of all, the education Eckhart received specifically as a *German* Dominican proved to be a fundamental influence upon his thought. The existence of a German Dominican school, centring upon the figure of Albert the Great, has only recently been fully established. It has been shown to be a radical form of Augustinianism, particularly in-debted to the neoplatonic influence of, among others, Proclus (a Greek), Avicenna (an Arab) and Maimonides (a Jew). It is this association, rather than the more general Dominican trends which Eckhart has in common with Thomas Aquinas, that makes Eckhart such a challenging thinker.

One of the foremost representatives of this German Dominican school was Dietrich of Freiberg. Dietrich belonged to the genera-tion before that of Meister Eckhart but, like him, he was an outstanding administrator and scholar, who also held a chair of theology at the University of Paris. Dietrich must have been Eckhart's mentor in the Dominican Order and, as Provincial of Teutonia, would have appointed the younger man Prior of the Dominican convent at Erfurt. The two works by his hand which are of most consequence to us are *On the Intellect* and *On the Beatific Vision*.[4] We do not find in Eckhart a treatise on the intellect as such, but the theory of intellect which is everywhere present in his works is virtually identical to that held by Dietrich and expounded in these two texts.

The key area that Eckhart has in common with Dietrich, and others of the German Dominican school, is an intense interest in the nature and meaning of 'intellect', by which is meant something that corresponds more to 'consciousness' than to 'intellect' in modern terminology. For our present purposes, Eckhart's chief debt was his belief that 'mind' or 'intellect' exists in so far as it is dynamically active. The degree to which the mind is active, and therefore the degree to which it exists, is determined by the actuality of that which it knows. Intellect therefore can be said to attain varying degrees of existence, and this depends on the extent to which it is activated, which depends in turn on the degree of actuality of the object with which it engages. Thus the concept of 'intellect' is an appropriate one to describe the nature of God, who is all-knowing and all-being. In the case of human beings, however, the intellect is locked in a body and in a world of objects whose reality is distinctly less than that of God and the divine realm. Accordingly, the human intellect is generally only partially actualized. Secondly, from Dietrich's *On the Beatific Vision* Eckhart took the idea that the human soul is itself intellect. In technical terms, this was the identification of the Augustinian 'ground of the soul' with the Aristotelian 'agent intellect', which meant that, for Eckhart, our essence, which is our innermost part, is itself intellect. Therefore in order to locate and explore 'mind' in this most dynamic and radical sense, we must look within to the most interior and intimate part of our being.

Although Meister Eckhart owed a great deal to his fellow German Dominicans, the tenor of his thought is markedly different from that of both Dietrich and Albert the Great. He does not share their encyclopedic and scientific tendencies; also, in Eckhart's case, a boldly speculative intellectualist philosophy takes on mystical and personal contours which are lacking in his contemporaries. The works of Dietrich or Albert, Ulrich of Strasburg or Hugh Ripelin, are for the specialist, while Eckhart's sermons still unfailingly excite, provoke and challenge the general reader. Nor are we alone in making that judgement, since Dietrich and Eckhart's contemporaries chose to preserve the sermons of the latter and not of the former. The difference between them can perhaps be summed up by the atmosphere of urgency which prevails in Eckhart's works and which makes us feel that he bears a great burden of truth. Indeed, we can feel in Eckhart the preacher a *sense of the presence of God* which underlies all his thinking and which lends it an astonishing communicative power. If the structure of Eckhart's thought is largely that of the philosophical movement which dominated German Dominican circles during the second half of the thirteenth and first half of the fourteenth centuries, the spirit which animates it is entirely his own.

MEISTER ECKHART'S THOUGHT

Oneness

To reduce a great thinker's work to a single idea is always to risk oversimplification. Nevertheless, in the case of Eckhart there is some justification for taking the view that one primary *perspective* is the controlling principle to which all else is in some degree subordinate: the concept of unicity or oneness.

A theology or philosophy of oneness has as its starting-point the belief that the ultimate principle of the universe is distinguished from all else by virtue of the fact that it is entirely one and undivided. All except this One is multiple, contingent and fractured. But, generally, the One is also understood to be in dynamic relation with the rest of the universe, which originates from it and which thus also 'looks back' to its source. The One is therefore everywhere present, since all exists only by reference to it, but it is also everywhere absent, since – for us – all objects of experience are multiple. The One alone is primal and permanent being (if indeed the term 'being' is attributable to it), while the being of all that is multiple shall inevitably decay. Redemption, for Neoplatonists such as Proclus or Plotinus, involves the ascent of the human mind away from the spheres of multiplicity and contingency back to a primal oneness which is grasped through an ecstasy of the mind. The challenge to Eckhart the Dominican is fundamentally to set a vigorous metaphysics of the One in the context of the Christian revelation, which in the doctrines of the Trinity and the Incarnation professes multiplicity precisely at the level of the Godhead.

Firstly, Eckhart affirms that he does indeed find the notion of the One the most adequate way of speaking of God. All else (God the 'good', the 'all-powerful', etc.) appears to 'add' something to him and therefore to conceal him. Oneness alone comes close to capturing something of God's essence in language, without clothing him in concepts which seem to owe more to our nature than to his.[5] But the doctrine of the Trinity, of course, demands multiplicity in God, and there are passages in which Eckhart appears to place the unity of God above his plurality, or at least to make his 'oneness' prior to his 'threeness'. Underlying such passages is Eckhart's belief that names and concepts belong essentially to the realm of created things: they denote specific and localized being. Among such concepts Eckhart includes 'threeness' but not 'oneness' (Sermon 30). But this tendency to prioritize God as One at the cost of God as Three must be set against another, which is also strongly present in Eckhart's thought: the belief that God is essentially *fertile*. God the Father constantly gives birth to God the Son. In other words, God is always dynamic and he always reproduces himself within the Trinity and within the human individual. Eckhart stresses that this generative function of God is not incidental to his nature but is his very essence.

It is not the case therefore that Meister Eckhart simply rejects Christian doctrine in favour of a neoplatonist metaphysic. Rather his thought seems a bold attempt to reconcile the neoplatonist inheritance with Christian orthodoxy in a way that parallels the fusion of Aristotelianism and Christianity that we find in the theology of Thomas Aquinas. That he should have ventured upon the task at all is a result of his strong Christian convictions together with his deeply held belief in the timeless veracity of neoplatonic philosophy. At one point he wrote that the pagan philosophers, Moses and Christ all professed the same truth, although each did so differently and at different levels of realization (thus the pagan – that is to say, neoplatonist – philosophers *taught* the truth while Christ *is* the truth). In any case, whether we judge the fusion to be successful, or whether we feel that there are residual tensions in Eckhart's exposition of the Trinity and the Incarnation, his work stands as one of the great theological and philosophical syntheses of the Middle Ages.

Creation

In common with most other medieval systematic theologians, Meister Eckhart has an intense interest in the processes of the Creation itself, which for him is both ongoing and outside time. This latter point, which Eckhart liked to emphasize, was typically daring, for it appeared to approximate to the (condemned) Aristotelian teaching that the world exists from eternity. Eckhart's meaning, however, was that the Creation must be considered eternal as it cannot be said to have occurred within time since time itself did not pre-exist the created order. Also, for Eckhart, the Creation is not an event located in the remote past whose consequences we experience today but is rather an ongoing and dynamic process. Also, like many other medieval theologians, Eckhart places great stress on the existence of creatures in the mind of God, as well as in their created state, and throughout his sermons he urges his audience to attain knowledge of things as they exist eternally in the mind of God and not as they exist temporally here below. In particular, he stresses that we should become fully united with the image or idea of ourselves that exists from eternity in the mind of God.

Similarly, Meister Eckhart shows a great concern with the typically medieval question of the nature of the relation between creatures and God. In technical terms this is the field known as the theory of analogy. According to the most influential system of analogy, which is that associated with the name of Thomas Aquinas, terms borrowed from the created order are not wholly without meaning when applied to God, but neither are they wholly accurate. Rather, they fall somewhere in between. Thus the alignment between the world and God is neither one of identity nor one of complete difference, but is rather one of a real, though imperfect, relation. A further feature of this system is that, although created qualities have their origin in God, they can truly be said to belong to creatures. Thus Thomas is always concerned to preserve the real being of creatures, while affirming the transcendence of their Creator.

But Meister Eckhart approaches these questions with a subtly different emphasis. He is concerned generally to stress the extent to which the created world remains within God, and so, for Eckhart, it can be said that being is only ever 'on loan' to creatures. It never becomes authentically their own possession, as it does for Thomas. Thus the individual quality of whiteness, justice, goodness, or whatever it may be, is identical with the universal principle of whiteness, justice and goodness, and remains within God. According to Eckhart, the philosophical principle which prevents the being of all creatures from collapsing into a pantheistic identity with God is the fact that properties exist in a mixed state in individual beings while they are wholly united within God. This is expressed as the *inquantum* maxim, which means 'in so far as'. Thus a man or woman who is 'good' is wholly identical with 'goodness' itself but only *in so far as* they are 'good'. In so far as we are 'just', we are 'justice' itself, but Eckhart well knows that 'justice' is only one among many elements which constitute the human person.

The general effect of Eckhart's thinking on the relation between God and his creation therefore is to stress the extent to which God can be said to be immanent within his creatures, since those properties which essentially combine to make things what they are still remain within God. Moreover, the use of the *inquantum* principle in order to distinguish between God and creatures can be seen in effect to be a subtle form of the oneness/multiplicity paradigm that we have discussed above. In God all properties are One, while in the created order they exist in combination. In other words, Eckhart knows that God is One, and so any or all his properties must exist in a state of unicity, while all that is not God partakes in multiplicity.

The one exception to this rule is a single element located within the human person which Eckhart sometimes calls the 'soul', a 'light', the 'ground of the soul', the 'spark of the soul' or, more generally, simply 'intellect'. In any case, it is this which, being unified and transcendent, sets us apart from other creatures and makes us a place of special interest to God. And it is this, a divine presence at the heart of our being, which is the foundation of our right action and the promise of our blessedness.

The Ground of the Soul

In his emphasis upon the importance of the divine image in the human person Meister Eckhart stands squarely within the Judaeo-Christian tradition, even if his insistence that the 'image' is to be equated with the human mind or intellect betrays his debt to Greek rationalism and the neoplatonic tradition. In one sermon (Sermon 23) Eckhart specifies what it is about the intellect that makes it the image of God within us. He tells us that it is 'detached from the here and now', that the intellect 'bears no likeness to anything else', that it is 'pure and unmixed with anything else' and that it is 'active or exploratory in itself'. In fact, these are remarkably close to the terms in which Eckhart speaks of God himself. And, like the deity, the 'image' or 'intellect' is higher than the angels, 'more nameless than with name' and 'more unknown than known' (Sermon 3). But most crucially, it is a 'single oneness', 'entirely one and simple, as God is one and simple' and is 'entirely spiritual' (Sermon 13). This means that the image-intellect belongs intrinsically to the unified, divine and spiritual realm of transcendent Oneness, and the many metaphors which Eckhart applies to it (i.e. the 'spark', the 'crown', the 'fortress', the 'ground of the soul') simply serve to underline that, like oneness itself, it is quite beyond conceptualization and that human thought can only delimit and negate it.

It is the immensely elevated terms in which Eckhart speaks of the divine image in us which have led some to believe that he is postulating that we contain a 'portion' of God within the self, as in the Brahman-Atman scheme of the vedantic tradition. But in the defence that he delivered in Cologne on 13 February 1327, Eckhart was careful to point out that he did not conceive of the divine spark as being in any sense something that was 'added' to the soul. We should read this statement as meaning that Eckhart conceived of the divine image as a *potentiality* within us: far from being substance, it is a transcendental potentiality within the soul through which the soul can enjoy a cognitive unity with God. In Dietrich's terms, this is the recognition that our human essence is 'intellect' or 'mind', as God is 'mind', and that the nature of 'mind' is a oneness that is above being. All 'intellect' in this sense therefore is one, and so the soul in its essence and God are one. But this is not to say that Eckhart taught that we are God, or anything of the kind. Rather, Eckhart's whole system rests upon the unremarkable observation that we are *not* God. His appeal is always to what we could be, to our potentiality, although he fully recognizes that as earthly creatures we cannot evade the confines of our embodied state (Sermon 21).

The chief way in which Eckhart anchors this transcendental symmetry between the human and divine mind is through his theory of the image. This forms the subject of one sermon in particular (Sermon 20) but it occurs widely throughout his work. The Christian notion of the image derives originally from two sources. The first is Genesis 1:26–7, which states that humanity is made 'in the image' of God, and the second is Trinitarian theology which asserts that the Son is the 'image' of the Father. The meaning of the latter is that the Son is generated by the Father but remains identical with him. By conflating the terms 'in the image' and 'image', Eckhart uses this same idea in order to articulate the connaturality between the Father and the human intellect. The latter is generated by the former but remains (potentially) identical with him. Eckhart states that the source of an image is fully present within that image; in his own metaphysical terms the image is 'in' its source and the source is 'in' the image. Thus, through the motif of the image, Eckhart is able to argue that even within our fallen state there is something in our human essence that enjoys a very special affinity with God, which is not paralleled by anything else in Creation.

The Birth of God in the Soul

The 'breakthrough' of the individual into a realization of God's immediacy is conveyed in Eckhart's work by the metaphor of the birth of God in the soul. This is a felicitous device, and as with the image metaphor above, it serves to combine his distinctively metaphysical and intellective sensibility with traditional Christian doctrine. Firstly, of course, the concept of the birth evokes the doctrine of the historical Incarnation: the birth of Christ in space and time. But, more generally, it refers to the birth, or generation, of the Son within the Trinity. Indeed, Eckhart's insistence upon the birth of the Son within the human soul serves to outline the possibility of our return to the Trinity, from which, according to Christian theology, we originally emerged. It is thus an image of our inner and essential union with God who, as the Father, gives birth to the Son in the Trinity and, as the same Father, gives birth to the same Son in the depths of the human soul.

But Eckhart's metaphor of the birth also tells us something about the nature of that union between the human and the divine. The Son is often referred to as the 'Word', and Eckhart tells us that the birth of God in the soul is God's uttering of his Word in the ground of the soul. The ground of the soul, which is 'intellect', is the 'image' of God in us, just as the Word (the Son) is spoken by the Father and is the 'image' of the Father within the Trinity. Now 'words' and 'images' have the same property in that they both 'go out' while 'remaining within' (Sermon 5). In other terms, both 'words' and 'images' belong to the divine-spiritual-intellective-unified realm. Thus, by hedging the metaphor of birth with terms such as 'Word' and 'image', Eckhart skilfully shows that the character of the birth is itself intellective, and succeeds in uniting 'birth' and 'intellect', which are his two principal images of transcendentality. Eckhart wishes us to understand that if the birth of God in us stands for a changed state of being, then it is also and fundamentally a changed state of *knowing*.

The metaphor of God's birth in us holds a central place in Eckhart's system in that it provides a place of unity for the many diverse strands in his thinking. Here transcendence and immanence are one, as are being and knowing, and the subjective dimension of personal interiority combines with the objective dimension of Christian doctrine. But we can discern a further principle within it: that of ethics and morality. Thus Eckhart tells us that only they 'who walk in the ways of God' can understand this birth, while those who are 'natural and undisciplined' are remote from it (Sermon W 1). Through the birth we are made 'like God', we are sanctified and established in virtue. It is not difficult to see this as a variation upon the traditional scholastic and patristic teaching on grace. Grace is the free action of God which causes the establishing of his moral order within us, whereby we are increasingly conformed to his nature.

Discussions of the nature of grace reached a high point during the thirteenth and fourteenth centuries, and Eckhart's teaching on the birth of the soul can be viewed as his contribution to this debate. In his metaphor of the birth, Eckhart, the Parisian master, strongly states his understanding of grace as the uncreated self-communication of God, which is to say as the transcendental union of the human and divine. He always remained scornful of the more orthodox notions of 'created' grace since this appeared to relegate God's activity to the world of finite entities, whereas, for Eckhart, God's essential nature is itself pure unified activity (as birth) and as such should be thought of as uncreated and as existing beyond the world.

If we view the metaphor of the birth as a veiled theology of grace, then several points emerge. The first is that it is in a sense mystical, being based upon the union of the human and divine. Secondly, it stresses the extent to which grace is God's initiative.

Few theologians have so wonderfully captured the urgency and the abundance of grace, which results from God's nature rather than our own. Eckhart tells us that God 'must' give birth to himself in us fully and at all times. He has no choice in the matter; this is simply his nature. If we do not receive the spiritual benefits of this birth, then that is because we are not content to allow God to act in us. Rather, we obstruct him with our false notions of self and the determination to cling to the nothingness which is the true reality of our own creaturely being.

Detachment

The convergence of metaphysics and ethics in Eckhart is most clearly shown in his concept of 'detachment'. This English word translates the Middle High German *abegescheidenheit* or sometimes *gelâzenheit*. The former means 'being cut off from', and expresses the freedom of the enlightened soul from attachment to things in the world. Of course, Christian asceticism had always stressed that the human person must shed his or her attachment to worldly things in order to progress in the spiritual life, but what is distinctive in Eckhart is the extent to which this moral liberation is seen as a liberation of the mind. 'Detachment' is simultaneously freedom from a libidinous attachment to things through our appetites and a cognitive freedom: that is, liberation from the images of physical things which serve to restrict the mind and alienate it from its own transcendental possibilities. Although not unique within the Christian tradition (there are parallels, for instance, in Evagrius of Pontus), such a metaphysical understanding of morality is unusual.

For Eckhart, the 'detached person' lives in the world but is not of it (cf. John 17:16). The 'birth of God' has taken place within them, and their 'knowing essence' is now engaged with God and not with the world. Since the metaphysical keynote of the spiritual and divine realities in which the human person now participates is oneness, the moral manifestation of this state is the practice of altruism, that is treating other people as if they were oneself (cf. Lev. 19:18). Thus we should be as concerned with the welfare of others as we are with our own, and all that we do will be conceived in the spirit of humility. Indeed, of all the virtues most associated with detachment humility is the most foundational. In one passage of great rhetorical brilliance Eckhart urges us to enter our own 'ground of humility', which is our *lowest* part, but it is also our *highest* part, since God is present there and raises us up, and it is no less our *innermost* part, for it is our own essence (Sermon W 46).

The second manifestation of detachment, which results from the birth of God within us, is indifference to suffering and to pain. Many of Eckhart's comments on this seem to be of an ideal and rhetorical type, as when he suggests that the mere fact of experiencing suffering means that God's birth has not taken place within us, or when he tells us that we should be indifferent to whether 'our friend lives or not' in the name of a general passivity to God's will. Such passages need to be read together with others, however, such as in Sermon 21, where he seems to be correcting precisely these views. We will comment further in a later section on Eckhart's rhetorical method of holding before his audience perspectives which derive from their potential and ultimate union with God rather than their present state of alienation from him.

If Eckhart's doctrine on the 'ground' or 'spark' of the soul appears to be an exploration through images of the traditional Christian teaching on the image of God within us, and if his teaching on the 'birth of God in the soul' is a similar presentation of a doctrine of grace, then Eckhart's teaching on 'detachment' can also be understood as a personal and expressive exposition of Christian virtue. The 'detached man or woman' is loving and humble, possessing serenity and wisdom, and with a will that is wholly taken up by God. And yet here too we find the distinctively Eckhartian emphasis upon intellectuality since the virtuous soul is one which has withdrawn from the 'multiplicity of its powers' into its unified ground. There it loses selfhood, which is the primary obstacle to the practice of virtue, and merges with the oneness of intellectual essence. It is this, the absence of distinction within the enlightened or detached self, which in Eckhart's system forms the metaphysical basis for the Christian life of virtue.

The chief consequence of Eckhart's understanding of virtue as an interior state, both existential and intellective, is his teaching on the role of devotional works. Eckhart lived in an age which gave great emphasis to explicit and visible piety, and the particular environment with which he chose to be closely associated, namely that of women's religious communities, reflected this trend in a high degree. According to the records of such communities, the religious women of the fourteenth century often practised a life of astonishing austerity as part of a culture of spiritual attainment. This is not to deny the great spiritual and literary achievements of women in the late Middle Ages, or indeed the fact that their sometimes extreme ascetical practices were rooted in the dominant misogyny and patriarchy of the age. But it is difficult not to read Eckhart's repeated and emphatic appeal to interiority and to interior *intention* with respect to devotional works as being a subtle critique of the widespread spiritual mores of his contemporary world. He does not attack the principle of devotional practices within the religious life as such, however (as some of the reformers were to do two centuries later), but always seeks to relativize them within the context of a personal and interior relationship with God. As he wisely reminds us: 'they do him wrong who take God just in one particular way. They take the way rather than God' (Sermon 19).

MEISTER ECKHART'S METHOD

The works of Eckhart included in the present volume reflect his activity as a preacher rather than a scholar. The Dominicans, or Friars Preacher as they are also known, are an evangelical Order who put great stress upon the role of preaching. Thomas Aquinas described this practice as 'conveying to others the fruits of meditation'. It is within this tradition of proclamation that Meister Eckhart stands, and his philosophical background serves largely to articulate, even to embody, his personal mystical vision. It is the coincidence of these two – boldly speculative philosophy/theology and the personal intuition of a transcendental state of consciousness – that forms the essential structures of Eckhart's thought and creates its compelling atmosphere. But it is the interaction of these two also which motivates Eckhart's particular use of language. Primarily in the German sermons, he exploits rhetorical imagery and radical linguistic strategies in order to effect a change in the minds of his listeners that conforms to his own understanding and experience. It is this *intentionality* which creates the rhetorical surface of the sermons, full of contradictions and flourish, metaphysical drama and hyperbole, and it is this too which has at times in the past caused the learned to believe that Eckhart is a confused thinker, and those less learned to believe that he preached a wildly mystical religion, freed from the trammels of Christian doctrine and institution.

One commentator has perceptively remarked that Eckhart is not so much a thinker who seeks after truth as one who articulates it.[6] And indeed, it is this element of proclamation which makes Meister Eckhart the most unsystematic of systematic theologians. There have been numerous attempts to impose system upon his thought but, as the great medieval scholar Etienne Gilson once remarked: 'Nothing is easier than to reduce Eckhart to a system founded upon one's own evidence; the problem is that having done so, one will see that one could just as easily have constructed an entirely different system, even though based on texts which are just as authentic as the other.'[7] Such attempts are ultimately futile, however, since the very truth which Eckhart was attempting to articulate is by definition one which defies systematization. The very last thing Eckhart wanted to cultivate in the minds of his listeners was the comfortable feeling that they now 'understood' what God was: for that, he was sure, would be the greatest error and ignorance of all (Sermon 28). Accordingly, an account of Eckhart's method is principally an account of the various strategies he employed in order to subvert the systematic process and to trigger in the minds of his listeners the possibility of truly transcendental knowledge.

Nevertheless, there are particular ways in which Eckhart was contradictory, imprecise and unsystematic which are themselves subject to some degree of systematization. The first such trend is his tendency to contradict himself when presenting a theology of God. This is true primarily in the Latin works, where God is described alternatively as 'being', 'naked, unveiled being', the 'purity of being', as 'oneness', and as 'intellect' or 'understanding', which (as he tells us in Sermon W 67) is as far above being 'as the highest angel is above a gnat'.[8] Taken together, such variations disrupt any premature complacency in the mind of the listener who is thus powerfully reminded of the fact that God transcends what can be said or thought about him. Eckhart uses a similar technique in the German sermons when he heaps a whole succession of metaphors upon the 'ground of the soul' as if to suggest that this too escapes the net of language.

In the German sermons, however, we find a different kind of 'confusion' which results in part from the fact that here Eckhart is responding to diverse scriptural texts which present to him a variety of images and theological concepts. He is always concerned to adapt these to the parameters of his own thinking and, in so doing, often adopts positions which are easily contradicted by statements he makes elsewhere. Thus he tells us that our union with God is not love but knowledge (Sermon W 72), not knowledge but love (Sermon W 77). Speaking also of the birth of God in the soul, he tells us that it is both intellect (Sermon 23) and not intellect (Sermon W 72), that it is to be identified with grace in one sermon (Sermon W 68) and not in another (Sermon W 41). Such imprecision underlines the extent to which Eckhart employs theological concepts and imagery relatively loosely. Even central figures such as 'the birth of God in the soul', or indeed 'the ground or spark of the soul', function as *metaphors* and not as calculated theological propositions. These serve not so much as details of an argument but as vehicles of expression to stir and move the imagination of Eckhart's audience.

A further element in the expressivity of Eckhart's style is his predilection for speaking from an *ideal* position. Time and again Eckhart makes statements which *would be true* if we were already united with God. As he himself tells us, it is his intention to adopt a 'God's-eye' view and to speak as though this were his audience's sole reality (Sermon 11). A sermon such as 'Blessed are the poor in spirit' (Sermon 22) abounds in such statements; as when Eckhart urges his audience to become as they were before they were created. These are not intended to be taken literally but are an attempt to hold before his listeners the transcendental possibilities of their own natures, and they too belong to what Eckhart himself at one point acknowledged to be his 'emphatic speech'.[9]

For Eckhart, breakthrough to God is a breakthrough in knowledge. Lower forms of knowledge serve to obscure God from the soul, and the soul from its own transcendent essence. And so we come to language itself, which (as Eckhart knows) is a fundamental part of the problem. Language mediates the world to us with all its finiteness in space and time. And when we use it of God, it gets in the way by making an object of him, clothing him in concepts and images which are inappropriate to his uncreated nature. But if language is the obstacle, it is also paradoxically the place of our redemption. Through purifying language into its most abstract and internal forms, through using wildly metaphorical language of God, Eckhart believes that he can aid the breakthrough into transcendental knowledge which, for him, is union with God. While knowing that God is – infinitely – beyond language, Eckhart also believes that he can be authentically proclaimed through a disruptive critique of language. Indeed, this is summed up in Eckhart's phrase: 'words come from the Word'. This formula also tells us *why* Eckhart believes that language can be redemptive: language belongs to the intellect. Like intellect, it belongs to the 'spiritual', 'mental', 'unified' sphere of 'word' and 'image' which is eternally opposed to the finite, coarse, pluralistic world of 'things' and the senses. That former reality is abstract and divine, and it is summed up in the Word, or Second Person of the Trinity, in the 'image' of which the human intellect was created and from which 'words come'.

However bewildering and confused the surface of Eckhart's thought might at times seem, the primary structures remain remarkably consistent. These may be described as divine oneness on the one hand and divine self-reproduction (the birth, the image) on the other. These two ideas, the first of which derives in the main from the neoplatonic and the second from the biblical tradition, can be restated as two further principles: the transcendence and immanence of God. God who is far away and near at hand; God who is beyond and within. It is between these two poles that Eckhart's thought turns and which together form a dialectic, of which he himself is well aware.[10] But the effect of that dialectic, which can be thought of as a particular momentum in all that Eckhart argued, is at times to distort the pattern of concepts and ideas that form the content of Eckhart's teaching as these are made to serve the ends of one or other of these two foundational and interrelated principles.

MEISTER ECKHART AND THE EUROPEAN INTELLECTUAL TRADITION

As we take stock of this complex figure, we can see that he stands at a critical point in the evolution of European intellectual life. Prior to Clement IV's injunction to the Dominicans in 1267 to take over the pastoral care of religious women's communities, which directly led to the use of German for the purposes of preaching, all intellectual thought was written down in the Latin language. Whatever the achievements of the first generation of Dominicans may have been (these are lost to us today), we have in the sermons of Meister Eckhart, who belonged to the second generation, the first substantial body of sophisticated philosophical and theological discussion in a European vernacular language. This then is the first context in which we must see Eckhart, as the father of a distinguished German philosophical and theological tradition which extends to the present day. Indeed, there is much in Eckhart that points down the centuries to later, distinctively German, schools of philosophical thought. The primacy of the intellect and human mind which is so characteristic of Eckhart and the German Dominican school anticipates nineteenth-century German Idealism, and Eckhart's recourse to the rhetorical resources of language in order to communicate his ideas is reminiscent of German thinkers of the modern period, such as Friedrich Nietzsche or Martin Heidegger.

Secondly, Eckhart's theology needs to be seen as one of the great medieval attempts to achieve a synthesis between Greek thought and Christian faith. If in the case of Thomas Aquinas it was the newly-translated Aristotle who mediated the Greek tradition, then for Eckhart it was the Neoplatonists, and particularly Proclus, who offered a philosophical inheritance he could claim as his own.

The coincidence moreover of neoplatonic and Christian thought in Meister Eckhart created a number of ideas and perspectives that have exercised a real fascination upon the minds of many leading modern thinkers. This modern response began with the rediscovery of Eckhart's works in Germany in the mid-nineteenth century. Hegel was intrigued by those elements in Eckhart which suggested a synthesis of philosophy and religion, while Schopenhauer saw in his teaching on the nothingness of creatures an affinity with Eastern religions and with his own pessimism. In the twentieth century this interest has extended from Ernst Bloch to Martin Heidegger (who made extensive and explicit use of Eckhart's term *Gelassenheit* – 'detachment') and Jacques Derrida.

If the philosophical world has been interested by Eckhart's treatment of themes such as being, spirit and negativity, then the Christian community has found in him a powerful advocate of religion based upon a sense of transcendent experience. He seems also to be largely free of the weight of theological language and thus able to present classical religious themes in a way that is both fresh and challenging.

Many of those who have read Meister Eckhart, whether Christian or not, have found in his work a geniality of style, profound speculation and spiritual vision that still move us today as they once did those who gathered in the churches and convents of medieval Germany to hear a Master who spoke in so strange a way of the 'God beyond words'.

A NOTE ON THE SELECTION AND TRANSLATION

The material presented in new translation for this volume derives overwhelmingly from the German works of Meister Eckhart since it is here that he lays aside the conventions of formal writing and seeks to speak to the hearts of those whom he is addressing. The first text, *The Talks of Instruction*, is a superb and relatively straightforward account of Eckhart's understanding of the spiritual life, while the two treatises of the later *Liber Benedictus* ('The Book of Divine Consolation' and 'On the Noble Man') are altogether more complex and are generally an exploration, in German, of Eckhart's theory of analogy. Among these treatises I have not included *On Detachment* since it is by no means clear that this is by the hand of Eckhart.

In selecting from the German sermons, I have sought to give an overall impression of Eckhart's thought, paying special attention to those texts in which he shows his most characteristic positions. Work on the critical edition of Eckhart's sermons is still in progress, and Sermons 29 and 30 are presented here in English for the first time.

The selection concludes with a number of Latin sermons, some of which (Sermons 1, 3 and 4) have not appeared in English translation before. These present familiar Eckhartian themes in a style which reflects the academic milieu in which they were originally preached.

Eckhart's highly original prose presents numerous challenges to his English translator. In particular, I have found difficulty with his use of spacial metaphors in order to describe metaphysical states (for example, 'going out of yourself', 'being in justice'). Generally, I have followed this same device in English; if the result is stylistically a little unconventional, then it is no more so than the original German. I have also experienced some difficulty with the verb *werken* and its cognates, which contain a whole range of diverse meanings. These range from 'active', 'act' and 'action' (often to be contrasted with passivity and receptivity) to specific 'works' of ascetical piety. Inevitably in such cases something of the consistency of the original is lost in English translation. I must also record that I have greatly profited from M. O'C. Walshe's translation of the complete German works. While not agreeing with all his judgements, and myself opting for a slightly different register of modern English, I have nevertheless found his work, on particular points, a valuable and consistent guide. Finally, I am indebted to Josef Quint and the Stuttgart edition of Eckhart's work for a number of points in the notes, which I have designated by square brackets.

The Talks of Instruction

These are the talks which the Vicar of Thuringia, the Prior of Erfurt, Brother Eckhart of the Order of Preachers, gave to those in his care who asked him many things concerning these talks as they sat together in evening discussions

I

On true obedience.

True and perfect obedience is a virtue above all virtues, and there is no work, however great it may be, that can take place or be performed without this virtue, and even the very least of works, whether it be saying or listening to Mass, praying, meditating, or whatever you can think of, is more usefully done when it is performed in true obedience.[1] Take any work you wish, however minor it may be, true obedience will make it nobler and better for you. Obedience always brings out the very best in all things. Indeed, obedience never undermines or forgets those things which we do out of true obedience, for it never neglects what is good. Obedience need never be anxious, for there is no form of goodness which it does not possess in itself.

When we go out of ourselves through obedience and strip ourselves of what is ours, then God must enter into us; for when someone wills nothing for themselves, then God must will on their behalf just as he does for himself. Whenever I have taken leave of my own will, putting it in the hands of my superior, and no longer will anything for myself, then God must will on my behalf, and if he neglects me in this respect, then he neglects himself. And so in all things in which I do not will for myself, God wills on my behalf. Now take note! What does he will for me, if I will nothing for myself? When I shed my own self, then he must of necessity will for me everything that he wills for himself, no more and no less, and in the very same way that he wills for himself. And if God did not do this, then by the truth which God is, he would not be just nor would he be God (which of course he is by his nature).

In true obedience there should be no 'I want this or that to happen' or 'I want this or that thing' but only a pure going out of what is our own. And therefore in the very best kind of prayer that we can pray there should be no 'give me this particular virtue or way of devotion'[2] or 'yes, Lord, give me yourself or eternal life', but rather 'Lord, give me only what you will and do, Lord, only what you will and in the way that you will'. This kind of prayer is as far above the former as heaven is above earth. And when we have prayed in this way, then we have prayed well, having gone out of ourselves and entered God in true obedience. But just as true obedience should have no 'I want this', neither should it ever hear 'I don't want', for 'I don't want' is pure poison for all true obedience. As St Augustine says: 'The true servant of God does not desire to be told or to be given what they would like to hear or see, for their prime and highest wish is to hear what is most pleasing to God.'[3]

2

On the most powerful prayer of all and the finest work.

The most powerful form of prayer, and the one which can virtually gain all things and which is the worthiest work of all, is that which flows from a free mind. The freer the mind is, the more powerful and worthy, the more useful, praiseworthy and perfect the prayer and the work become. A free mind can achieve all things. But what is a free mind?

A free mind is one which is untroubled and unfettered by anything, which has not bound its best part to any particular manner of being or devotion and which does not seek its own interest in anything but is always immersed in God's most precious will, having gone out of what is its own. There is no work which men and women can perform, however small, which does not draw from this its power and its strength.

We should pray with such intensity that we want all the members of our body and all its faculties, eyes, ears, mouth, heart and all our senses to turn to this end; and we should not cease in this until we feel that we are close to being united with him who is present to us and to whom we are praying: God.

3

On undetached people who are full of self-will.[4]

People say: 'O Lord, I wish that I stood as well with God and that I had as much devotion and peace with God as other people, and that I could be like them or could be as poor as they are.' Or they say: 'It never works for me unless I am in this or that particular place and do this or that particular thing. I must go to somewhere remote or live in a hermitage or a monastery.'

Truly, it is you who are the cause of this yourself, and nothing else. It is your own self-will, even if you don't know it or this doesn't seem to you to be the case. The lack of peace that you feel can only come from your own self-will, whether you are aware of this or not. Whatever we think – that we should avoid certain things and seek out others, whether these be places or people, particular forms of devotion, this group of people or this kind of activity – these are not to blame for the fact that you are held back by devotional practices and by things; rather it is you as you exist in these things who hold yourself back, for you do not stand in the proper relation to them.

Start with yourself therefore and take leave of yourself. Truly, if you do not depart from yourself, then wherever you take refuge, you will find obstacles and unrest, wherever it may be. Those who seek peace in external things, whether in places or devotional practices, people or works, in withdrawal from the world or poverty or self-abasement: however great these things may be or whatever their character, they are still nothing at all and cannot be the source of peace. Those who seek in this way, seek wrongly, and the further they range, the less they find what they are looking for. They proceed like someone who has lost their way: the further they go, the more lost they become. But what then should they do? First of all, they should renounce themselves, and then they will have renounced all things. Truly, if someone were to renounce a kingdom or the whole world while still holding on to themselves, then they would have renounced nothing at all. And indeed, if someone renounces themselves, then whatever they might keep, whether it be a kingdom or honour or whatever it may be, they will still have renounced all things.

St Peter said, 'See, Lord, we have left everything' (Matt. 19:27), when he had left nothing more than a mere net and his little boat, and a saint[5] comments that whoever willingly renounces what is small, renounces not only this but also everything which worldly people can possess or indeed even desire. Whoever renounces their own will and their own self, renounces all things as surely as if all things were in that person's possession to do with as they pleased, for what you do not wish to desire, you have given over and given up to God. Therefore our Lord said,

'Blessed are the poor in spirit' (Matt. 5:3), which is to say those who are poor in will. Let no one be in any doubt about this: if there were a better way, then our Lord would have told us, who said, 'If anyone would follow me, he must first deny himself' (Matt. 16:24). This is the point which counts. Examine yourself, and wherever you find yourself, then take leave of yourself. This is the best way of all.

4

On the value of the renunciation that we should practise inwardly and outwardly.

You should know that no one has ever renounced themselves so much in this life that there was nothing left of themselves to renounce. But there are few people who are properly aware of this and who remain constant in their efforts. It is a fair trade and an equal exchange: to the extent that you depart from things, thus far, no more and no less, God enters into you with all that is his, as far as you have stripped yourself of yourself in all things. It is here that you should begin, whatever the cost, for it is here that you will find true peace, and nowhere else.

People should not worry so much about what they *do* but rather about what they *are*. If they and their ways are good, then their deeds are radiant. If you are righteous, then what you do will also be righteous. We should not think that holiness is based on what we do but rather on what we are, for it is not our works which sanctify us but we who sanctify our works. However holy our works may be, they do not in any way make us holy in so far as they are works, but it is we, in so far as we are holy and possess fulness of being, who sanctify all our works, whether these be eating, sleeping, waking, or anything at all. Little comes from the works of those whose being is slight. This teaches us then that we should make every effort to be good, and should worry not so much about what we do or the character of our actions, but we should be concerned rather about their ground.

5

Take note of what makes our essence and our ground good.

The reason why a person's essence and ground, which lends goodness to their works, is wholly good is that their mind is wholly turned to God. Make every effort then to let God be great and to ensure that all your good intentions and endeavours are directed to him in all that you do and in all that you refrain from doing. Truly, the more you do this, the better your works will be, whatever they are. If you hold to God, then he will give you goodness. If you seek God, then you will find both God and all goodness. Indeed, if you trod on a stone while in this state of mind, it would be a more godly act than if you were to receive the body of our Lord while being concerned only for yourself and having a less detached attitude of mind. Whoever holds to God, holds to both God and all virtue. And what was previously the object of your seeking, now seeks you; what you hunted, now hunts you, what you fled, now flees you. This is so because the things of God cling to those people who cling to God, and all those things flee them, which are unlike God and are alien to him.

6

On detachment and possessing God.

I was once asked: 'Some people like to withdraw from company and prefer always to be alone. That is where they find peace, when they enter a church. Is this the best thing?' My answer was 'No!', and this is the reason why.

That person who is in the right state of mind, is so regardless of where they are and who they are with, while those who are in the wrong state of mind will find this to be the case wherever they are and whoever they are with. Those who are rightly disposed truly have God with them. And whoever truly possesses God in the right way, possesses him in all places: on the street, in any company, as well as in a church or a remote place or in their cell. No one can obstruct such a person, if only they possess God in the right way, and possess him alone. Why is this so?

This is the case because they possess God alone, intend God alone, and all things become God for them. Such a person bears God with them in all that they do and wherever they go, and it is God who acts through them. For a deed belongs more truly to whoever is its cause than to whoever carries it out. And so if we truly intend God alone, then he must be the one who acts in what we do and nothing, neither the crowd nor any place, can stand in his way. No one can obstruct this person, for they intend and seek nothing but God and take their pleasure only in him, who is united with them in all their aims. And so, just as no multiplicity can divide God, in the same way nothing can scatter this person or divide them, for they are one in the One in whom all multiplicity is one and is non-multiplicity.

We should grasp God in all things and should train ourselves to keep God always present in our mind, in our striving and in our love. Take note of how you are inwardly turned to God when in church or in your cell, and maintain this same attitude of mind, preserving it when you go among the crowd, into restlessness and diversity. And, as I have often said, when we speak of sameness, we do not mean that we should regard all works as being the same, or all places and people. That would be wrong, for it is better to pray than to spin and a church is a worthier place than the street. But you should maintain the same attitude of mind in whatever you do, the same trust and love for your God and the same seriousness of intent. Truly, if your attitude were always the same, then no one could prevent you from enjoying the presence of God.

But whoever does not truly have God within themselves, but must constantly receive him in one external thing after another, seeking God in diverse ways, whether by particular works, people or places, such a person does not possess God. The least thing can impede them, for they do not *have* God and do not seek, love and intend him alone. It is not only bad company but also good company that can obstruct them, not only the street but also the church, not only evil words and deeds but also good words and deeds, for the obstruction lies within themselves, since in them God has not become all things. If this were the case, they would be at peace in all places and with all people, for they would possess God, and then no one would be able to take him away from them nor impede them in his work.

But where is this true possession of God, whereby we really possess him, to be found? This real possession of God is to be found in the heart, in an inner motion of the spirit towards him and striving for him, and not just in thinking about him always and in the same way. For that would be beyond the capacity of our nature and would be very difficult to achieve and would not even be the best thing to do. We should not content ourselves with a God of thoughts for, when the thoughts come to an end, so too shall God. Rather, we should have a living God who is beyond the thoughts of all people and all creatures. That kind of God will not leave us, unless we ourselves choose to turn away from him.

Whoever possesses God in their being, has him in a divine manner, and he shines out to them in all things; for them all things taste of God and in all things it is God's image that they see. God is always radiant in them; they are inwardly detached from the world and are in-formed by the loving presence of their God. It is the same as when someone has a great thirst and, although they may be doing something other than drinking and their minds may be turned to other things, the thought of a drink will not leave them for as long as they thirst, whatever they do, whoever they are with, whatever they strive for, whatever their works or thoughts; and the greater their thirst, the greater, the more intense, immediate and persistent the thought of a drink becomes. Or if someone loves something passionately with all their might, so that nothing else pleases them or touches their heart, and they desire that alone and nothing else, then certainly whoever it may be, or whoever they may be with, whatever they are doing or are setting out to do, the object of their love will never be extinguished in them, but they will find its image in all things, and the greater their love becomes, the more present to them it will be. Such a person does not seek peace, for it is already theirs.

This person is far more praiseworthy in God's eyes because they grasp all things in a divine way and make of them something more than they are in themselves. Truly, this demands hard work and great dedication and a clear perception of our inner life and an alert, true, thoughtful and authentic knowledge of what the mind is turned towards in the midst of people and things. This cannot be learned by taking flight, that is by fleeing from things and physically withdrawing to a place of solitude,[6] but rather we must learn to maintain an inner solitude regardless of where we are or who we are with. We must learn to break through things and to grasp God in them, allowing him to take form in us powerfully and essentially. It is the same as when someone wants to learn to write; if they wish to acquire this skill, then they must practise hard and often, however difficult it may seem, even to the point of impossibility. If they do that, they will master the art of writing, although of course they will at first have to concentrate on every letter and commit it to memory. But then, when they have acquired this skill, they will no longer have any need for the image or the concentration, but will write freely and spontaneously. The same is true of learning to play the violin or anything else which is based on the acquisition of a skill. All that is necessary is that someone should desire to perform their art, and then, whether they are concentrating upon it or not, they are able to perform on the basis of the skill which they have acquired.

Thus we should be permeated with the sense of a divine presence and be in-formed with the form of our beloved God and be so established in him that we see his presence effortlessly and, more than this, remain unencumbered by anything, free of all things. But this will initially demand of us much application and concentration, as any art does of one who will learn it.

7

How we should perform our works in the most rational way.

There are many people (and we can ourselves easily be among them, if we wish) who are not impeded by those things with which they come into contact and in whom such things do not create a permanent image; for creatures can neither have nor find a resting place in a heart which is filled with God. But we should not rest content with this: we should also derive great profit from all things, whatever they may be, wherever we may be, whatever we see or hear and however alien and strange to us they are. It is then, and only then, that we are in the right state of mind. And no one can ever come to the end of this process, but rather we should grow in it without end and come to achieve ever more.

We should make good use of our reason in all our works and

in all things and have a clear understanding of ourselves and our inner nature, grasping God in all things and in the highest possible manner. For we should be as our Lord told us: 'You should be like those who at all times watch and wait for their Lord' (Luke 12:36). Truly, such vigilant people are alert and on the watch for their Lord for whom they wait; they look to see if he is not by chance concealed in what befalls them, however strange it may be to them. So we too should consciously look out for our Lord in all things. This demands much effort, and must cost us all that our senses and faculties are capable of. But this is the right thing for us to do, so that we grasp God in the same way in all things and find him equally everywhere.

Works are different in kind, but whatever is done in the same spirit will be of equal value. For those who are in the right frame of mind, and for whom God has become their own, God will truly shine out just as clearly from their worldly acts as he does from their most sacred ones. But of course this is not to be understood as meaning that we should do things which are either worldly or wrong, but rather that we should offer to God whatever we see or hear of things in the world. Only those for whom God is present in all things and who make the very best use of their reason, know what true peace is and truly possess heaven.

For those who want to achieve this, one of two things must always happen: either they must learn to grasp and to hold God in what they do, or they must stop doing things altogether. But since we cannot abandon all activity in this life, which is part of being human and which takes so many different forms, we must learn to possess God in all things, while remaining free in all that we do and wherever we are. Thus, if the beginner is to achieve something in company, then he or she must first enlist God's help, fixing him firmly in their hearts and uniting all their intentions, thoughts, desires and faculties with him so that nothing else can take form in them.

8

On constant effort in spiritual progress.

No one should ever judge what they do so positively or as having been done so well that they become so casual or self-confident in their actions that their reason grows lazy or slumbers. But they should always elevate themselves with the twin faculties of reason and will, thus activating the very best in themselves and protecting themselves against all harm by means of understanding in matters both internal and external. Thus they will not fail in anything anywhere but will make constant spiritual progress.

9

How the temptation to sin always aids our progress.

You should know that the impulse to sin always brings great benefit for someone who is righteous. Now listen to this. Imagine two individuals, one of whom is the type of person who experiences little or no temptation while the other is the type who is much troubled by temptation. The mere presence of certain things rouses their outer self so that they are moved to anger, to vanity or to sensuality, according to the nature of the stimulus. But with their higher powers they remain steadfast and unmoved, and determined not to give in to their weakness, whether it be losing their temper or any other sin, and they strongly resist it. Perhaps it is a question of a weakness which is rooted in their own nature, just as certain people are irascible or vain or whatever but do not wish to commit the sin. These are far worthier of praise and deserving of a far greater reward, and are far nobler than the first type, for the perfection of virtue is born in struggle, as St Paul says: 'virtue is perfected in weakness' (2 Cor. 12:9).

It is not being tempted to sin which is sinful, but consenting to sin; it is wanting to lose your temper which is sinful. In fact, if someone who is in the right state of mind had the power to make the temptation to sin go away, then they would not exercise that power, for without temptation we would be untried in all things and in all that we do, unaware of the dangers of things, and without the honour of battle, victory and reward. The assault and stimulation of vice bring virtue and our struggle's reward. Temptation makes us work harder in the practice of virtue, and it drives us forcefully into the arms of virtue and is a sharp lash which teaches us vigilance and virtue; for the weaker someone is, the more they should arm themselves with strength and victory, since virtue, like vice, is a matter of the will.

10

How the will can do all things and how all the virtues reside in the will, if only it is righteous.

Nothing should terrify us as long as we will the good, nor should we be depressed if we cannot fulfil our will in what we do. And in that case we should not regard ourselves as being far from the virtues, for virtue and all that is good reside in a good will. You can lack nothing, neither love nor humility nor any other virtue, if only your will is good and true. But rather, what you desire with the whole of your will, that is your possession, and neither God nor any creature can take it from you, as long as your will is undivided and is a truly godly will which is fixed in the present moment. Do not say then: 'I should like to do it later', which would refer to the future, but rather 'I wish it to be so now.' Note this: when I want something even if it is a thousand miles away, then it is more truly mine than something in my lap which I do not want to have.

Good is no less powerful a force for good than evil is for evil. Take note: even if I were never actually to perform an evil act, but still willed what is evil, then sin would be as much in me as if I had carried out the deed. With a will concentrated upon evil I could commit as great a sin as if I killed everyone in the world, without ever killing anybody. Why should this not be true also of a good will – incomparably more so, in fact?

Truly, with the will I can do all things. I can share the sorrows of all men and women, feed all the poor, perform everyone's actions, and whatever else you can think of. If you do not lack the will to do something, but only the capacity to carry it out, then truly in God's eyes you have done it, and no one can take it away from you or obstruct you even for a moment; for wanting to do something as soon as you can and actually doing it are the same thing in God's eyes. Moreover, if I wanted to possess as much will as the whole world has, and if I desired this perfectly and wholeheartedly, then I would indeed possess it; for what I desire is already mine. Similarly, if I truly wanted as much love as everyone in the world has ever possessed, and if I wanted to praise God as much as everyone has ever praised him, or if I wanted whatever else you can think of, then you would truly possess it, as long as your will is perfect.

But now you might ask: 'When is the will a right will?' The will is perfect and right when it has no selfhood[7] and when it has gone out of itself, having been taken up and transformed into the will of God. Truly, the more this is so, the more the will is right and true. And with such a will you can achieve all things, whether this be love or whatever you wish.

Now I hear you ask: 'How can I have this love so long as I neither feel it nor am aware of it as that which I observe in many people who perform great works and in whom there is great devotion and marvellous things which I do not have?'

There are two things which you must consider here: the first is the essence of love, and the second is the work, or outflow of love. Love resides essentially in the will alone, so that whoever has more will, has more of love. But no one knows who has the more, for it is hidden in the soul, for as long as God is hidden in the soul. This love resides entirely in the will, and whoever has more will, has more of love.

But there is a something else, which is the outflow and work of love. This is easily visible as inwardness and devotion and celebration, although it is not always the best thing, for it comes sometimes not from love but from nature that some people experience such sweetness and delight, or it might result from heaven's influence[8] or be conveyed by the senses. And those who experience this more frequently are not always the best people, for, even if it comes from God, our Lord grants it to such people as an enticement and way of leading them on as well as a way of keeping them apart from other people. But as such people grow in love, it may well be that they have less sense and awareness of it, and then it can be seen whether they truly have love by the extent to which they remain wholly faithful to God without feelings of this kind.

Assuming that it is fully and wholly love, then still it is not the best thing, which follows from the fact that you must sometimes leave your state of exaltation for the sake of something better out of love[9] and sometimes to perform an act of love where this is needed, either spiritually or physically. As I have already said: even if you are in such ecstasy as St Paul was, and knew of a sick person who asked for a bowl of soup from you, then I would consider it far better for you to leave your ecstasy for the sake of love and to administer to the needy person in a love that is greater.

Nor should we suppose that we are thus losing out on grace, for what we give up willingly for the sake of love will be given back to us more gloriously, as Christ said: 'Whoever leaves anything for my sake will receive again a hundredfold in return' (Matt. 19:29). Truly, whatever we give up and deny ourselves for God's sake – even if we willingly give up for God's sake the consolations and inwardness which we have greatly desired and sought and which God has not granted us – we will truly find again in God just as if we had all the good things in our possession that there have ever been and, having chosen to give them up for God's sake, received them back in a hundredfold. For whenever we give up what we desire for God's sake, be it something physical or spiritual, we will find it again in God just as if we had actually possessed it and had given it up for God; for we should suffer the loss of all things for God's sake and deprive ourselves of all consolation in love for the sake of love.

Paul, who is full of love, teaches us that we should sometimes abandon such feelings for the sake of love when he says: 'I have wished to be separated from the love of Christ for love of my brothers' (Rom. 9:3). He does not mean here love in its first sense, from which he did not wish to be separated even for a moment for the sake of anything in heaven or on earth, but rather the consolation of love.

You should know that the friends of God are never without consolation, for their greatest consolation is what God wills for them, whether it be for their comfort or not.

II

What we should do when God hides himself and we cannot find him.

You should know too that a good will cannot fail to find God, although the mind sometimes feels that it misses him and often believes that he has departed. What should you do then? Do exactly the same as you would if you were experiencing the greatest consolation: learn to do the same in the greatest suffering, and behave in exactly the same way as you did then. There is no better advice on how to find God than to seek him where we left him: do now, when you cannot find God, what you did when last you had him, and then you will find him again. But a good will can never lose God or fail to find him. Many people say that their will is good when they do not have God's will but wish to have their own will and to instruct our Lord to do this or that. But that is not a good will. We should seek from God what his most precious will is. And it is God's wish in all things that we should give up our own will. Although St Paul spoke at length with our Lord and our Lord with him, this availed him nothing until he gave up his own will and said: 'Lord, what is it that you wish me to do?' (Acts 9:6). And our Lord well knew what it was that he should do. It was the same when the angel appeared to our Lady: nothing which they said to one another could have made her the mother of God, but as soon as she gave up her will, she immediately became a true mother of the Eternal Word and conceived God straight away; he became her natural son. And nothing makes us true so much as the giving up of our will. Truly, without giving up our will in all things, we can achieve nothing at all for God. Indeed, if we went so far as to give up the whole of our will, daring to abandon all things for God's sake, both inner and outer, then we would have accomplished everything, and not before.

There are not many people who – whether they know it or not – do not wish to be in this state of mind and to experience great things on account of it, desiring both the method and the good that it brings; and yet all this too is nothing but self-will. You should give your all to God, and then worry no more about what he may do with what is his. There are thousands of people who have died and are now in heaven, who never renounced their will to perfection. A perfect and true will can only exist when we have been entirely taken up into God's will and no longer have our own will; whoever does this the more, the more and the more truly they are rooted in God. Indeed, a single Ave Maria spoken in this spirit, when we have stripped ourselves of ourselves, is worth more than the repetition of a thousand psalters without it. In fact, a single step would be better with it than to cross the sea without it.

If someone were to go entirely out of themselves with all that is theirs, then truly they would be so rooted in God that if anyone were to touch them, they would first have to touch God. They would be so entirely in God, and God would surround them as my hood surrounds my head, so that if anyone wants to touch me they must first touch my clothing. Or similarly, if I want to drink something, then it must first pass over my tongue, which is where the drink acquires its taste. Now if my tongue is coated with bitterness, then however sweet the wine may be in itself, it must always be made bitter by that through which it must pass in order to come to me. Truly, if someone were to go out of what is theirs entirely, then they would be so enfolded in God that no creature could touch them without touching God first, and whatever came to them, would first have to pass through God on the way to them and would thus take on the taste and colour of God. However great your suffering may be, if it first passes through God, then he must first endure it. Indeed, in the truth which God is, no suffering which befalls us is so minor, whether it be a kind of discomfort or inconvenience, that it does not touch God infinitely more than ourselves and does not *happen* to him more than to us in so far as we place it in God. But if God endures it for the sake of the benefit for you which he has foreseen in it, and if you are willing to suffer what he suffers and what passes through him to you, then it takes on the colour of God, and shame becomes honour, bitterness is sweetness and the deepest darkness becomes the clearest light. Then everything takes its flavour from God and becomes divine, for everything conforms itself to God, whatever befalls us, if we intend only him and nothing else is pleasing to us. Thus we shall grasp God in all bitterness as well as in the greatest sweetness.

The light shines in the darkness, and then we become aware of it. But what good is the teaching or the light for people unless they use it? It is when they are in darkness or suffering that they will see the light.

Indeed, the more we are our own possession, the less we are God's possession.[10] If someone has gone out of what is theirs, then they can never fail to find God in all that they do. But if such a person were to make a slip or speak out of turn, or unjust things were to happen to them, then, if it was God who was the origin of the deed, it is he who would have to take the hurt upon himself; although in no way should you let up in your efforts. We find an example of this in St Bernard and many other saints. In this life we can never be entirely free of such assaults. But just because tares sometimes grow among the corn is no reason to throw away the good corn. Truly, whoever is in the right state of mind and knows God's ways, all such suffering and assaults will prove to be for their profit, since for the good all things work to the good, as St Paul (Rom. 8:28) and St Augustine say: 'Yes, even sins.'[11]

12

Concerning sin and our proper attitude when we find ourselves in sin.

Truly, to have committed a sin is not sinful if we regret what we have done. Indeed, not for anything in time or eternity should we *want* to commit a sin, neither of a mortal, venial or any other kind. Whoever knows the ways of God should always be mindful of the fact that God, who is faithful and loving, has led us from a sinful life into a godly one, thus making friends of us who were previously enemies, which is a greater achievement even than making a new earth. This is one of the chief reasons why we should be wholly established in God, and it is astonishing how much this inflames us with so great and so strong a love that we strip ourselves entirely of ourselves.

Indeed, if you are rightly placed in the will of God, then you should not wish that the sin into which you fell had not happened. Of course, this is not the case because sin was something against God but, precisely because it was something against God, you were bound by it to greater love, you were humbled and brought low. And you should trust God that he would not have allowed it to happen unless he intended it to be for your profit. But when we raise ourselves out of sin and turn away from it, then God in his faithfulness acts as if we had never fallen into sin at all and he does not punish us for our sins for a single moment, even if they are as great as the sum of all the sins that have ever been committed. God will not make us suffer on their account, but he can enjoy with us all the intimacy that he ever had with a creature. If he finds that we are now ready, then he does not consider what we were before. God is a God of the present. He takes you and receives you as he finds you now, not as you have been, but as you are now. God willingly endures all the harm and shame which all our sins have ever inflicted upon him, as he has already done for many years, in order that we should come to a deep knowledge of his love and in order that our love and our gratitude should increase and our zeal grow more intense, which often happens when we have repented of our sins.

Therefore God willingly tolerates the hurtfulness of sin and has often done so in the past, most frequently allowing it to come upon those whom he has chosen to raise up to greatness. Now listen! Was there ever anyone dearer to or more intimate with our Lord than the apostles? And yet not one of them escaped mortal sin. They all committed mortal sin. He showed this time and again in the Old and New Testament in those individuals who were to become the closest to him by far; and even today we rarely find that people achieve great things without first going astray. And thus our Lord intends to teach us of his great mercy, urging us to great and true humility and devotion. For, when repentance is renewed, then love too is renewed and grows strong.

13

On the two kinds of repentance.

There are two kinds of repentance, one which belongs to time and the senses and another which is supernatural and of God. The temporal kind always draws us downwards into yet greater suffering, plunging us into such distress that it is as if we were already in a state of despair. And so repentance can find no way out of suffering. Nothing comes of this.

But the repentance which is of God is very different. As soon as we become ill at ease, we immediately reach up to God and vow with an unshakeable will to turn away from all sin for ever. Thus we raise ourselves up to a great trust in God and gain a great sense of certainty. This brings a spiritual joy that lifts the soul out of her suffering and distress and binds her to God. For the more inadequate and guilty we perceive ourselves to be, the more reason we have to bind ourselves to God with an undivided love, who knows neither sin nor inadequacy. And so if we wish to approach God in complete devotion, the best path that we can follow is to be without sin in the power of that kind of repentance which comes from God.

And the greater we feel our sin to be, the more prepared God is to forgive our sin, to enter into the soul and drive sin away. Everyone is keenest to rid themselves of what is most hateful to them, and so the greater and graver our sins, the more God is immeasurably willing and quick to forgive them, since they are hateful to him. And when the repentance which comes from God rises up to him, all our sins vanish more quickly in the abyss of God than the eye can blink, and are eradicated so totally that it is as if they had never existed, provided only that we have perfect contrition.

14

On true confidence and on hope.

We should be able to recognize true and perfect love by whether or not someone has great hope and confidence in God, for there is nothing that testifies more clearly to perfect love than trust. Wholehearted love for another creates trust in them, and we will truly find in God everything that we dare hope for in him, and a thousand times more. Just as we can never love God too much, neither can we have too much trust in him. Nothing we may do can ever be so appropriate as fully trusting in God. He has never ceased to work great things through those who have great trust in him, and he has clearly shown in all such people that their trust is born of love, for love possesses not only trust but also true knowledge and unshakeable certainty.

15

On the two kinds of certainty of eternal life.

In this life there are two kinds of certainty concerning the life which is eternal: the one consists in those occasions when God tells us of it either himself or through an angel or special revelation, although this happens rarely and only to a few. The other kind of knowledge is better and more beneficial and falls frequently to those whose love is perfect. This happens to those whose love for and intimacy with their God is so great that they trust him completely and are so sure of him that they can no longer have any doubts, their certainty being founded on their love for him in all creatures without distinction. And if all creatures were to reject and abjure him, even if God himself were to do so, then they would not cease to trust, for love is not capable of mistrust but can only trust all that is good. And there is no need for anything to be said to either the lover or the beloved, for as soon as God senses that this person is his friend, he immediately knows all that is good for them and that belongs to their well-being. For however devoted you are to him, you may be sure that he is immeasurably more devoted to you and has incomparably more faith in you. For he is faithfulness itself – of this we can be certain as those who love him are certain.

This type of certainty is far greater, more perfect and true than the other and it cannot deceive us, while the first kind can be deceptive and can easily be an illusion. Indeed, the second type is experienced in all the faculties of our soul and cannot deceive those who truly love God; indeed they no more doubt it than they doubt God himself, for love drives out all fear. 'Love knows no fear' as St John[12] (1 John 4:18) says, and it is also written: 'Love covers a multitude of sins' (1 Peter 4:8). For where there is sin, there can be neither complete trust nor love, since love completely covers over sins and knows nothing of them. Not in such a way as if we had not sinned, but rather it wipes them away and drives them out, as if they had never existed. For all God's works are so utterly perfect and overflowing that whoever he forgives, he forgives totally and absolutely, preferring to forgive big sins rather than little ones, all of which creates perfect trust. I hold this kind of knowledge to be incomparably better, more rewarding and more authentic than the other, since neither sin nor anything else can obstruct it. For when God finds people in the same degree of love, then he judges them in the same way, regardless of whether they have sinned greatly or not at all. But those to whom more is forgiven, should have a greater love, as our Lord Jesus Christ said: 'They to whom more is forgiven must love more' (Luke 7:47).

16

On true penance and the holy life.

Many people think that they are achieving great things in external works such as fasting, going barefoot and other such practices which are called penances. But true penance, and the best kind of penance, is that whereby we can improve ourselves greatly and in the highest measure, and this consists in turning entirely away from all that is not God or of God in ourselves and in all creatures, and in turning fully and completely towards our beloved God in an unshakeable love so that our devotion and desire for him become great. In whatever kind of good work you possess this the more, the more righteous you are, and the more there is of this, the truer the penance and the more it expunges sin and all its punishment. Indeed, in a short space of time you could turn so firmly away from all sin with such revulsion, turning just as firmly to God, that had you committed all the sins since Adam and all those which are still to be, you would be forgiven each and every one together with their punishment and, were you then to die, you would be brought before the face of God.

This is true penance, and it is based especially and consummately on the precious suffering in the perfect penance of our Lord Jesus

Christ. The more we share[13] in this, the more all sin falls away from us, together with the punishment for sin. In all that we do and at all times we should accustom ourselves to sharing in the life and work of our Lord Jesus Christ, in all that he did and chose not to do, in all that he suffered and experienced, and we should be always mindful of him as he was of us.

This form of penance is a mind raised above all things into God, and you should freely practise those kinds of works in which you find that you can and do possess this the most. If any external work hampers you in this, whether it be fasting, keeping vigil, reading or whatever else, you should freely let it go without worrying that you might thereby be neglecting your penance. For God does not notice the nature of the works but only the love, the devotion and the spirit which is in them. For he is not so much concerned with our works as with the spirit with which we perform them all and that we should love him in all things. They for whom God is not enough are greedy. The reward for all your works should be that they are known to God and that you seek God in them. Let this always be enough for you. The more purely and simply you seek him, the more effectively all your works will atone for your sins.

You could also call to mind the fact that God was a universal redeemer of the world, and that I owe him far greater thanks therefore than if he had redeemed me alone. And so you too should be the universal redeemer of all that you have spoiled in yourself through sin, and you should commend yourself altogether to him with all that you have done, for you have spoiled through sin all that is yours: heart, senses, body, soul, faculties, and whatever else there is in you and about you. All is sick and spoiled. Flee to him then in whom there is no fault but rather all goodness, so that he may be a universal redeemer for all the corruption both of your life within and your life in the world.

17

*How we should remain at peace when not confronted with
the outward oppression which Christ and many of the
saints endured, and how we should follow God.*

Many people are daunted and troubled by the toughness and
severity of our Lord Jesus Christ's life and that of his saints, as
they are by the fact that they lack the strength to emulate them
and are not called upon to do so. Seeing themselves as unequal to
the task, many thus regard themselves as being far from God,
whom they are not strong enough to follow. But no one should
think this! We should in no way regard ourselves as being far
from God, neither on account of our weakness or our failings or
anything else. And if your great sins have ever driven you so far
from him that you regard yourself as not being close to God,
then you should still regard God as being close to you. It can be
very destructive if we regard God as being distant from us since,
whether we are far from or near to him, he is never far from us
and is always close at hand. If he cannot remain within, then he
goes no further than the door.

The same applies to the discipline of following God. Note the
form which your discipleship takes. You should observe, and
have observed, in which direction God urges you most of all to
go, for, as St Paul says, not all people are called to follow the
same path to God. If you find then that the shortest way for you
does not lie in many outward works, great endurance and priva-
tion (which things are in any case of little importance unless we
are particularly called to them by God or unless we have
sufficient strength to perform them without disrupting our inner
life), if you do not find these things right for you, then be at
peace and have little to do with them.

But then you might say: if they are not important, why

did our forebears, including many saints, do these things?

Consider this: if our Lord gave them this particular kind of devotional practice, then he also gave them the strength to carry it through, and it was this which pleased him and which was their greatest achievement. For God has not linked our salvation with any particular kind of devotion. Any one devotional practice has things which others lack, but the effectiveness of all good practices comes from God alone and is denied to none of them, for one form of goodness cannot conflict with another. Therefore people should remember that if they see or hear of a good person who is following a way which is different from theirs, then they are wrong to think that such a person's efforts are all in vain. If someone else's way of devotion does not please them, then they are ignoring the goodness in it as well as that person's good intention. This is wrong. We should see the true feeling in people's devotional practices and should not scorn the particular way that anyone follows. Not everyone can follow the same way, nor can all people follow only one way, nor can we follow all the different ways or everyone else's way.[14]

Everyone should maintain their own good devotional practice, embracing in it all other ways and thus grasping in their own way all goodness and all ways. Changing a devotional practice unsettles both the mind and the practice. The benefits that one way gives you are present also in others, if they are good and praiseworthy and are performed for God alone; it is not possible for everyone to follow the same way. It is the same with following the severe life-style of such saints. You should love their way and find it appealing, even though you do not have to follow their example.

Now you might say: 'Our Lord Jesus Christ always had the highest way. We should always follow him by rights.'

This is true. We should indeed follow our Lord, but not in all ways. Our Lord fasted for forty days, but no one should attempt to imitate him in this. Christ performed many works, whereby he intended that we should follow him in the spiritual rather than physical sense. Thus we should strive to follow him spiritually, for our love was more important to him than our works. We should follow him always in our own way.

But how?

Take note of this: in all things.

How and in what way?

As I have often said: I regard a work of the spirit as being far better than a work of the body.

Why?

Christ fasted for forty days. You should follow him in this by considering what you are most inclined or ready to do, and then you should give yourself up in that, while observing yourself closely. It is often better for you to go freely without that than to deny yourself all food. And sometimes it is more difficult for you to refrain from uttering one word than it is to refrain from speaking altogether. Sometimes it is more difficult for us to endure a single word of insult, which is insignificant in itself, than a heavy blow for which we have prepared ourselves, and it is far more difficult to be solitary in a crowd than it is in a desert, and it is often more difficult to give up a small thing than a big one, or to perform a small work rather than one which we regard as major. Thus we can easily follow our Lord in our weakness, and we neither can nor should believe ourselves to be distant from him.

18

How we can appropriately enjoy good food, fine clothes and cheerful company as these come our way in the natural course of things.

You should not worry yourself about food or clothing, feeling that these things are too good for you, but train your mind and the ground of your being to be above them. Nothing should rouse your mind to love and delight but God alone. It should be above all other things.

Why?

It would be a sickly form of inwardness which needed to be put right by external clothing; rather, as long as it is under your control, what is inside should correct what is outside. And if the latter comes to you in a different form, then you should accept it as being good from the ground of your being, but in such a way that you would accept it just as willingly if it were different again. It is just the same with the food, the friends and relatives and with everything that God may give you or take from you.

And so in my view the most important thing of all is that we should give ourselves up entirely to God whenever he allows anything to befall us, whether insult, tribulation or any other kind of suffering, accepting it with joy and gratitude and allowing God to guide us all the more rather than seeking these things out ourselves. Willingly learn all things from God therefore and follow him, and all will be well with you. Then we will be able to accept honour and comfort, and if dishonour and discomfort were to be our lot, we could and would be just as willing to endure these too. So they can justifiably feast who would just as willingly fast.[15]

And that must also be the reason why God relieves his friends of both major and minor suffering, which otherwise his infinite faithfulness could not allow him to do, for there is so much and such great benefit in suffering and he neither wishes nor ought to deny his own anything which is good. But he is content with a good and upright will, or else he would spare them no suffering on account of the inexpressible benefit which it contains.

As long as God is content, you too should be content, and

when it is something else in you which pleases him, then you should still be content. For we should be so totally God's possession inwardly with the whole of our will that we should not be unduly concerned about either devotional practices or works. And in particular you should avoid all particularity, whether in the form of clothes, food or words – as in making grand speeches, or particularity of gesture, since these things serve no useful purpose at all. But you should also know that not every form of particularity is forbidden to you. There is much that is particular which we must sometimes do and with many people, for whoever is a particular person must also express particularity on many occasions and in many ways.

We should have grown into our Lord Jesus Christ inwardly and in all things so that all his works are reflected in us together with his divine image. We should bear in ourselves all his works in a perfect likeness as far as we can. Though we are the agents of our actions, it is he who should take form in them. So act out of the whole of your devotion and your intent, training your mind in this at all times and teaching yourself to grow into him in all that you do.

19

Why God sometimes allows people who are genuinely good to be hindered in the good that they do.

God, who is faithful, allows his friends to fall frequently into weakness only in order to remove from them any prop on which they might lean. For a loving person it would be a great joy to be able to achieve many great feats, whether keeping vigils, fasting, performing other ascetical practices or doing major, difficult and unusual works. For them this is a great joy, support and source of hope so that their works become a prop and a support upon which they can lean. But it is precisely this which our Lord wishes to take from them so that he alone will be their help and support. This he does solely on account of his pure goodness and mercy, for God is prompted to act only by his goodness, and in no way do our works serve to make God give us anything or do anything for us. Our Lord wishes his friends to be freed from such an attitude, and thus he removes their support from them so that they must henceforth find their support only in him. For he desires to give them great gifts, solely on account of his goodness, and he shall be their comfort and support while they discover themselves to be and regard themselves as being a pure nothingness in all the great gifts of God. The more essentially and simply the mind rests on God and is sustained by him, the more deeply we are established in God and the more receptive we are to him in all his precious gifts – for human kind should build on God alone.

20

On frequently receiving our Lord's body, on the manner of our receiving it and the devotion we should feel.

Whoever wants to receive the body of our Lord does not need to scrutinize what they are feeling at the time or how great their piety or devotion is, but rather they should note the state of their will and attitude of mind. You should not place too much weight on your feelings but emphasize rather the object of your love and striving.

Whoever both wishes to and can approach the Lord freely should firstly have a conscience which is free of all the suffering of sin. Secondly, their will should be turned to God so that they intend nothing and desire nothing but him and all that is his and find the things which are unlike God distasteful. For it is this which tells us how far from God or how near to him we are, precisely whether this is our own attitude of mind to a greater or lesser degree. Thirdly, we should find that the love we have for the sacrament and for our Lord grows ever stronger and that the awe we feel is not diminished by frequent attendance. For often what is death for one person is life for another. Thus you should observe within yourself whether your love for God is growing as is your fear of him. Then the more often you attend the sacrament, the better you will become and the better and more valuable it will be for you. Do not let anyone tell you the contrary, in sermons or otherwise, for the more often you go, the better it is and the more pleasing to God. After all, our Lord desires to dwell in and with his people.

Now you might say: sir, I find that I am so empty and cold and worn out that I do not dare go to our Lord.

And I shall say: then all the greater is your need to go to your God, for he shall inflame you and make you burn with zeal and in him you shall be sanctified, joined and made one with him alone. For only in the sacrament and nowhere else shall you so truly find such grace that your bodily powers are so united and gathered together by the noble power of the physical presence of our Lord's body that your mind and all your scattered senses, which were previously separated from each other and were too inclined to tend downwards, are now united and gathered together and thus are raised up and properly offered to God.[16] Through the God who dwells within, the senses become attuned to inwardness and are weaned from the physical hindrances which result from temporal things. Strengthened by his body, your body too will be renewed. For we should be transformed into him and wholly united with him so that what is his becomes ours and all that is ours is his, our heart one heart with his and our body one body with his. Thus our senses and our will, our intentions, powers and members should be established in him so that we feel his presence in all the powers of our body and soul.

Now perhaps you will say: sir, I am aware of nothing great in myself but my own great poverty. How can I dare then to approach him?

Truly, if you wish to transform all your poverty, then go to the abundant treasure of wealth beyond measure, and you shall be made rich. For you should know within yourself that he alone is the treasure that can fill you and make you replete. 'Therefore,' you should say, 'I wish to come to you so that your wealth shall fill my poverty, your infinity shall fill my emptiness, and your immeasurable, incomprehensible Godhead shall fill my base and wretched humanity.'

'Sir, I have committed many sins and cannot atone for them.'

Go then to him, for he has worthily atoned for all guilt. In him you may offer the precious sacrifice to our heavenly Father for all your sins.

'Sir, I would like to praise him, but I cannot.'

Go then to him, for he alone is an acceptable offering of thanks to the Father and an infinite, true and perfect expression of praise for all his divine goodness.

In short, if you wish to shed all your defects, to be clothed with virtue and grace and to be led joyfully back to the source with all virtue and grace, then make sure that you can receive the sacrament worthily and frequently. Thus you shall be united with him and made noble through his body. Indeed, in the body of our Lord the soul is so united with God that none of the angels, neither Cherubim nor Seraphim, can distinguish or discover a difference between them; for where they touch God, they touch the soul and where they touch the soul, they touch God. There has never been such an absolute union, for the union of the soul with God is far closer than that of the body with the soul, which makes a person. And this union is far closer than when someone pours a drop of water into a barrel of wine: the latter would be water and wine, whereas the former are so united with each other that no creature can find a difference between them.

Now you could say: how can that be? This is certainly not my experience!

But does that matter? The less you feel and the more firmly you believe, the more laudable is your faith and should be esteemed and praised all the more, for perfect faith is far more than mere opinion in a person. In faith alone do we have true knowledge. In fact, true faith is all we need. That we should think one thing is far better for us than another derives from external criteria and is true neither of the one thing nor of the other. Thus whoever has equal faith, receives all things equally and possesses all things equally.[17]

Now you may say: how can I believe in higher things when I do not find myself in this attitude of mind but find that I am weak and inclined to many things?

See, there are two things about yourself which you must be aware of and which were also true of our Lord. He too had higher and lower faculties, and their respective functions were different. His higher faculties possessed and enjoyed eternal blessedness while at the same time his lower faculties found themselves in the greatest suffering and struggle on earth, and neither of these two interfered with the other. In you too the higher faculties should be raised to God, offered up to him and united with him. Indeed, we should assign all suffering wholly to the body, the lower faculties and the senses, whereas the spirit should rise up with all its power and immerse itself freely in its God. But the suffering of the senses and of the lower faculties do not affect the spirit, any more than these temptations do, for the greater and more fierce the struggle, the greater and more praiseworthy is the victory and the honour of victory. The greater the temptation and the more fierce the assault of vice which we are able to overcome, then the more virtue we have and the more pleasing it is to God. Therefore, if you wish to receive your God worthily, ask yourself whether your higher faculties are orientated to him and your will seeks out his will, what it is that you want from him, and whether you are being faithful to him.

We can never receive the precious body of our Lord in this state without receiving an exceptional degree of grace; and the more frequently we do so, the greater the benefit. Indeed, we can receive the body of our Lord with such devotion and so intently that if we were ordained to enter the lowest choir of angels, we would immediately be promoted to the next. In fact, we can receive it with such great devotion that we would be judged worthy of the eighth or ninth choir of angels. Therefore, if there were two people who had led identical lives, and if one of them had worthily received the body of our Lord one more time than the other, then that person would be like a radiant sun beside the other and would enjoy a special union with God.

This receiving and blessed savouring of the body of our Lord is not a matter of physical enjoyment alone but also of a spiritual savouring with a mind filled with desire and united with him through devotion. We can receive this so trustingly that we become richer in grace than anyone on earth. And this spiritual communion is something which we can do a thousand times a day, or more frequently still, wherever we may be and whether we are ill or in good health. But we should prepare ourselves for it as for the sacrament, by good and wise discipline and according to the strength of our desire. If we have no desire, then we should motivate ourselves, preparing ourselves for it and acting accordingly, and thus we will become holy in time and blessed in eternity; for to submit to God and to follow him, that is eternity. May the teacher of truth grant us this, who loves chastity and is himself life eternal.

21

On spiritual endeavour.

Whenever someone wishes to receive the body of our Lord, then they need not be afraid to draw near. It is fitting and of great advantage to make your confession beforehand, even if you are not suffering any pangs of conscience, for the sake of the benefits of the sacrament. If it is the case that we are guilty of something but cannot find the opportunity to go to confession, then we should turn to God and acknowledge our guilt in great repentance before him, being content with this until we are able to make our confession. If the consciousness or reproach of sin passes from us in the meantime, then we can consider that God too has forgotten it. We should make our confession to God rather than to men and, if we are guilty, we should take our confession before God very seriously and chastise ourselves soundly. Neither should we lightly turn from this and cast it aside on account of our external penances when we finally attend the sacrament, for it is only the attitude of mind we have in our works which is righteous and godly and good.

We must learn to be inwardly free in the works that we do. But for those who are unschooled in this, striving to achieve a state where they are unhindered by either crowds or works and where God is present to them and shines steadily upon them without concealment at all times and in all company, is an unfamiliar task and is something which calls for much perseverance. This requires vigorous commitment and two things in particular. The first is that we should have sealed ourselves off internally so that our minds are protected from external images which thus remain outside and do not unfittingly associate with us or keep our company or find a place to lodge in us. The second is that neither in our inner images, whether these be representations of things or sublime thoughts, nor in external images or whatever is present to us, should we allow ourselves to be dissipated or fragmented or externalized through multiplicity. We should apply and train all our faculties to this end, maintaining our inwardness.

Now you could say: we must turn outside in order to perform external works, for works can be carried out only in their appropriate form.

This is certainly true. But the external character of their form is not external for someone who is practised in this since, for the inward person, all things possess an inward and divine manner of being.

And it is this which above all is necessary: that we should properly and completely train the mind in its orientation to God so that our interior being is made divine. Nothing is as proper, present or as close to the mind as God. It never turns in any other direction. It never turns towards creatures unless it suffers violence and injustice which damages and distorts it. When the intellect is corrupted in a young person, or in anyone at all, then it must be trained again with great effort, and we must apply all we have to restoring it and bringing it back. For however much it may enjoy a natural affinity with God, as soon as it is wrongly directed and becomes fixed on creatures, growing used to them and being filled with their images, then it becomes so weak in this part and so dispossessed of itself and hindered in its noble striving that we lack the strength, regardless of our best efforts, to win it back completely. And even if we give our all to this, we still need to maintain constant vigilance.

We must ensure above all that we school ourselves properly in this. If someone who is unpractised and untrained wished to behave as if they were not so, then they would cause damage to themselves and nothing would come of them. Once we have weaned ourselves from things and have distanced ourselves from them, we can begin to perform actions prudently, freely delighting in them or choosing not to do them. Further, if there is something which we like and enjoy and which we indulge in with the assent of our will, whether in what we eat or drink or whatever it may be, then this is something an unpractised person cannot do without being damaged in some way.

We must train ourselves not to seek or strive for our own interests in anything but rather to find and to grasp God in all things. For God does not give us anything in order that we should enjoy its possession and rest content with it, nor has he ever done so. All the gifts which he has ever granted us in heaven or on earth were made solely in order to be able to give us the *one* gift, which is himself.[18] With all other gifts he simply wants to prepare us for that gift which is himself. And all the works which God has ever performed in heaven or on earth served solely to perform the *one* work, that is to sanctify himself so that he can sanctify us. And so I tell you that we should learn to see God in all gifts and works, neither resting content with anything nor becoming attached to anything. For us there can be no attachment to a particular manner of behaviour in this life, nor has this ever been right, however successful we may have been. Above all, we should always concentrate upon the gifts of God, and always do so afresh.

I shall tell you briefly about someone who greatly desired something from our Lord, but I told her that she was not properly prepared and that, if God gave her the gift in this unprepared state, it would then be lost.

Now you may ask: in what way was she not properly prepared? Her will was righteous and you say that a righteous will is capable of all things, that it contains all things and all perfection.

That is true, but we must understand that the word 'will' means two things: the first is an accidental and insubstantial will while the other is a will that is decisive, creative and disciplined.

Indeed, it is not sufficient for us to have a detached attitude of mind at a specific point in time when we wish to bind God to ourselves, but rather we should have a practised detachment which exists both before and after. Only then can we receive great things from God and find him in them. But if we are unprepared, the gift will be spoiled and God with the gift. That is also why God cannot always give us what we ask for. This is not due to a deficiency on his part, for he is a thousand times more eager to give than we are to receive. But we do violence to him and wrong by obstructing him in his natural work through our unpreparedness.

We must learn to free ourselves of ourselves in all our gifts, not holding on to what is our own or seeking anything, either profit, pleasure, inwardness, sweetness, reward, heaven or our own will. God never gives himself, or ever has given himself, to a will that is alien to himself, but only to his own will. Where he finds his own will, he gives himself and enters in with all that he is. And the more we cease to be in our own will, the more truly we begin to be in God's will. Thus it is not enough for us to give ourselves up just once, together with all that we have and are capable of, but we must renew ourselves constantly, thus preserving our freedom and simplicity in all things.

It is also very beneficial for us if we do not content ourselves with maintaining virtues such as obedience, poverty and the rest in the mind alone, but ourselves practise the works and fruits of virtue, testing ourselves while wishing and desiring to be exercised and tested by other people too. It is not enough for us to perform the works of virtue, exercising obedience, accepting poverty or disgrace or practising humility or detachment in some other way; rather we should strive ceaselessly until we attain the essence and ground of virtue. And we can tell if we have attained this or not by asking whether we find ourselves inclined to virtue above all else and perform the works of virtue without prior preparation of the will, practising virtue without the ulterior motive even of a great and good cause, so that the virtuous act in fact happens spontaneously on account of love of virtue and without asking 'what for?'. Then and only then do we have the perfect possession of virtue.

We must train ourselves in self-abandonment until we retain nothing of our own. All turbulence and unrest comes from self-will, whether we realize it or not. We should establish ourselves, together with all that is ours and all that we might wish or desire in all things, in the best and most precious will of God through a pure ceasing-to-be of our will and desire.

A question: should we also voluntarily abandon the sweetness of God that we feel? Can this not also be the result of lukewarmness and a lack of love for him?

Yes, indeed, if we do not know the difference. For, whether it comes from lukewarmness or from true detachment or serenity, we must note whether, when we are inwardly so detached, we find ourselves in a state in which we are just as faithful to God as when we experience him most strongly, and that we do in this state all those things which we do in the other and no less so, and that we are as detached with regard to all consolation and all support as we are when we feel God's presence.[19]

22

On how we should follow God and on finding the right path.

Whoever wishes to begin a new life or work should turn to their God, desiring with all their strength and devotion that he should send them the best thing of all, that which is most precious to him and worthy, while they themselves desire and intend nothing of self but only the most precious will of God and that alone.

They should then accept what God sends them as being directly from him, holding it to be the very best thing of all, and they should be wholly content with it.

Even if an alternative spiritual way later appeals to them more, they should consider: God has given you this way and for him it is the best one of all. They should trust God in this, and should find all good paths in this one path, receiving all things in and according to it, whatever their nature. For the good that God has invested in one way is present in all others. We should make all good ways our own in the one way, and not be attached to the particular character of the way. For we should only ever do the one thing, since we cannot do all things. It must only ever be a single thing, and in that single thing we must make all things our own. For if we wished to do all things, this and that, abandoning our own path for that of another which seems to us for the moment to be a better one, then this would lead to great instability. Similarly, someone who leaves the world and enters a religious order once and for all, will attain perfection more swiftly than that person ever could who moves from one order to another, however holy they may have been. This comes from changing one way for another. We should make one way our own and stick with it, drawing into it all other good ways and regarding it as having been given by God. We should not start one thing today and another tomorrow without worrying that we might thus be missing something. For with God we can miss nothing. We can no more miss anything with God than God can. Accept the one way from God then, and draw all that is good into it.

But if it turns out that they are incompatible, that the one clashes with the other, then this is a sure sign that it is not from God. One form of the good cannot oppose another for, as our Lord said, 'A kingdom divided against itself will not stand' (Luke 11:17) and also, 'Whoever is not with me is against me, and he who does not gather up with me, scatters' (Luke 11:23). Let this be a sure sign for you then, that if one form of good opposes or destroys another, even if this be a lesser one, then it cannot come from God. It should not be destructive but constructive.

To state the matter briefly: there is no doubt that God, in his faithfulness, takes every individual at their best. This is certainly the case, and he never takes someone lying down whom he could take standing up, for the goodness of God looks for the very best in all things.

But why then, someone once asked me, does God not cause those people to die in childhood, before they reach the age of reason, who he knows will fall from the grace of their baptism, since he knows that they will fall and will not pick themselves up again? That would be the best thing for them.

I replied that God does not destroy anything that is good, but rather he perfects it. God does not destroy nature, but perfects it. Neither does grace destroy nature, but perfects it.[20] If God were to destroy nature thus in its very foundation, then this would be an act of violence and injustice against it, which he does not do. We have a free will with which we can choose either good or evil. God shows us that our evil-doing leads to death and the good which we do leads to life. We should be free and the master of our deeds, knowing neither hindrance nor compulsion. Grace does not destroy nature but perfects it. Glory does not destroy grace but perfects it, for glory is perfected grace. And so it is not in God to destroy anything which has being, but he perfects all things. And so we should destroy nothing that is good in ourselves however small, nor any minor spiritual practice on account of one that is greater, but we should bring them to the very summit of perfection.

This is what someone said who wanted to begin a new life afresh and I replied: we must become somebody who seeks and finds God in all things and at all times, in all places, in all company and in all ways. Then we shall always be able to grow and increase unceasingly and without end.

23

On inner and outer works.

Supposing someone wanted to withdraw into themselves with all their faculties, both inner and outer, and they were in this state in such a way that there were neither any images nor impulses in them and they were thus without any form of activity, either inner or outer, then they would have to note carefully whether there are not in them any spontaneous promptings to action. If nothing impels them to act and they do not wish to undertake anything, then they should energetically force themselves to act, whether internally or externally, for we should rest content with nothing, however good it may seem or be, so that, when we find ourselves under pressure or constraint, it will be apparent that we are more worked than working, and so that we may learn to enter into a relationship of cooperation with our God. It is not that we should abandon, neglect or deny our inner self, but we should learn to work precisely in it, with it and from it in such a way that interiority turns into effective action and effective action leads back to interiority and we become used to acting without any compulsion. For we should concentrate on this inner prompting, and act from it, whether through reading or praying or – if it is fitting – some form of external activity. Though if the external activity destroys the internal one, we should give priority to the latter. But if both are united as one, then that is best for cooperating with God.

The question now arises: how can we be said to cooperate when we have abandoned ourself and all our works and so all images and forms of activity, praise and thanksgiving or whatever else we may do, fall away? As St Denys says: they speak most beautifully of God who can maintain the deepest silence concerning him in the fullness of their inner wealth.[21]

The answer is that there is one work which is right and proper for us to do, and that is the eradication of self. But however great this eradication and reduction of self may be, it remains insufficient if God does not complete it in us. For our humility is only perfect when God humbles us through ourselves. Only then are they and the virtue perfected, and not before.

But how can God destroy somebody through themselves? Does it not seem as if this destruction of the person is at the same time their elevation by God, for the Gospel says: 'He that humbles himself shall be exalted' (Matt. 23:12)?

The answer to this question is both yes and no. That person must 'humble' themselves, which cannot happen adequately unless God does it. And they are to be 'exalted' but not in such a way as if being brought low were one thing and being raised on high another. Rather, the highest point of the elevation lies in the deep ground of humility. For the deeper and lower the ground, the higher and more immeasurable is the elevation and the height. The deeper the well, the higher it is, for the height and the depth are one. Thus whoever can humble themselves the more, the greater is their exaltation. This is why our Lord says: 'He who desires to be the greatest, let him be the least among you' (Mark 9:34). Whoever wishes to be the former must become the latter, for this being is found only in that becoming. Whoever becomes the least, is in truth the greatest, while whoever has become the least, is already the greatest one of all. And thus the word of the Gospel is fulfilled: 'whoever humbles themselves will be lifted up' (Matt. 23:12). For our entire being is founded purely on a process of becoming nothingness.

It is written: 'They have become rich in all virtues' (1 Cor. 1:5). Truly, this cannot happen unless they first become poor in all things. Whoever desires to be given everything, must first give everything away. This is a fair trade and an equal exchange, as I said some time ago. God wishes to give us himself and all things for our own free possession, and therefore he wishes to strip us completely of all that is ours. Indeed, God wills that we should possess no more than could lodge as a speck in the eye. For all the gifts which he ever gave us, those both of nature and of grace, were given with the sole intention that we should possess nothing of our own, and he has made no gift to his mother, or to any person or creature in any other way. In order to educate us and to warn us he often takes from us both physical and spiritual belongings, for the possession of honour should be his and not ours. Furthermore, we should keep all things only as if they had been merely lent and not given to us, without any sense of possessiveness, whether it be our body or soul, our senses, faculties, worldly goods or honour, friends, relations, house or home or anything whatsoever.

But what is God's intention in this, since he is so keen that it should be so? It is that he wishes to be our sole possession. This is what he wills and intends, and he strives for one thing only, that he can and may be this. Here lies his greatest bliss and delight. The more he can be this and the more completely, the greater is his bliss and joy, for the more we are in possession of other things, the less he is our possession. And the less love we have for all things, the more we possess him together with all that he can do for us. Therefore, when our Lord wished to speak of all the beatitudes, he put poverty of spirit at their head, and it came first in order to show that all blessedness and perfection have their beginning wholly in poverty of spirit. And indeed, if there were a single foundation upon which all goodness could be built, then it would have to include this.

In return for keeping ourselves detached from things which are outside us, God wishes to give us for our own possession all that is in heaven, even heaven itself together with all its powers, indeed with everything which ever flowed from it and which all angels and saints enjoy, so that all this may be ours too, far more than any *thing* has ever been ours. In return for stripping myself of myself for his sake, God will be wholly my own possession with all that he is and can do, as much mine as his, no more and no less. He will belong to me a thousand times more than anything ever belonged to anyone which they keep in their chest, or than he was ever his own possession. Nothing was ever my own as much as God will be mine, together with all that he is and all that he can do.[22]

We should earn this possession of God by not being in possession of ourselves here on earth or of all those things that are not him. The more perfect and naked this poverty, the greater this possession. We should not intend this reward or have it in mind, nor should we direct our gaze at a possible gain or gift, but we should be motivated solely by love of virtue. For the more detached we are in the possession of something, the more truly it is ours, as St Paul says: 'We should have as if we had nothing, and yet possess all things' (2 Cor. 6:10). They do not possess self who neither desire nor wish to have anything, either of themselves or of anything which is outside them, even of God or of anything at all.

Do you want to know what a truly poor person is? They are truly poor in spirit who can easily do without everything which is not strictly necessary. That is why the man who sat naked in his tub said to Alexander the Great, who ruled the whole world: 'I am a greater lord than you are, for I have spurned more than you have seized. What you think it is a great thing to possess, is too trivial for me to scorn.'[23] They who can go without all things, not needing them, are far more blessed than they who possess them in their need. That person is the best who can do without what they do not need. Therefore, whoever can do without and spurn the most, has given up the most. It seems a major event if someone gives away a thousand gold crowns for God, building many convents and monasteries with their money and feeding all the poor; and this is indeed a great thing. But whoever can spurn just as much for God's sake is even more blessed. Someone would possess heaven itself if they could renounce all the things for God's sake which God gives or does not give.

Now you say: yes, sir. But would I not obstruct this with my failings?

If you have failings, then ask God frequently in prayer if it may not be to his honour and pleasure to take them from you, for you can do nothing without his help. If he does so, then thank him, and if he does not, then bear them for his sake, though not as the failings of sin but as a great exercise in which you can earn a reward and practise patience. You should be content whether he grants you the gift or not.

He gives to each according to what is best for them and most suitable. If we are to make new clothes for someone, then we must make them according to their dimensions, and those which fit one will not fit another. We measure everyone to see what fits them. So too God gives everyone the best thing of all according to his knowledge of what is most suitable for them. Indeed, whoever trusts him entirely in this, receives and possesses in the least of things as much as they do in the greatest. If God wished to give me what he gave St Paul, then I would receive it gladly, if this were his will. But since he does not wish to give it to me, for he wills that only very few people should attain to such knowledge in this life as Paul, if he does not give it to me, then he is still as precious to me and I am just as grateful to him and I am just as content that he should withhold it from me as I am that he should give it to me. It satisfies me just as much, and is just as welcome, as if he had given it to me, as long as I am in a proper state of mind in other respects. Truly, this is how the will of God should be enough for me: in all things in which God wished to act or to give, his will should be so dear and precious to me that this is no less meaningful to me than if he had given me the gift and had acted in me. Then all God's gifts would be mine and all his works and, if all creatures were to do their best or their worst, they could not deprive me of this. How can I then complain if everyone's gifts are mine? In fact, I am so content with what God might do to me, give me or withhold from me that I would not pay a penny for the best possible life which *I* could conceive for myself.

Now you say: I am afraid that I do not apply myself enough to this and do not persist as I should.

This is properly the cause of regret. Bear it with patience. Regard it as an exercise, and be at peace. God is happy to endure scorn and discomfort and to go without service and praise so that those who intend him and belong to him have peace in themselves. Why then should we not have peace whatever he gives us or withholds from us? It is written, and our Lord tells us, that they are blessed who suffer for the sake of justice (Matt. 5:10). Indeed, if a thief who was on the point of being hanged and justly so on account of their crime, or if someone who had committed a murder was to be justifiably broken on the wheel, could find it in them to say to themselves, 'Look, you are going to suffer this for the sake of justice, for you are being justly punished', then they would be immediately blessed. Indeed, however unjust we may be, if we receive from God what he does or does not do for us as being justly given and suffer for the sake of justice, then we too will be blessed. So do not complain but complain rather that you do still complain and find no peace. Complain only of an excess of this. For whoever has the right attitude will receive as much in loss as they do in gain.

Now you say: But look, God works such great things in many people and they are transformed in their essence by the divine essence and it is not they but God who works this in them.

Then thank God for their sakes and if he grants it to you, accept it gladly. If he does not grant it to you, then you should willingly go without it. Intend only him and have no thought as to whether it is you or God who performs things in you, for this is what God must do if you intend him alone, whether he wishes to or not.

Do not be concerned either with the nature or the manner which God has given someone else. If I were good and holy enough to be elevated among the saints, then the people would discuss and question whether this was by grace or nature and would be troubled about it. But this would be wrong of them. Let God work in you, acknowledge that it is his work, and do not be concerned as to whether he achieves this by means of nature or beyond nature. Both nature and grace are his. What is it to you which means he best uses or what he performs in you or in someone else? He should work how and where and in what manner it suits him to do so.

A man wanted to channel a spring into his garden and said: 'As long as I get the water, I am not concerned with the type of channel used, whether it is of iron or wood or bone or rusty metal, provided I get the water.' Thus those people are quite wrong who worry as to how God performs his work in us, whether it is by nature or grace. Just let him act, and be at peace.

As far as you are in God, thus far you are in peace, and as far as you are outside God, thus far you are outside peace. If only something is in God, then it has peace. It is in peace in so far as it is in God. And you can tell how far you are in God, or not, by the extent to which you have peace or not. For where you lack peace, you must necessarily lack peace, since lack of peace comes from the creature and not from God. Nor is there anything to fear in God, for all that is in him can only be loved. Similarly there is nothing in him to cause us sadness.

They who have all that they want and desire, know joy. But no one has this except those whose will is one with God's will. May God grant us this union! Amen.

The Book of Divine Consolation

Benedictus deus et pater domini nostri Jesu Christi (2 Cor. 1:3f.)

The noble apostle Paul says this: 'Blessed be God and the Father of our Lord Jesus Christ, the Father of mercies and God of all consolation, who comforts us in our tribulation.' There are three kinds of tribulation which affect and oppress us in this place of exile. The first comes from damage to our worldly goods, the second from the harm which befalls our relatives and friends and the third comes from the injury we suffer when we become the object of others' disdain, when we experience hardship, physical pain and emotional distress.

Therefore it is my intention in this book to record certain precepts with which men and women can find consolation in all their distress, grief and suffering. And this book has three parts. In the first there are a number of truths from which it can be deduced what can and will give us appropriate and complete consolation in all our suffering. Following this, there are some thirty extracts and maxims in every one of which we can find complete consolation. Finally, the third part of this book contains examples of words and deeds which wise people have spoken and done in the face of suffering.

I

First of all we should know that a wise man and wisdom, a true man and truth, a just man and justice, a good man and goodness relate to one another in the following way. Goodness is neither created nor made nor begotten, but it is generative and gives birth to a good man. Thus a good man, in so far as he is good, is himself unmade and uncreated though he is still the child and son of goodness. Goodness reproduces itself and all that it is in a good man. It pours being, knowledge, love and activity into a good man, and a good man receives the whole of his being, knowledge, love and activity from the heart and core of goodness and from it alone. A good man and goodness are nothing but a single goodness, wholly one in all things, except for the giving birth on the one side and the being born on the other, while the giving birth of goodness and the being born in a good man are wholly one essence and one life.[1] A good man receives everything which belongs to him from the goodness in goodness. He is, lives and dwells there. It is there that he knows himself and knows all the things that he knows, and loves all the things that he loves, and acts with the goodness in goodness, and goodness performs all her works with and in him in accordance with Scripture, where the Son says: 'It is the Father who dwells in me doing his own work' (John 14:10), 'the Father works until now and I work' (John 5:17) and 'all that belongs to the Father is mine, and all that is mine and pertains to mine is the Father's: his in the giving and mine in the receiving' (John 17:10).

Further, we should know that, when we speak of the 'good', the name or the word signifies or includes nothing other, neither more nor less, than goodness, pure and simple, but goodness which overflows. When we say 'good', then we understand that its goodness is given to it, poured into it and born into it by the unbegotten goodness. Therefore the gospel says: 'As the Father has life in himself, so he has given to the Son to have the same life in himself' (John 5:26). He says 'in himself' and not 'of himself', for it is given to him by the Father.

Everything which I have just said concerning a good man and goodness is no less true of a true man and truth, a just man and justice, a wise man and wisdom, God the Son and God the Father, indeed of all that is born of God and has no father on earth, in which nothing created is born and in which there is no image but only God, naked and pure. For John in his gospel states, 'To all of them is given power and strength to become sons of God, who were not born of blood nor of the will of the flesh or of the will of man, but of God and from God alone' (John 1:12f.).

By 'blood' he means everything within us which is not subject to the will. By the 'will of the flesh' he means everything within us which, while being subject to the will, is so only with struggle and conflict, which inclines to the desires of the flesh and which properly belongs to both the soul and the body together and not to the soul alone, on account of which these lower powers of the soul grow old, tired and enfeebled. By the 'will of man' John means the highest powers of the soul, whose nature and activity is wholly independent of the flesh and which are located in the purity of the soul, detached from all time and space and from all those things which look to time and space or have any taste for them: that is, powers which have nothing in common with anything else at all, in which we are formed in the image of God and are members of God's race and family. And yet, since they are not God himself, being created in and with the soul, they must lose their own form and be transformed into God alone and be born into and out of God so that he will be their sole father, since they will thus also be the sons of God and God's only begotten son. For I am the son of all that forms me and gives birth to me as identical to itself according to and in itself. In so far as such a person, God's son, who is good as the son of goodness and is just as the son of justice, is the son solely of justice, to that extent justice is unbegotten-begetting, and the son to whom it gives birth has the same being as justice has and is, and possesses all the properties of justice and of truth.

It is all this teaching, which is written in the sacred scriptures and is known with certainty in the natural light of the rational soul, which gives us true consolation in all our suffering.

St Augustine says: 'There is nothing which is far or remote from God.'[2] If you wish that nothing should be far or remote from you, then join yourself to God, for then a thousand years will be like a single day. Thus I say that in God there is neither sadness, nor suffering, nor distress, and if you wish to be free of all distress and suffering, then turn to God and fix yourself on him alone. It is certain that all your suffering comes from the fact that you do not turn to God or not to him alone. If you were formed and born solely in justice, then truly nothing could cause you pain, any more than justice can cause God pain. Solomon says: 'The just will not grieve whatever may befall' (Prov. 12:21). He does not say: 'the just man' or 'the just angel' or this or that. He says: 'the just'. Whatever belongs to the just man or woman, whatever it is that constitutes his or her justice in particular and the fact that he or she is just, that is the son with an earthly father, and is a creature, both created and made, since its father is a creature, either created or made. But suffering and distress can no more affect 'the just' pure and simple than they can God, for it has no father, whether created or made, since God and justice are entirely one and justice alone is its father. Justice can cause no suffering to the just since all joy, delight and bliss are justice. Indeed, if justice were to cause the just pain, then it would be causing itself pain. Nothing which is dissimilar to itself or unjust, which is created or made, can cause the just pain, for all that is created is as far beneath them as it is beneath God, and it cannot affect or influence the just nor reproduce itself in those whose father is God alone.[3] Thus we should strive to shed our own form and the forms of all creatures, knowing no father but God alone. Then nothing shall be able to cause us pain or oppress us, neither God nor any creature, neither things created or uncreated, and our whole being, life, understanding, knowledge and love will be from God and in God and will actually *be* God.

And there is something else which we should know and which can give us consolation in all our suffering. This is that someone who is just and good certainly rejoices and delights immeasurably, unspeakably more in the works of justice than they do, or than the highest angel does, in their natural life and being. That is why the saints gladly gave their lives for the sake of justice.

Now I say: when it happens that a good and just person who has suffered an outward misfortune remains unmoved in serenity and peace of heart, then indeed, nothing that befalls them will distress them, as I have said. If the contrary should prove the case, and they are disheartened by their outward misfortune, then it is only right and proper that God should have permitted the misfortune to befall such a person who thought that they were just, even though such insignificant things could weigh on them so heavily. And if it is God's right so to do, they should not allow themselves to be troubled, but rather they should rejoice in it more than they do in their own lives, which everyone delights in and values more than they do the whole world. After all, what would the whole world profit us if we did not have life?

The third thing we can and should know is this, that according to natural truth God is the sole fount and vein of all goodness, essential truth and consolation, and that everything which is not God has its natural bitterness, despair and suffering from itself, adding nothing to goodness, which stems from God and is God. Rather, its bitterness reduces, veils and conceals the sweetness, bliss and consolation which God gives.

Now I say further that all suffering comes from our love for what misfortune takes from us. If the loss of external things causes me pain, then this is a clear sign that I love external things and thus, in truth, love suffering and despair. Is it surprising then that I suffer, since I love and seek suffering and despair? My heart and my affections assign to creatures that goodness which is God's possession. I turn to creatures which, by their nature, are the source of suffering and turn my back on God, from whom all consolation comes. Is it then surprising that I suffer and that I am sad? Truly, it is impossible for God or for the whole world to console someone who seeks consolation from creatures. But they who love only God in the creature and the creature only in God, will find true, just and constant consolation in all places. Let this be enough for the first part of the book.

2

In this second part of the book there now come some thirty precepts, each one of which ought to provide comfort for a rational person in their suffering.

The first is this, that no hardship and loss is without some gain, and there is no harm which is wholly negative. Therefore St Paul says that the faithfulness and goodness of God do not allow any trial or tribulation to become unbearable. He always creates and gives some consolation with which to aid ourselves for – as the saints and the pagan masters also tell us – neither God nor nature allows such a thing as unadulterated evil or suffering.

Let us suppose that someone has one hundred marks, forty of which they lose and sixty of which remain in their possession. Now if they think constantly of the forty which they have lost, then this person will remain disconsolate and depressed. Indeed, how could they be comforted and forget their suffering when they cling to their loss and their suffering, brooding on it,[4] gazing upon it, as it gazes upon them, talking and conversing with it, the loss, as the loss does with them, staring each other in the eyes. But if they were to consider the sixty marks which they still have, turning their back on the forty which are lost, sinking themselves into the sixty, staring *them* in the eyes and talking to them, then they would certainly be comforted. What exists and is good can offer us comfort, while what does not exist or is not good, what remains 'mine' and 'of me', must necessarily cause distress, suffering and disappointment. Thus Solomon says: 'In the days of adversity, do not forget the days of prosperity' (cf. Ecclus. 11:25). This means: when you are in suffering and distress, then consider the good and pleasing things which you still possess. We will be comforted too if we consider how many thousands of people there are who, if they had the sixty marks, would consider themselves lords and ladies, thinking themselves to be very rich and rejoicing from the bottom of their hearts.

And there is something else which can console us. If we are ill and in great pain, we still have a roof over our head, the essential requirements of food and drink, the advice of doctors and the services of nurses, the sympathy and support of our friends: what should we do? What do poor people do who have to endure the same or an even worse illness and hardship who have no one even to give them a sip of cold water? They have to seek their crust in rain, snow and cold, going from door to door. And so, if you want to be comforted, then forget those who are better off than you are and think always of those whose fate is worse.

I say further that all suffering comes from attachment and affection. Therefore, if I suffer on account of transitory things, my heart still has attachment to and affection for transitory things, so that I do not love God with all my heart nor that which God wants me to love together with himself. Is it surprising then that God rightly permits me to suffer hardship and pain?

St Augustine says: 'Lord, I did not wish to lose you, but in my greed I wanted to have creatures as well as you, and thus I lost you for you do not allow us to possess the falsity and deception of creatures together with you, who are truth.'[5] Elsewhere he also says that 'they are too greedy who are not content with God alone' and 'how can God's gifts to creatures satisfy someone who is not content with God himself?'.[6] For a good person, all that is alien to God, unlike him and other than him should be the cause of suffering and not consolation. They should constantly say: Lord God, my comfort, if you send me away from you to something else, then let it be another you, so that I pass from you to you, for I want nothing but you. When our Lord promised Moses all that is good and sent him into the Promised Land, which stands for heaven, Moses said: 'Lord, send me nowhere but where you will go with me' (cf. Ex. 33:15).

All predilection, attachment and affection come from what is similar to us, since all things incline to and like what is the same as themselves. A pure person likes all purity, a just person likes and inclines to justice. A person's lips speak of what is within them, as our Lord says: 'Out of the fullness of the heart the mouth speaks' (Luke 6:45). And Solomon says that 'All the labour of a man is in his mouth' (Eccles. 6:7). And so it is a clear sign that it is creatures and not God which live in our hearts if we incline to external things and find comfort in them.

Therefore a good man or woman should be ashamed before God and themselves if they realize that God is not in us and that God the Father is not active in us but it is rather wretched creatures that act within us, living in us and determining our affections. Thus King David laments in the psalter: 'Tears are my food day and night, while all day long people ask me, "Where is your God?"' (Ps. 42:3). For an inclination towards external things, the finding of comfort in what is comfortless and the delighting in much talk about these things are a clear sign that God is not manifest in us and that he is neither alert nor active in us. Furthermore, a good person should feel shame before other good people if the latter perceive that this is the case. And so they should never complain on account of injury or suffering but rather lament their own lamentation and their realization of the fact that they do lament.

The masters say that there is an extended layer of blazing hot fire immediately beneath the heavens and yet the heavens are in no way affected by it.[7] Now it says in one text that the lowest part of the soul is nobler than the highest part of the heavens.[8] How then can someone claim to be a heavenly being with their heart in heaven if they are troubled and pained by such trivial things?

Now I will tell you something else. No one can be good who does not will exactly what God wills, for it is impossible that God should will anything other than the good. Something necessarily becomes good and is good and is the best thing of all, precisely in and through the fact that God wills it. That is why our Lord taught the apostles, and us through them, to pray every day that God's will be done. And yet, when God's will is done, we complain.

Seneca, a pagan master, asks 'What is the best consolation in suffering and distress?' and gives this answer: 'It is this, that we should accept everything as if we had desired it and prayed for it, for you would have desired it, if you had known that all things happen from, with and in the will of God.'[9] A pagan master says: 'Lord, supreme father, master of the highest heavens, I am ready for all that you will. Give me the will to will what you will!'[10]

A good person should trust God, believe in him and be sure of him, knowing his goodness to be such that it is impossible for God with his goodness and love to permit any suffering or sorrow to befall someone unless they are either spared some greater suffering thereby or God wishes to give them more perfect consolation on earth or to make something better out of the situation, whereby God's honour will be more fully and visibly manifest. Yet, be that as it may, for the simple reason that it is God's will that it should happen, a good person should be so entirely united in their will with God's will that they desire the same thing that God desires, even when this entails injury to themselves or indeed their own damnation. Thus St Paul wished to be separated from God for God's sake, for the sake of God's will and for his glory (cf. Rom. 9:3). For someone who is truly perfect should be so accustomed to being dead to themselves, stripped of their own form in God and transformed in God's will, that their whole happiness lies in not being aware of themselves or of anything else, but rather knowing only God, without willing anything or knowing any will other than God's will, and desiring to know God, in St Paul's words, 'as God knows me' (cf. 1 Cor. 13:12). God knows everything that he knows, loves and wills everything that he loves and wills, in himself and in his own will. Our Lord himself says: 'This is eternal life: to know you the only true God' (John 17:3).

Therefore the masters say that the blessed in heaven know creatures without the images of creatures, which they perceive rather in a single image, which is God and in which God knows, loves and desires himself and all things.[11] God himself teaches us to pray for and to desire this when we say 'Our Father, hallowed be your name', which means to know only him; 'your kingdom come', so that I shall possess nothing which I hold precious but you alone who are all-precious. Therefore the gospel says 'blessed are the poor in spirit' (Matt. 5:3), which means those who are poor in will, and we ask God that his will 'be done on earth', which means in us 'as it is in heaven', that is as it is in God himself. Such a person is so united with God's will that they will everything that God wills and in the way that God wills it. Therefore, since God in a certain way wills that I should have committed sins, I cannot wish that I had not committed them, for thus it is that God's will is done 'on earth', which is to say in misdeeds, 'as it is in heaven', which is to say in right doing. Therefore such a person desires to renounce God for the sake of God and to be free of God for God's sake, which is the sole true repentance of our sins, and so we grieve at our sins without grief, just as God grieves at evil but without grief. I know regret, and the greatest regret, on account of sin, since I would not wish to sin for all that is or can be created, even if there were to be a thousand worlds throughout all eternity, yet my regret is free of grief, and I accept and receive it in and from God's will.[12] Only this kind of grieving at sin is perfect, for it comes from and originates in pure love of the purest goodness and joy of God. Thus what I have said in this little book becomes true and is seen to be true, namely that a good person, in so far as they are good, enters into the very property of goodness itself, which God is in himself.

Now notice what a wonderful and blissful life this person has in God himself 'on earth as in heaven'. Discomfort serves them as comfort, and suffering as joy. But note also their special consolation, for if I possess the grace and goodness of which I have just spoken, then at all times and in all things my consolation and contentment are complete. But if I do not have these, then I should give them up for God's sake and in his will. If it is God's will that I should have what I desire, I shall have it and shall be happy; but if it is not God's will that I should have it, then I shall gain it by renouncing it in God's same will, in that his will is to withhold it from me, and so I receive it by renouncing it rather than by being given it. Where is the problem then? Indeed, I come into the possession of God more truly by renouncing him than by receiving him, for when we receive something, the gift has that in itself which brings us delight and comfort. But if we do not receive something, then we neither have nor discover nor know anything other than God and his will.[13]

And here is another kind of consolation. If someone has lost an external possession of theirs, a friend or relative, an eye, a hand or whatever it might be, they should know that if they patiently suffer this loss for God's sake, they will at least possess before God all that for which they would not have wished to lose it. If, for instance, someone loses their sight in one eye and if they would not have wished to lose the use of this eye for a thousand or six thousand marks or more, then they will certainly possess with God and in God all that they would have given in order not to endure such a loss or suffering. And this must be what our Lord meant when he said: 'It is better for you to enter into eternal life with one eye than to be lost with two' (Matt. 18:9). This must also have been what God meant when he said: 'He who leaves father and mother, sister and brother, farm and fields or anything else, shall receive a hundredfold and eternal life' (Matt. 19:29). Certainly, I dare to say by God's truth and by my salvation that whoever leaves their father and mother, brother and sister or whatever it may be, for the sake of God and goodness, will receive the hundredfold in two ways. The first is that their father, mother, brother and sister will become a hundred times dearer to them than they are now, and the second is that not only a hundred people but everyone will become incomparably more precious to them than either their father, mother or brother are precious to them at present on account of the family bond. The fact that someone is not aware of this can only mean that they have not yet left their father and mother, sister and brother, and all things for the sake of God and goodness. How can they have left their father and mother, sister and brother for God's sake if they still have them on earth in their heart, if they still become depressed and troubled about what is not God and attentive to it? How can that person have abandoned all things for God's sake who still considers and regards this or that good thing? St Augustine says that if you remove this or that form of the good, then pure goodness remains in itself in its simple extent, which is God.[14] For, as I said above, neither this nor that particular form of the good adds anything to goodness as such, but they cover and conceal the goodness in us. Only those who know and see in truth shall know and understand this, since it is true in truth and that is where we too must be if we are to understand it, and nowhere else.

But you should know that there are different degrees of possessing virtue and the will to suffer, just as we see in nature that one person is bigger, or more attractive in form, complexion, knowledge or skills than another. And I say too that someone can be good and yet be swayed to a greater or lesser degree by their natural love for father, mother, sister and brother, though not falling away from God and from goodness. They are good and better to the extent that to a lesser or greater degree they are consoled and affected by, and are conscious of, their natural love and affection for father and mother, sister and brother, and for themselves.

And yet, as I have written above, if someone could accept this in God's will (since it is God's will that human nature should be flawed in this way specifically because of God's justice with respect to the sin of the first human), and if on the other hand they were willing to do without it if this were not in fact the case, again in God's will, then all would be well with them and they would certainly receive consolation in their suffering. This is what St John means when he says that the true 'light shines in the darkness' (John 1:5) and when St Paul says that 'virtue is perfected in weakness' (2 Cor. 12:9). If the thief were able to endure his death entirely, truly, perfectly, willingly and happily out of love for God's justice, in which and according to which God wills in his justice that the criminal should be put to death, then he would certainly be saved and would be blessed.

But consolation comes from this too: there is hardly anyone who would not wish to see someone else live to the extent that they would be prepared to go without the use of an eye or to be entirely blind for the period of one year, as long as they could have their sight back at the end of the year and could thereby save their friend's life. If therefore someone were willing to go for a year without the use of an eye in order to save the life of someone else who will necessarily die within a few years in any case, then they should be even more prepared to give up the ten, twenty or thirty years which they perhaps still have left in order to become blessed for ever and to contemplate God eternally in his divine light and themselves in God together with all creatures.

Here is another consolation: for a good person, in so far as they are good and are born only from goodness and are an image of goodness, that which is created and which is either this or that is distasteful and is the source of bitter suffering and harm. To lose this therefore is to be free of pain, discomfort and harm, and to be free of suffering is indeed a true consolation. Therefore we should not bewail our loss. Rather we should lament the fact that our consolation is still unknown to us, that comfort cannot comfort us, just as sweet wine is unpleasant for those who are ill. We should regret, as I have written above, that we cannot strip ourselves entirely of the forms of creatures, being transformed into goodness with all that is ours.

We should also consider in our suffering that God speaks the truth and that his promises are founded upon himself as truth. If God failed in his word, in his truth, then he would fail also in his own divinity and would no longer be God, for he *is* his word, his truth. And his word is that our sorrow shall be turned into joy (Jer. 31:13; John 16:20). Now, truly, if I knew for certain that all the stones in my possession were going to turn to gold, then the more stones I had and the bigger they were, the happier I would be. Indeed, I would ask for more stones and, if I could, would get big ones and many of them. The more I had of them and the bigger they were, the happier I would be. In this way we would certainly be greatly consoled in all our grief.

And another point, similar to the last one. No barrel can hold two different drinks. If it is to contain wine, then the water must be poured out so that the barrel is quite empty. Therefore, if you wish to be filled with God and divine joy, then you must pour the creatures out of yourself. St Augustine says: 'Pour out, so that you may be filled. Learn not to love in order that you may learn to love. Turn away, so that you may be turned towards.'[15] In short, if anything is to be receptive and to receive, it must be empty. The masters say that if the eye had its own colour when it perceives, then it would see neither that colour nor any other. But since it is not itself any particular colour, it can perceive all colours. The wall has its own colour, and thus it can see neither that colour nor any other and takes no pleasure in colour, neither in gold nor sky blue nor the colour of coal. But the eye has no colour and yet does possess it in the truest sense, for it recognizes colour with delight and pleasure and joy.[16] The more perfect and pure the powers of the soul are, the more perfectly and comprehensively they can receive the object of their perception, embracing and experiencing a greater bliss, and the more they become one with that which they perceive, to such a degree indeed that the highest power of the soul, which is free of all things and which has nothing in common with anything else at all, perceives nothing less than God himself in the breadth and fullness of his being. And the masters prove that nothing can be compared in terms of bliss and delight with this union, this interpenetration and ecstasy. Therefore our Lord says: 'Blessed are the poor in spirit' (Matt. 5:3). They are poor who have nothing. 'Poor in spirit' means this: just as the eye is poor and bereft of colour, and is thus receptive to all colours, so too those who are poor in spirit are receptive to all spirit, and the spirit of all spirits is God. Love, joy and peace are the fruits of the spirit. Possessing nothing, being naked, poor and empty, transforms nature. Emptiness draws water uphill and causes many other miracles of which we cannot speak here.

Therefore, if you wish to discover and to possess complete joy and consolation in God, you must ensure that you are free of all creatures and of all the consolation which they provide. Certainly, for as long as the creature can comfort you and does so, you will never find true consolation. But when nothing can console you except God alone, then indeed he will console you and with him and in him all that gives delight. If you are comforted by what is not God, you will find no consolation either in this life or the next. But if creatures do not give you comfort or pleasure, then you will find consolation both now and hereafter.

If it were possible for us to empty a cup completely and to keep it empty of all that might fill it, even air, then the cup would without doubt deny and forget its own nature and would be drawn up to heaven by its emptiness. In the same way, being naked and poor and empty of all creatures draws the soul up to God. Likeness and warmth also draw us upwards. We attribute likeness to the Son in the Godhead, warmth and love to the Holy Spirit.[17] Likeness or identity in all things, but especially and primarily in the divine nature, represents the birth of the One, while the likeness of the One, in the One and with the One is the origin and source of flowering and fiery love. The One is origin without beginning. Likeness is the origin of the One alone and receives this, the fact that it exists and that it exists as origin, from and in the One. Love by nature flows and springs forth from Two as One. One as One does not produce love, any more than Two as Two does, while Two as One necessarily produces according to its nature a powerful and fiery love.

Now Solomon says that all the waters, which means to say all creatures, flow back and return to their origin (Eccles. 1:7). Thus what I have said is necessarily true: likeness and fiery love draw us upwards, raising the soul to the primal origin of the One, which is 'Father of all that is in heaven or earth' (cf. Eph. 4:6). Thus I say that likeness, born of the One, draws the soul into God, as he is One in his hidden unity, for that is what the One means. We have a visible analogy for this when material fire ignites wood, for then a spark takes on the nature of fire and becomes identical to the fire which is attached to the lower part of the heavens.[18] It immediately forgets about and gives up its father and mother, brother and sister on earth and shoots upwards to its heavenly father. Fire is the father of the spark here below, while its mother is the wood, and its brother and sister are other sparks, for which the first spark does not wait. It goes speedily upwards to its true father, which is the sky, for whoever knows the truth, knows that fire, in so far as it is fire, is not the real father of the spark. The real father of the spark and of all that has the nature of fire is the sky. Furthermore, we should note that this spark not only takes leave of father and mother, brother and sister on earth, but rather takes leave of, forgets and denies its very self for the sake of the loving drive it feels to come to its true father, the sky, for it must necessarily be extinguished in the cold of the air. Yet it wants to proclaim the natural love it has for its true and heavenly father.

Just as before we spoke of emptiness and bareness, saying of the soul that the more she is pure, naked and poor, the fewer creatures she possesses and the emptier of all things she is which are not God, then the more purely she grasps God and does so in him, becoming one with God and gazing upon him as he gazes upon her, face to face, being transformed into his likeness, as St Paul says (2 Cor. 3:18). I now say exactly the same of likeness and the fire of love for, to the extent that something is more like something else, to that extent it rushes towards it, and does so more swiftly and is filled with greater happiness and joy on account of its movement. The further it departs from itself and from everything which is not that towards which it hastens, and the more unlike itself it becomes and unlike all that is not its goal, to that extent it becomes ever more like the thing to which it is drawn. Since likeness flows from the One and attracts and draws by and in the power of the One, neither peace nor satisfaction comes to that which attracts or to that which is attracted until they become one in the One. Therefore our Lord spoke through the prophet Isaiah to the effect that there is no sublime likeness nor peace of love that satisfies me until I am myself revealed in my Son and I am myself consumed and burned in the love of the Holy Spirit (cf. Isaiah 62:1). Our Lord asked his Father that we should be one with him and in him and not just united. We have a clear analogy for this passage and this truth in nature, which is even a visual one. When the fire acts, igniting the wood and setting it ablaze, then the fire reduces the wood to something small, quite unlike its former self, removing from it its bulk, coldness, mass and moistness, and making the wood more and more like itself. And yet neither the fire nor the wood is satisfied or contented with any warmth, heat or likeness until the fire has given birth to itself in the wood and has conveyed to it its own nature and its own being so that all becomes a single fire, equally one, without distinction and knowing neither increase nor decrease. And this is why, until the process is complete, there is always smoke, crackling and contention between the fire and the wood. But when all the differences between them have been removed, the fire is still and the wood is silent. I also say in truth that the secret power of nature hates hidden likeness in so far as this contains distinction and duality, and that it seeks in it the One, which nature loves in likeness solely for its own sake, just as the mouth seeks and loves the taste or sweetness in and of wine. If water had the taste which wine has, then the mouth would not prefer wine to water.

This is why I said that a soul in a state of likeness hates likeness and does not love it in itself and for its own sake. She loves it rather on account of the One which is concealed within it and which is her true 'father', the origin without beginning of 'all that is in heaven and earth'. Therefore I say that so long as likeness can be found between fire and wood and is manifest, there can never be true delight or silence, rest or satisfaction. This is why the masters say that fire comes through conflict, anger and unrest, and that it happens within time, while the birth of fire and desire is beyond time and space. No one finds that joy and delight either go on too long or are too remote. Our Lord meant all the things I have described when he said: 'A woman giving birth to a child endures sorrow, pain and suffering, but when the child is born, she forgets the pain and woe' (John 16:21). Therefore God too urges us in the gospel to ask our heavenly Father that our joy might be complete (cf. John 15:11), and St Philip said: 'Lord, show us the Father and it will suffice us' (John 14:8), for 'Father' indicates birth and not likeness, and it denotes the One in which likeness is reduced to silence and all that desires to be is still.

Now we can clearly see why and how it is that we remain unconsoled in all our suffering, hardship and injury. This comes always and solely from the fact that we are far from God and are not free of creatures, being unlike God and lacking in divine love. But now there is another point, and whoever wishes to consider this will fittingly receive consolation in their external injury and pain.

If someone were to take a particular path or set about a particular task, or even abandon one, and then were to suffer an injury of some kind (perhaps they might break a leg or an arm, or lose the sight of an eye, or fall ill), then if they constantly think to themselves, 'If only you had taken another path, or set about another task, this would never have happened to you', they shall remain without consolation and will necessarily be grief-stricken. Therefore they should think to themselves, 'If you had taken another path or if you had set about or had abandoned another task, then you might easily have suffered greater injury and misfortune.' And thus they will be comforted.

Now take another case. Suppose that you have lost a thousand marks. Do not lament their loss but rather thank God, who gave you a thousand marks in the first place and who has allowed you to earn eternal life through the practice of the virtue of patience, which many thousands of people have been denied.

Another point which can bring us consolation. If it were the case that someone who had possessed honour and comfort for many years were now to lose these by divine decree, then this person should reflect wisely and thank God. When they become aware of their present injury and hardship, they will realize for the first time how great was their earlier advantage and security and they should thank God now for the security which they previously enjoyed without really being aware of how well off they were, and should refrain from complaining. They should consider that by their natural being men and women possess nothing other than wickedness and weakness. All that is good and goodness has been given on loan to them by God and not for their own possession. For whoever knows the truth, knows that God, the heavenly Father, gives all that is good to the Son and the Holy Spirit, while he does not give but rather only lends goodness to creatures. The sun gives warmth to the air, but it only lends air light. Therefore when the sun sets, the air loses light but warmth remains in it, since it has been given to the air as its own possession. Thus the masters say that God, the heavenly Father, is Father and not Lord either of the Son or the Holy Spirit. But God-Father-Son-and-Holy-Spirit is one Lord and is the Lord of creatures. And we say that God was Father from eternity but, from that point on when he made creatures, he was also Lord.

Now I say: since all that is good, consoling or existent in time is only on loan to us, what right do we have to complain if he who lent it to us, wishes to take it back again? We should thank God that he has lent it to us for such a long time. And we should thank him for not taking back all that he has lent us, for it would be perfectly fair for God to take back all that he has lent us if we become indignant when he takes from us just a part of what has never been ours and of which we have never been the true owner. Thus Jeremiah the prophet, when he was in great suffering and lament, well says: 'How great and manifold are God's mercies that we are not destroyed' (Lam. 3:22). If someone who had lent me their jacket, fur-coat and cloak took back their cloak, while leaving me the jacket and fur-coat in the cold, then I should properly be grateful to them and relieved. Note how wrong it would be of me to get angry and to complain when I lose something, for if I wish that the good I have should be given and not lent, then I should desire myself to be Lord and the Son of God both perfectly and by nature, though I am not yet even God's Son by grace, since it is the property of the Son of God and of the Holy Spirit to respond to all things in the same way.

We should also know that natural human virtue has without doubt such excellence and power that there is no external work which is too difficult or indeed which is sufficiently demanding for this virtue to express itself fully in it and by it and to prove its own worth. Therefore there is an inner work which neither time nor space can support or contain and in which there is something which is divine and akin to God and which, similarly, is beyond time and space. It is equally present in all places and at all times, and is like God in this, whom no creature can wholly embrace and whose goodness no creature can possess in itself. Therefore there must be something more inward and elevated, something uncreated, with neither dimension nor mode of being, on which our heavenly Father can imprint himself, pouring himself forth, and in which he can reveal himself: as Son and Holy Spirit.[19] Also we cannot impede the inner activity of virtue any more than we can God. This activity shines out day and night. It extols God, praising him and singing a new song, as David says: 'Sing

God a new song' (Ps. 95:1). But the activity which is external, which is constrained by time and space, which is hemmed in, which can be impeded or restricted, which becomes weary and aged through passage of time and usage, sings praise that is earthbound and is not pleasing to God. But the former activity means to love God and to desire the good and goodness, whereby all that we wish and intend to do with a pure and undivided will in all our good works is already achieved, just as is the case with God, of whom David writes: 'All that he has intended, he has already done and performed' (cf. Ps. 135:6).

We have a visible proof of this teaching in the stone, whose external work it is to fall to the ground and to lie there. This work can be impeded, and it does not fall on every occasion nor does it always fall the whole way. But the stone has another, more internal, work: its tendency to move downwards, which is innate and which neither God nor creature nor anyone else can take from it. The stone performs this work without ceasing, day and night, and if it were to lie for a thousand years in a high place, then it would not incline downwards any more or any less than it did on the first day.

In the same way I say of virtue that she has an inner work, which is a striving and inclination towards all that is good, and a fleeing from and resistance to all that is wicked and evil because of its unlikeness to goodness and to God. And the more the work is evil and alien to God, the greater is her resistance to it, while the more significant and similar to God the work is, the easier, more congenial and delightful it becomes. It is virtue's sole complaint and sorrow – in so far as virtue can experience sorrow – that this suffering for the sake of God and all her external work within time is far too restricted for her to find full expression and self-realization within it. Through practice she becomes strong, and she becomes rich by showing generosity. It is not having suffered and having survived suffering in the past that she desires but rather that she should always suffer for the sake of God and righteousness without ceasing. All her joy lies in suffering, and not in having suffered, for God's sake. Therefore our Lord says pointedly: 'Blessed are those who suffer for righteousness' sake' (Matt. 5:10). He does not say: 'those who *have* suffered'. A person of this kind hates suffering which is in the past, for having suffered is not the suffering which they love, but is rather the loss and relinquishing of that suffering for God which they love. Thus I say that such a person also hates suffering in the future, for it too is not actual suffering. However, they hate suffering in the future less than suffering in the past because having suffered is more remote from and alien to suffering since it is entirely past. But if someone is going to suffer in the future, then this does not entirely remove from them the suffering that they love.

St Paul says that he wishes to lose God for the sake of God in order that the glory of God should be increased (Rom. 9:3). It is maintained that St Paul said this when he was not yet perfect. But I say that these words sprang from a perfect heart. It is also maintained that he only wished to be separated from God for a moment, but I say that someone who is perfect would be equally unwilling to be separated from God for an hour as for a thousand years. But if being separated from him were God's will and to his glory, then it would be as easy to be apart from him for a thousand years or even the whole of eternity as it would for a day or an hour.

The inner work is also divine, God-like and possessed of divine qualities in that, even if there were a thousand worlds, all creatures together would not amount to more than God on his own by so much as a whisker, and so I say, as I have already said, that the external work, its size and extent, its length and breadth, cannot increase the goodness of the inner work to any degree whatever, since this contains its goodness in itself. Thus the outer work can never be minor, when the inner work is a major one, and the outer work can never be major or good when the inner work is a minor one and without value. The inner work always determines in itself all the dimensions of the outer work, its whole breadth and extent. The inner work receives and draws the whole of its being from nowhere but the heart and in the heart of God: it receives the Son and is born as Son in the womb of the heavenly Father. But this is not the case with the outer work, which receives rather its divine goodness through the inner work as something given and poured out in a descent of the Godhead which then becomes clothed with distinction, number and divisibility, all of which properties however, together with their like, are remote from God and alien to him, as is likeness itself. All these things inhere and rest in the individual instance of the good, which is illumined and is creature and is entirely blind to goodness and the light *as such* and to the One in which God gives birth to his only begotten Son and, in him, to all those who are the children, the begotten sons, of God. It is there that we find the origin and flowing-out of the Holy Spirit, and from him alone, in so far as he is the spirit of God and God himself is spirit, the Son is conceived in us.[20] The Spirit flows forth from all those who are the sons of God, according to whether they are born purely of God to a greater or lesser degree, transformed within God and after his likeness and are removed from all multiplicity (which can still be found in even the highest angels according to their nature), removed in fact even from goodness and truth and from all that permits the merest hint or shadow of distinction by being thought or named, and are devoted to the One which is free of all multiplicity and distinction, in which God-Father-Son-and-Holy-Spirit sheds and is stripped of all distinctions and properties, and is One. This One makes us blessed, and the further we are from the One, the less we are the sons and Son of God and the less perfectly the Holy Spirit rises up in us and flows forth from us; while, on the other hand, the closer we are to the One, the more truly we are God's sons and Son, and the more truly God-the-Holy-Spirit flows forth from us. It is this which is meant when our Lord, the Son of God in the Godhead, says: 'Whoever drinks from the water that I give, in him a fountain of water shall arise, springing up to everlasting life' (John 4:14), in which, according to St John, he was referring to the Holy Spirit.[21]

In accordance with his nature, the Son in the Godhead bestows nothing other than sonship, that is being born of God, the source, origin and flowing-out of the Holy Spirit, of God's love, and the full, true and perfect savour of the One, who is the heavenly Father. Thus the voice of the Father says to the Son from heaven: 'You are my beloved son in whom I am beloved and well-pleased' (cf. Matt. 3:17), for certainly no one loves God with a pure and sufficient love who is not God's son. For love, which is the Holy Spirit, springs and flows from the Son, and the Son loves the Father for his own sake, the Father in himself and himself in the Father. Thus our Lord says very rightly: 'Blessed are the poor in spirit' (Matt. 5:3), which means: those who have shed their own, human spirit and who approach God in a state of nakedness. And St Paul says: 'God has revealed it to us in his spirit' (Col. 1:8).

St Augustine says that they who are stripped of their own spirit best understand Holy Scripture, seeking the meaning and truth of Scripture in itself, that is in the Spirit in which it was written and spoken: in the Spirit of God. St Peter says that all holy people have spoken in God's Spirit (2 Pet. 1:21). St Paul says that no one can ascertain and know what there is in men and women but the Spirit which is in them, and no one can know the Spirit of God and what is in God but the Spirit which is of God and which is God (1 Cor. 2:11). Thus one text, a gloss, says properly that no one can understand or teach St Paul's writings unless they possess the same Spirit in which St Paul spoke and wrote.[22] And this is my constant complaint, that unintelligent people who neither possess nor have any part of the Spirit of God wish to understand with their primitive human reason what they hear or read in Scripture, which was spoken and written down by the Holy Spirit and in the Holy Spirit, and so do not consider the words: 'What is impossible for men, is possible for God' (Matt. 19:26). And this is no less true of the natural sphere: what is impossible for our lower nature is customary and natural for our higher nature.

Now add to this what I have said before: namely that a good person, born in God as the son of God, loves God for his own sake and in himself, as well as many other things which I have said. To understand this better, we should know, as I have said often enough before, that someone who is good, who is born of goodness and born in God, enters into the complete nature of God. Now, according to Solomon, it is part of God's nature that he performs all things for his own sake, which means that he considers no 'why' outside himself but considers rather the 'for his own sake'; he loves and performs everything for his own sake. When therefore someone loves themselves and all things and carries out their works not for the sake of a reward, for honour or convenience, but only for the sake of God and his glory, then this is a sign that such a person is the son of God.

Furthermore, God loves for his own sake and performs all things for his own sake, which means to say that he loves for the sake of love and he acts through his works for the sake of acting, for without doubt if God had never given birth to his only begotten Son in eternity, then having given birth in the past would not be the same as giving birth in the present. Thus the saints say that the Son is born eternally and that he will continue to be born without ceasing. Neither would God have created the world, if having created were not the same as still creating. Therefore, God created the world in such a way that he still creates it without ceasing.[23] All that belongs to the past and future is alien and remote to God. Accordingly, they who are born of God as the son of God, love God for his own sake, which means that they love God for the sake of loving God and they act through their works for the sake of acting. God never tires of loving and acting, and all that he loves is for him a single love. Thus it is true that God is love. This is why I have said above that the good person always desires to suffer for love, not to *have suffered* for love: it is suffering in the present that brings them what they love. Such a person loves suffering for the sake of God and does suffer for the sake of God. Thus they are God's son, formed in God and in his image, who loves for his own sake, which means to say that he loves for the sake of love and acts for the sake of acting, and so God loves and acts without ceasing. God's acting is his very nature, his being, his life, his blessedness. And truly, suffering for God's sake, acting for God's sake is the life, activity and blessedness of the son of God, that is to say of a good person in so far as they are the son of God, since our Lord says: 'Blessed are they who suffer for righteousness' sake' (Matt. 5:10).

Moreover, I say in the third place that a good person, in so far as they are good, possesses the nature of God not only in the fact that they love all that they love and do all that they do for the sake of God, whom they love therein and for whose sake they act, but they who love do so also for their own sake, for it is the God-Father-Unborn that they love and it is the God-Son-Born who does the loving. Now the Father is in the Son and the Son is in the Father: Father and Son are one. In the book that follows this one you can read of how the innermost and highest part of the soul finds and receives God's Son, and the process of becoming God's Son, in the bosom and heart of the heavenly Father. There I have written 'On the nobleman, who went into a distant country to gain a kingdom for himself, and returned' (Luke 19:12).[24]

We should know too that in the natural realm the impress and influence of the highest and noblest nature is more blissful and delightful for every being than its own nature and essence. It is the nature of water to flow downwards into the valley, and that is its essence. But under the impress and influence of the moon in the sky above, it abandons and forgets its own nature by flowing uphill, and it finds this far easier than flowing downhill. We can ascertain if we are in the right spiritual state by whether we would have bliss and joy in abandoning and taking leave of our own natural will and in going out of ourselves entirely in all those things which God wills us to endure.

And this is the proper meaning of our Lord's words when he says: 'Anyone who wishes to be a follower of mine must renounce self; he must take up his cross and follow me' (Matt. 16:24), which means that they should shed and lay down everything which belongs to the cross and to suffering.[25] For truly, whoever has abandoned themselves and gone entirely out of themselves, for such a person nothing can be a cross, or pain or suffering, but for them all is bliss, joy and the heart's delight and they will come and follow God truly. For just as nothing can oppress God or cause him suffering, neither can anything cause them pain or suffering. Thus when our Lord says, 'Anyone who wishes to be a follower of mine must renounce self; he must take up his cross and follow me', then this is not only a commandment, as is usually said, but it is also a promise and a divine instruction as to how the whole of our suffering, action and life can be turned to bliss and joy, and it is more a reward than a commandment. For such a person has everything that they desire, since they desire nothing which is bad, and this is blessedness. Therefore once again our Lord rightly says: 'Blessed are they that suffer for righteousness' sake.'

Moreover, when our Lord, the Son, says 'he must take up his cross and follow me', he means: become a son, as I am Son,

God-begotten, and become the same One that I am and that I receive, dwelling and abiding in the bosom and heart of the Father. Father, says the Son, I desire that whoever follows me, whoever comes to me, should be where I am (John 12:26). No one really comes to the Son, as far as he is Son, but they who themselves become a son, and no one comes to where the Son is, who is One in One in the bosom and heart of the Father, but they who are a son.

'I,' the Father says, 'will lead her into the wilderness and speak to her heart' (Hos. 2:14). Heart to heart, one in one, is how God loves. God hates all that is alien or remote from this; God draws and entices to the One. All creatures seek the One, even the lowest, and the highest perceive the One: taken beyond their own natures and transformed, they seek the One in the One, the One in itself. Thus the Son can say: in the Godhead the Son is in the Father, and where I am, there too shall be those who serve me, follow me and come to me.[26]

But there is another consolation. We should know that it is impossible for the whole of nature to break, spoil or even to touch something, without meaning to improve what is touched. Nature is not content with creating something which is only as good, and she always wishes to make something which is better. But how? A wise doctor never touches the damaged finger of his patient, thus causing them pain, if he does not wish to make the finger or the whole patient better and thus bring relief. If he can make the person and the finger better, then he does so; and if he cannot, he amputates the finger in order to improve the condition of the person. And it is very much better to give up the finger in order to save the person than to lose both the finger and the person. A single loss is better than a double loss, especially when the one would be incomparably greater than the other. We should know too that by their nature the finger and the hand and every limb of our body far prefer the person of which they are a member to themselves and that they willingly and cheerfully accept pain and travail for that person's sake. I can say confidently and truthfully that such a member of the body does not love itself at all except for the sake of that and in that of which it is a part. Therefore, it would be entirely appropriate and natural for us not to love ourselves in any way except for the sake of God and in God. And if this is the case, we will find everything that God wants from us and in us to be both easy and delightful, especially if we are certain that God could much less tolerate any deficiency or loss if he did not intend or recognize in it a far greater advantage. Truly, if someone does not put their trust in God in this respect, then it is only right that they should experience suffering and pain.

Now there is a further consolation. St Paul says that God punishes all those who he accepts and receives as sons (cf. Heb. 12:6). Suffering is part of being a son. Since God's Son could not suffer in the divinity and in eternity, the heavenly Father sent him into time so that he should become human and could suffer. Therefore, if you wish to be a son of God but do not wish to suffer, you are in the wrong. In the Book of Wisdom it is written that God tests and examines to see who is righteous, just as we test and examine gold, melting it in an oven (cf. Wisd. 3:5–6). It is a sign of the trust that a king or prince places in a warrior when he sends him into battle. I once saw a ruler who at times would send a man out, who he had newly received into his retinue, and would then attack him himself and fight with him. Once it happened that he was almost killed by one man, who he wished to test in this way, and he held this servant in greater regard than before.

We read that the evil spirits once caused especially great suffering to St Anthony in the desert, and when he had overcome the pain, our Lord appeared to him visibly and joyfully. Then the holy man said: 'O Lord, where were you just now when I was in such great need?' Our Lord replied: 'I was here, as I am now. But I wished, I desired to see, how devout you are.'[27] A piece of silver or gold is pure and yet, if we wish to make a container from it for the king to drink from, then we heat it far more than we normally do. Thus it is written of the apostles that they rejoiced to be found worthy to suffer ignominy for God's sake (Acts 5:41).

God's Son by nature wished to become human by grace in order that he could suffer for your sake, while you wish to become a son of God, who is more than human, in order that you neither can nor need to suffer for the sake of God or for your own sake!

If only we would remember and consider how great is the joy that God himself in his way, all angels and all those who know and love God, have in the patience of someone who endures suffering and harm for God's sake, then truly this thought alone should by rights bring us consolation. After all, we give our goods away and experience hardship in order to please even our friend and to show him a kindness.

We should consider too that if we had a friend who was suffering for our sake, who was experiencing pain and hardship, then it would be right for us to be with them and to comfort them with our presence, offering them all the consolation that we could. Therefore in the psalms our Lord says that he is with a good person in their suffering (Ps. 34:17). From these words we can extract seven points and seven reasons for consolation.

Firstly, there is St Augustine's comment that to show patience when we suffer for God's sake is better, more precious, more noble and sublime than all that could be taken from someone against their will, which is to say merely their outward possessions.[28] God knows, we will find no one who loves this world who is so rich that they would not gladly and willingly experience great pain and tolerate it for a long time in order subsequently to become the powerful ruler of the whole world.

Secondly, not only on the basis of what God says do I deduce that he is with us in our suffering, but I take it from and in the text, and say: if God is with us in our suffering, then what more do we want, what else do we want? I desire nothing other than God and nothing more than him, if I am as I should be. St Augustine says: 'They who are not satisfied with God lack wisdom and are greedy', and elsewhere he says: 'How can we be satisfied with God's outward and inward gifts if God himself does not satisfy us?'[29] Therefore he says again in another place: 'Lord, if you reject us, then give us another You, for you are all we desire.'[30] Therefore the Book of Wisdom says: 'All good things have come to me at once together with God, the Eternal Wisdom' (Wisd. 7:11). In one way this means that nothing is or can be good that comes without God, and all that comes with God is good, and is so since it comes with God. Of God himself I shall be silent. If all the creatures of the whole world were to be robbed of the being that God gives them, they would be a pure nothingness: unpleasing, valueless and hateful. This statement that all good things come with God conceals other, precious meanings, which we cannot pursue here.

Our Lord says: 'I am with those who suffer' (Ps. 91:15). Concerning this St Bernard says: 'Lord, you are with us when we suffer, so make me suffer always so that you will always be with me, and so that you shall always be mine.'[31]

Thirdly, I say the fact that God is with us when we suffer means that he himself shares our suffering. Indeed, whoever knows what truth is knows that what I say is true. God shares our suffering, indeed he suffers in his own way more readily and incomparably more than they do who suffer for his sake. Now I say that if God himself desires to suffer, then it is only right and proper that I too should suffer, for I desire what God desires, if my attitude of mind is right. Every day I pray, and God commands me to pray, 'Lord, may your will be done'. And yet, when it is

God's will that I should suffer, I complain at the suffering, which is quite wrong. I affirm too that God so wishes to suffer with us and for us when we suffer only for his sake, that he suffers without suffering. Suffering is so blissful for him that suffering is not suffering for him at all. And so, if we were rightly disposed, suffering would not be suffering for us either, but rather delight and consolation.

In the fourth place, I say that a friend's compassion naturally lessens our suffering. If I am consoled when another person shares in my suffering, then I will be comforted even more if it is God who suffers with me.

In the fifth place, if I can be ready and willing to suffer with someone whom I love and who loves me, then it is right and proper that I should readily suffer with God, who suffers with me and for me on account of the love he bears me.

In the sixth place, I say if it is the case that God suffers before I do when I suffer for his sake, then all my suffering, however great it may be, will easily turn into consolation and joy. It is a natural truth that when someone undertakes a task with another purpose in mind, then the final goal for the sake of which they begin the work is more precious to them and their labour less important, touching them only with respect to that for the sake of which they do it. He who builds, hewing wood and dressing stone in order to erect a house which will stand against the summer heat and winter cold, has his heart set first and foremost on the house, and would never chisel the stone and get down to the work if it were not for the sake of the house. Now we well know that when a sick person drinks sweet wine, they pronounce it bitter, and rightly so, for the wine loses all its sweetness on the outside in the bitterness of the tongue before it can penetrate within, to where the soul discerns taste and forms a judgement. The same is true, although to an incomparably higher degree, when someone performs all their works for the sake of God alone, when God is the mediator who enfolds the soul most closely, when nothing can touch the soul or heart of the person which has not first lost its bitterness through God and his sweetness, and has had necessarily to lose it, becoming pure sweetness before ever being able to touch their heart.

But there is another example and comparison, for the masters say that there is fire beneath the heavens, all around, and so no rain or wind or any storms or tempests can approach the heavens from below so that they come into contact with them in any way.[32] Everything is burned up and consumed by the heat of the fire before it reaches the heavens. In the same way, I say, everything that we suffer and do for God's sake is sweetened by his sweetness before it reaches the heart of him or her who acts and suffers for the sake of God. For this is the meaning of the words 'for God's sake', since nothing can reach the heart which does not first pass through the sweetness of God, where it loses all its bitterness. It too is burned by the hot fire of God's love which enfolds within itself the good person's heart.

Now we can clearly see how easily and in how many different ways a good man or woman receives consolation on all sides when they act, suffer or are in pain. This happens in one way if they act and suffer for God's sake and in another when they are immersed in divine love. We can also tell whether we are doing all our works for God's sake and whether we are immersed in divine love since truly, in so far as we are full of grief and without consolation, to that extent we have not acted for God's sake alone nor – take note – have we been constant in God's love. 'A fire,' says King David, 'comes with God and before God, that burns up all around whatever God finds opposed to him and unlike him' (Ps. 97:3), which is to say grief, despair, unrest and bitterness.

There still remains the seventh reason for consolation in the statement that God is with us in our suffering and indeed that he suffers with us. The nature of God can be the source of great consolation for us since he is pure oneness, being free of any accretive multiplicity of distinction even at a conceptual level, and since everything which is in him is God himself. This being true, I say that everything which the good person suffers for the sake of God, he or she endures in God and God suffers with them in their suffering. If my suffering is in God and God shares in it, how then can suffering be grievous for me, when suffering loses its grievousness and my suffering is in God and is God? Truly, just as God is truth and wherever I find the truth I find my God, who is truth, so too, in the same way exactly, when I find pure suffering in God and for God's sake, I find God *as* my suffering. Whoever does not realize this should blame their own blindness rather than me or the truth and loving kindness of God.

Let your suffering be like this therefore for the sake of God, since this is such a great source of benefit and blessing. 'Blessed are they,' our Lord said, 'who suffer for righteousness' sake' (Matt. 5:10). How can our God, who loves goodness, allow his friends, who are good people, *not* constantly to suffer? If someone had a friend who accepted suffering over a period of a few days in order to gain great benefit, honour and advantage for a long time, and if the first person wished to prevent this, or if it were their wish that someone else should prevent it, then you would not say that they were the friend of the second person or that they loved them. For this reason, God could easily not allow his friends, that is good people, ever to be without suffering if it were not the case that they can suffer without suffering. All the goodness of external suffering comes and flows from the goodness of the will, as I have stated above. Therefore, the good person does actually suffer in God, before the face of God and for his sake, everything which they might wish and be willing to endure, even hunger to endure for God's sake. King David says in the psalter: 'I am ready in all distress, and my sorrow is ever present in my heart and in my face' (cf. Ps. 38:18). St Jerome says that a pure wax which is soft and pliable enough to twist into whatever shapes we desire already contains within itself all that can be made from it, even if no one is actually making anything from it at the time.[33] I have also written above that the stone is no less heavy when it is not actually lying on the ground; all its weight results from the fact that it tends downwards and is inclined in itself to drop. And I have also described above how the good person has already done in heaven and on earth everything that he or she has wished to do, and in this respect is like God.

Now we can see the stupidity of those who are generally struck by the fact that good people suffer pain and hardship, and who have the idea that this is the result of such people's hidden sins. Sometimes they even say: 'Oh, I thought that so-and-so was a good person. How is it that they suffer so much pain and hardship, and I thought that they had no vices?' I agree with this, and say that if such a person really did feel pain and if this pain really were a suffering and misfortune for them, then they would indeed not be good and without sin. But if they are good, their pain is neither suffering nor misfortune but is rather a great good fortune for them and is blessedness. God, who is truth, says: 'Blessed are they who suffer for righteousness' sake' (Matt. 5:10). Thus we read in the Book of Wisdom that 'the souls of the righteous are in God's hand. Foolish people think and believe that they die and perish ... but they are at peace' (Wisd. 3:1–3). When Paul writes of how many saints have sometimes had to endure many different kinds of pain, he says that the world was unworthy of them (Heb. 11:32–38). And these words, if correctly understood, have three meanings. The first is that this world is not worthy of the presence in it of many good people. But the second meaning is better and is that the goodness of the world seems worthless and hateful; God alone has value, and therefore they are precious to God and are worthy of him. The third meaning is this, that the world, that is to say those who love this world, are not worthy to suffer pain and hardship for the sake of God. Therefore it is written that the holy apostles rejoiced that they were found worthy to suffer in God's name (Acts 5:41).

Enough of words. In the third section of this book I shall write about the different kinds of comfort with which a good person should be able to console themselves in their suffering and which are to be found not only in what the good and the wise have said but also in what they have done.

3

We read in the Book of Kings how a man cursed King David and hurled abuse at him. Then one of the friends of David said that he was going to strike the dog dead. But the King answered: 'No! For it may be that God intends my welfare by this insult' (2 Sam. 16:5–12).

In the Book of the Fathers we read of how a man complained of his sufferings to a holy father, who replied: 'Do you wish, my son, that I should ask God to take them away from you?' The other said: 'No, father. They are good for me, that I well know. But ask God to give me his grace in order to suffer them willingly.'[34]

A sick man was once asked why he did not beseech God to make him well again. He replied that he was unwilling to do that for three reasons. The first was that he was convinced that God in his love could not permit him to be ill if it were not for his own good. A second reason was that a good person necessarily desires what God wills and not that God should will what it is that they want, for that would not be right. Therefore, if it was God's desire that he should be ill (and if God did not wish this, it would not be so), then he too should not wish to be well again. For without doubt, if it were somehow possible for God to make him better without this being his divine will, then being healed would have no point or value for him. Desiring something comes from love, and not desiring something comes from a lack of love. It was much better, preferable and advantageous for him to be ill with the love of God, than to be physically well but without God's love. What God loves, has existence, while what God does not love, has no existence, as the Book of Wisdom says (Wisd. 11:25). This also contains the truth that all that God wills is good merely by virtue of the fact that God wills it. Indeed, personally speaking, I would prefer it if someone who is rich and powerful, a king perhaps, loved me but gave me nothing for a while than if he immediately gave me something while withholding his love from me: if he gave me nothing for the time being out of love, that is, because he wished to shower gifts upon me at a later point in time. But supposing even that the man who gives me nothing for the moment does not intend to give me anything later on either, he might still change his mind and give me something. I should patiently wait and see, especially as his gift is one of grace and is unearned. It is also certain that if I care nothing for someone's love, and my will is opposed to theirs except in so far as I want them to give me something, then such a person is doing the right thing if they do not give me anything, disliking me rather and abandoning me to my misfortune.

The third reason why it would be pointless and demeaning for me to ask God to make me better again is that I am reluctant to ask the rich, loving and generous God for something as insignificant as this. Supposing I travelled to see the Pope one or two hundred miles away, and said as I stepped before him, 'Holy Father, I have made a difficult and costly journey of two hundred miles to see you and I beseech you, whatever the reason for my coming here, to give me a single bean!' Indeed, he himself and anyone who was near by would justifiably say that I was a fool. But now it is a certain truth that everything good, even the whole of creation, is less beside God than a single bean is beside the whole of the physical world. That is why I should rightfully disdain to ask God to make me better, if I am good and wise.

I say too that it is the sign of a weak spirit if the passing things of this earth cause someone joy and despair. We should be thoroughly ashamed of ourselves before God, his angels and our fellow men and women if we ever become aware of this in us. After all, we feel great shame if we have a facial disfigurement which is only visible on the outside. What more can I say? The books of the Old and New Testament, as well as those both of the saints and pagans, are full of accounts of how devout men and women have sacrificed their lives or willingly denied themselves for the sake of God or because of their own natural virtue.

Socrates, a pagan master, says that virtues make impossible things possible, even pleasant and easy to do.[35] Nor let us forget that pious woman of whom the Book of Maccabees speaks, who one day saw and heard the terrible, barbaric and hideous tortures which were inflicted on her seven sons and who did so cheerfully and with self-restraint, urging each individually not to be afraid but willingly to give up body and soul for the sake of God's justice (2 Macc. 7). With this the present book comes to an end, although I wish to make two further points.

The first is that a good and godly person should be heartily ashamed of ever having succumbed to pain when we consider that in the hope of only a small reward and trusting to his luck, a merchant often journeys so far abroad over such difficult paths, over mountain and dale, desert and sea, his life and goods constantly threatened by robbers and murderers, suffering a lack of food, drink and sleep, and other discomforts, and yet does all this willingly for the sake of such small and uncertain profit.[36] A knight in battle risks his possessions, his life and his soul for the sake of a glory that is brief and passing, and yet enduring just a little suffering for God and for eternal blessedness seems such a big thing to us!

The other point I wish to make is that a number of unintelligent people will say that many things I have written in this book and elsewhere are not true.[37] I answer such people by quoting from the first book of St Augustine's *Confessions* where he says that God has already made everything that lies in the future, one or two thousand years away, for as long as the world exists, and that he will still create today all that lies several thousand years in the past. Is it my fault if someone does not understand that? And elsewhere he says again that those people evidently love themselves too much who wish to blind others in order to hide their own blindness.[38] For me it is enough to say that what I say and what I write is true in me and in God. Whoever sees a piece of wood which has been dipped into water, sees it as being bent, although it is actually perfectly straight. This comes from the fact that water is denser than air. Therefore the stick is not bent but is straight both in itself and in the eyes of those who see it in the purity of the air.

St Augustine says: 'Whoever inwardly perceives, without any concepts, impressions or visual images, what no external sight has mediated, knows what is true. But they who know nothing of this, laugh out loud and mock at me, and I pity them. Meanwhile, such people want to see and know eternal things and divine works and wish to stand in the light of eternity, while their heart still flies about in yesterday and in tomorrow.'[39]

A pagan master, Seneca, says: 'We should speak of things that are great and sublime with minds that are great and sublime and with an exalted soul.'[40] They will say that such teachings should not be spoken and written down for unlearned people. To this I say that if we do not teach the unlearned, then no one will be learned and no one will be able to speak or write. The unlearned are taught so that they may become learned. If there were nothing new, then there could be nothing that is old. 'Those who are healthy,' says the Lord, 'do not need healing' (Luke 5:31). The doctor is there in order to heal the sick. But if there is someone who does not understand these words aright, then what can that person do who rightly speaks these right words? St John preaches the holy gospel to all believers as well as to unbelievers, so that they too may be believers, and yet he begins his gospel with the most sublime things that we can say about God in this life; and both his words, and those of our Lord, have been misunderstood.

May the loving and merciful God, who is Truth itself, allow myself and all those who read this book to find and realize the truth which is in us. Amen.

On the Noble Man

Our Lord says in the Gospel: 'A certain nobleman went away to a distant country to gain a kingdom for himself, and returned' (Luke 19:12). Our Lord is teaching us in these words of the nobility of our created nature, how divine the end is to which we can come through grace and also how we should attain it. These words also touch on a great part of Scripture.

We should know first of all that we possess in ourselves two natures, one that is body and the other spirit, as is evident to all. Thus one book states: whoever knows themselves, knows all creatures, for all creatures are either body or spirit.[1] Thus the Scriptures say of us that there is in us an outer man and another, inner man (cf. 2 Cor. 4:16). To the outer man there belongs everything which, while it adheres to the soul, is nevertheless enclosed by flesh and mixed up with it and which cooperates with each and every member of the body, such as the eye, the ear, the tongue, the hand and so forth. All this Scripture calls the old, the earthly, the outer, the hostile or the slavish man.

The other person in us is the inner man, which Scripture calls the new, the heavenly, the young, the noble man, or the friend. And this is the one which is meant when our Lord says that 'a certain nobleman went away to a distant country to gain a kingdom for himself, and returned'.

We should know furthermore that St Jerome says, as do the masters in general, that everyone has from the very beginning of their existence a good spirit, which is an angel, and an evil spirit, which is a devil. The good spirit counsels and ceaselessly impels us to what is good and divine, to what is virtuous, heavenly and eternal, while the evil spirit counsels us and impels us towards what is temporal and passing, to what is immoral, wicked and of the devil. The same evil spirit maintains a constant dialogue with the outer man and, through him, it ceaselessly and secretly waylays the inner man, just as when the serpent beguiled Eve and, through her, beguiled Adam. The inner man is Adam. The man in the soul is the good tree which constantly brings forth good fruit, of which our Lord speaks (cf. Matt. 7:17).[2] He is also the field in which God sows his image and likeness and in which he plants the good seed, which is the root of all wisdom, all skills, all virtues and all goodness: the seed of divine nature. And the seed of divine nature is God's Son, God's Word (Matt. 13:24).

The outer man is the hostile and wicked man who has sown and cast tares on the field. Of him St Paul says, 'I find in me that which hinders me and is opposed to what God commands and what God counsels and what God has spoken and still speaks in the highest, in the ground of my soul' (cf. Rom. 7:23). And elsewhere he complains: 'Wretched man that I am! Who will deliver me from this body of death?' And he says again that our spirit and flesh are constantly at odds with one another. The flesh is immorality and evil, while the spirit counsels love of God, joy, peace and every kind of virtue (cf. Gal. 5:17–23). Whoever follows the spirit and lives according to him and his counsel, shall have eternal life (cf. Gal. 6:8). The inner man is the one of whom our Lord speaks when he says: 'A certain nobleman went away to a distant country to gain a kingdom for himself.' That is the good tree of which our Lord says that it always produces good fruit, never bad, since it wills the good and inclines to it, to goodness as it exists freely in itself, untouched by this or that. The outer man is the evil tree, from which good fruit can never come.

Even pagan masters, such as Cicero and Seneca, speak of the nobility of the inner man, that is the spirit, and the worthlessness of the outer man, that is the flesh, saying that no rational soul can exist without God and that the seed of God is in us.[3] With a good, wise and industrious farmer, that seed would flourish all the more and would grow up towards God, whose seed it is, and the fruit would be akin to God's nature. The seed of a pear tree grows into a pear tree, that of a nut tree into a nut tree, and the seed of God grows into God. But if the good seed has a foolish and wicked farmer, then weeds will grow, smothering the good seed and pushing it out, so that it cannot reach the light or grow to its full height. But as the great master Origen says: since it is God himself who has engendered this seed, sowing and implanting it, it can never be destroyed or extinguished in itself, even if it is overgrown and hidden. It glows and gleams, shines and burns and always seeks God.[4]

Augustine says that the first stage of the inner or new man is achieved when we live according to the example of good and holy people, even though we still clutch at chairs and lean against the walls and we still drink at the breast.[5]

The second stage comes when we no longer consider external images, even those of good men and women, but run and hasten towards the teaching and counsel of God and divine wisdom, turning our back on the world and our face towards God. Then we clamber off our mother's lap and smile at our heavenly Father.

The third stage is reached when we increasingly withdraw from our mother, removing ourselves more and more from her lap, shedding concern and fear so that even if it were in our power to inflict evil and injustice on all people without difficulty, we would not desire to do so, since through our love we are so bound to God in eager devotion that he finally establishes and leads us in joy and sweetness and blessedness to where all that is unlike God and alien to him is hateful to us.

The fourth stage comes when we grow and become ever more

rooted in love and in God, so that we are prepared to take upon ourselves any trial, temptation, unpleasantness and suffering willingly and gladly, eagerly and joyfully.

The fifth stage is when we live altogether at peace in ourselves, quietly resting in the overflowing wealth of the highest and unutterable wisdom.

The sixth stage comes when we are stripped of our own form and are transformed by God's eternity, becoming wholly oblivious to all transient and temporal life, drawn into and changed into an image of the divine, and have become God's son. Truly, there is no stage higher than this, and here eternal peace and blessedness reign, for the end of the inner man and the new man is eternal life.

For this inner and noble man, in whom God's seed has been sown and planted, and for the way in which God's seed and the image of the divine nature and essence, God's Son, becomes manifest so that we become aware of him, or is even sometimes hidden from us, for all this the great master Origen has a metaphor when he says that the image of God, God's Son, is in the ground of the soul like a spring of living water. But when someone throws earth upon it, that is earthly desire, then it becomes choked and blocked so that we no longer see it or know that it is there. And yet it still remains active and living in itself, and if we remove the earth with which it has been covered, then it appears again and we can see it. And he says that this truth is spoken of in the Book of Genesis, where we read that Adam dug springs of living water in his field which wicked people covered over, and that when the earth was later removed, the springs of living water appeared again (Gen. 26:15ff.).[6]

And there is another metaphor for this, which is that of the sun that shines without end. But whenever a cloud or mist comes between us and the sun, we can no longer see the sunshine. In the same way, when the eye is impaired, diseased or veiled, then the sunshine is no longer visible. And I have sometimes presented another clear analogy: when a master sculpts a figure from wood or stone, he does not place the figure in the wood but cuts away the sections that cover and conceal it. He gives the wood nothing but rather takes from it, cutting away the overlay, scraping off the rust and then polishing what lay hidden beneath. This is the treasure which lay hidden in the field, as Our Lord says in the Gospel (Matt. 13:44).

St Augustine says that when the human soul is turned fully upwards towards eternity, towards God alone, then the image of God shines brightly.[7] But when the human soul is turned outwards, even towards the practice of external virtues, this image is completely hidden. This is why women cover their heads, while men have their heads uncovered, according to the teaching of St Paul (cf. 1 Cor. 11:4ff.). Therefore, everything to do with the soul which tends downwards receives from that to which it tends an overlay or headscarf, but that part of the soul which strives upwards is the pure image of God, the birth of God, revealed in a soul laid bare. Speaking of the nobleman, and of how the image of God, God's Son, the seed of divine nature, is never destroyed within us, that even if it is sometimes covered up, King David says in the Psalter: Even if many kinds of vanity, suffering and adversity befall us, we still remain in the image of God with his image in us. The true light shines in the darkness, though we may not be aware of it (cf. John 1:5).

'Do not consider that I am brown,' says the Song of Solomon, 'I am black but lovely; it is the sun that has burnt me' (S. of S. 1:5–6). The 'sun' is the light of this world and signifies that even what is best and highest in us, having been created and made, obscures and discolours God's image in us. Solomon says: 'From silver remove the dross and it emerges wholly purified' (Pro. 25:4), meaning God's image, his Son, in the soul. And that is also what our Lord means when he says that 'a nobleman went away', for we must take leave of all images and of ourselves, becoming distant from them and unlike them, if we are really to receive and become the Son in the bosom and heart of the Father.

Every kind of mediation is alien to God. God says, 'I am the first and the last' (Rev. 22:13). There is neither distinction in the nature of God nor in the Persons of the Trinity according to the unity of their nature. The divine nature is One, and each Person is both One and the same One as God's nature. The distinction between essence and existence is apprehended as One and is One. Distinction is born, exists and is possessed only where this Oneness no longer obtains. Therefore it is in Oneness that God is found, and they who would find God must themselves become One. 'A man,' our Lord says, 'went away . . .'.[8] In distinction we shall find neither Oneness, essence, God, rest, blessedness or contentment. Be One then, so that you shall find God! And truly, if you are properly One, then you shall remain One in the midst of distinction, and the multifold will be One for you and shall not be able to impede you in any way. The One remains equally One in a thousand times a thousand stones as it does in four stones, and a thousand times a thousand is just as certainly a simple number as four is a number.

A pagan master says that the One is born from the all-highest God.[9] It is his nature to be one with the One. Whoever seeks it at a point beneath God, deceives themselves. And, fourthly, the same master says that this One has a special affinity with virgins or maids, as St Paul says: 'I have given you in marriage, pure virgins, to the One' (cf. 2 Cor. 11:2). This is exactly how we should be, for our Lord says: 'A man went away . . .'.[10]

One meaning of the Latin for 'man' or 'human being' in the true sense of the word is that person who entirely submits to God, together with all that they are and possess, turning their face up to God and not to their own possessions which they know to be behind, beneath and beside them. This is true and perfect humility; its name comes from the earth. But I do not wish to speak further of this now. When we say 'man', then this word also signifies that which is above nature, above time and above everything which leans towards time or itself smacks of time, and the same is true with respect to space and corporality. Moreover, this 'man' has in a certain sense nothing in common with anything else, that is, he is neither formed nor made like this or that, and knows nothing of 'nothingness' so that nowhere can we find or ascertain any nothingness in him, and nothingness has been so removed from him that we can find only pure life, essence, truth and goodness in him. Whoever is made like this, is a 'nobleman' indeed, no more and no less.

But there is another explanation and elucidation of what our Lord means by 'nobleman'. We should realize that those who know God in his bare essence also know all creatures; for knowledge is a light of the soul, and all people have a natural desire for knowledge since even the knowledge of evil things is good. Now the masters say: when we know a creature in its own essence, then this is an 'evening knowledge' in which we see creatures in images of multiplicity and distinction. But when we know creatures in God, then that is called a 'morning knowledge', and in this way we see creatures without any distinctions, stripped of images and likeness in the Oneness which God himself is.[11] This too is the 'nobleman' of whom our Lord says: 'A nobleman went away'. He is noble because he is One, knowing God and creature in Oneness.

I want to turn now to yet another meaning of the term 'nobleman'. I say that when the self, the soul, the spirit sees God, then it knows itself also as knowing subject: that is, it knows that it sees and knows God. Now it has been the opinion of some, and indeed seems credible, that the seed and flower of blessedness reside in that knowledge in which the spirit knows that it knows God, for if I possessed all bliss and had no knowledge of it, then what good would it do me and what kind of bliss would it be?[12] But I say that this is definitely not the case. Even if it is true that the soul would not be blessed without this, it does not follow that this is blessedness, for blessedness consists primarily in the fact that the soul sees God in himself. It is in this that the soul receives the whole of her nature and life and all that she is from the ground of God, knowing nothing of knowledge nor of love nor of anything else at all. Only in God's essence does she become wholly still. There she knows nothing but essence and God. But when she knows and understands that she sees, knows and loves God, then this both results from and is a reflex back to the former, according to the natural order of things.[13] After all, no one knows themselves to be white except those who are white. Therefore, whoever knows themselves to be white builds and supports themselves on *being* white, deriving their knowledge not directly and unreflectingly from the colour in itself but rather from that which is white in the present, not deriving their knowledge from the colour alone in itself but rather from coloured or white objects, thus knowing themselves to be white. The colour white is something far less substantial and far more superficial than *being* white. A wall and the foundations upon which a wall stands are two different things.[14]

The masters say that the power through which the eye sees is quite different from that through which it knows that it sees. The former, the seeing, is something which it takes from the colour, rather than from that which is coloured. Thus it is of no consequence whether that which is coloured is a stone or a piece of wood, a person or an angel: the essential thing is only that it has colour.

In the same way I say the nobleman derives his whole essence, life and blessedness solely from God, with God and in God, and not from knowing, seeing or loving God or anything of that kind. Therefore our Lord says truthfully that eternal life consists in this, in knowing God as the one true God (John 17:3) and not in knowing that we know God. For how should we know ourselves to know God when we do not even know ourselves? Indeed, it is not ourselves and other things that we know, but rather God alone, if we are blessed in the root and ground of blessedness. But when the soul knows that she knows God, then she has knowledge simultaneously of God and of itself.

But now there is one power, as I have said, through which we see and another through which we know and understand the fact that we see. It is true that here below, in this life, that power by which we know and understand that we see is nobler and better than that power by which we see, since nature begins her work at the weakest point while God begins his at the point of perfection. Nature makes a man or woman from a child and a chicken from an egg, while God makes the man or woman before the child and the chicken before the egg. Nature first makes the wood warm and then hot, and only then does she generate fire, while God first gives all creatures being and only later, within time and yet timelessly and individually, he gives them all that belongs to being. Similarly, God bestows on us the Holy Spirit before he gives us the gifts of the Spirit.

Thus I say that although there cannot be blessedness without us consciously knowing that we see and know God, God forbid that our blessedness should be founded on this. If someone else is happy with this, then all well and good, but I do not want it. The heat of fire and the essence of fire are quite different from each other and are astonishingly far apart by nature, although they exist in close proximity within time and space. Seeing God and seeing ourselves are wholly separate from each other and distinct.

Therefore our Lord rightly says that 'A certain nobleman went away to a distant country to gain a kingdom for himself, and returned'. For we must be One in ourselves and must seek it in ourselves and in Oneness and must receive it in Oneness, which means to say that we must first simply look upon God and that when we know that we know and see God, then this is our 'return'.

All that has been stated here was prophesied by Ezekiel when he said that 'a mighty eagle with great wings, long-pinioned, rich with many-coloured plumage, came to the pure mountain and, taking the pith or marrow of the highest tree, plucked off its crown of leaves and brought it down' (Ezek. 17:3–4). What our Lord calls a nobleman, the prophet calls a great eagle. Now what is nobler than that which is born, on the one hand, from all that is highest and best in the creature and, on the other, from the most inward ground of divine nature and the divine desert? In the prophet Hosea our Lord says: 'I will lead the noble soul into a wilderness and there I will speak into her heart' (Hos. 2:14). One with One, one from One, one in One and one in One in all eternity. Amen.

Selected German Sermons

SERMON I (DW 33, W 81)

Sancti per fidem vicerunt regna (Heb. 11:32)

St Paul says: 'the saints have conquered heaven with their faith'. The saints have conquered four kingdoms with their faith, and we should conquer them too. The first kingdom is the world, which we should overcome with poverty of spirit. The second kingdom is our body, which we should overcome with hunger and thirst. The third is the kingdom of the devil, which we should conquer with grief and pain, and the fourth is the kingdom of our Lord Jesus Christ, which we should conquer with the power of love.

Even if we possessed the whole world, we should nevertheless consider ourselves to be poor and should reach out to the door of our Lord and God, beseeching the gift of our Lord's grace, for it is grace that makes us children of God. Therefore David says: 'Lord, my whole desire is for you and is before you' (Ps. 37:10). St Paul says: 'I count all things as refuse in order to gain my Lord, Jesus Christ' (Phil. 3:8). It is impossible for a soul to be without sin unless God's grace has entered it. The effect of grace is to make the soul buoyant and responsive to all the works of God, for grace flows forth from the divine spring; it is a likeness of God that has the savour of God and makes the soul like God. Now when this grace and this savour enters the will, we call it love, and when this grace and savour enters our intelligence, we call it the light of faith. When the same grace and savour enters the irascible part, which is the dynamic power in us, then we call it hope.[1] That is why they are called the divine virtues, since they have divine effects in the soul, just as we can tell by the power of

III

the sun that it quickens the earth, since it enlivens all things and sustains their being.[2] If this light were to disappear, then all things too would pass and it would be as it was before they existed. It is just the same with the soul: where there is grace and love, it is easy for us to do all godly works, and it is a sure sign of the absence of grace if we find it difficult to perform godly works. Therefore a master says:[3] I do not condemn those people who wear fine clothes or eat well, as long as they have love. I do not regard myself as being any better when my life is demanding than when I see that there is more love in me. It is nonsensical for some people to fast and pray a good deal, to perform great works and seek constant solitude if they do not also improve their moral behaviour, but remain restless and irritable. They should take note of where they are weakest, and should apply themselves to overcoming this. If their way of life is right, then God will be pleased with whatever they do.

Thus it is that we can 'conquer' the 'kingdoms'. Let us pray.

SERMON 2 (DW 38, W 29)

In illo tempore missus est angelus Gabriel a deo: ave gratia plena, dominus tecum
(Luke 1:26, 28)

St Luke writes these words: 'At that time the angel Gabriel was sent by God'. At what time? 'In the sixth month', when John the Baptist was in his mother's womb.

If someone were to ask me: why do we pray, why do we fast, why do we all perform our devotions and good works, why are we baptized, why did God, the All-Highest, take on our flesh? – then I would reply: in order that God may be born in the soul and the soul be born in God. That is why the whole of Scripture was written and why God created the whole world and all the orders of angels: so that God could be born in the soul and the soul in God. It is the nature of every grain of corn to become wheat and every precious metal to become gold and all procreation to lead to the procreation of the human race. Therefore a master says that there is no animal which does not possess some likeness to human beings.

'At that time.' Firstly, when a word is conceived in my intellect, it is so pure and subtle there that it is a true word before it subsequently takes form in my thought. Thirdly, it is physically uttered by my mouth, and then it is nothing but a revelation of the inner word. In the same way the Eternal Word is spoken internally in the heart of the soul, in the most interior and purest part, in the head of the soul, of which I have recently spoken, in the *intellect*. That is where the birth takes place. Whoever has only an intimation of and hope for this, may wish to know how this birth takes place and what aids it.

St Paul says: 'In the fullness of time God sent his only Son' (Gal. 4:4). St Augustine explains the meaning of 'fullness of time' here when he says 'where there is no more time, there is "fullness of time"'.[4] For the day is full when there is no more of the day left. It is a necessary truth that all time must disappear where this birth begins, for there is nothing that so impedes it as time and creatures. It is a certain truth that time by its nature can touch neither God nor the soul. If the soul could be touched by time, she would not be the soul, and if God could be touched by time, he would not be God. If the soul could be touched by time, then God could never be born in her, and she could never be born in God. All time must fall away from that place where God is to be born in the soul, or she must have fallen away from time through her intentions or desires.

And here is another meaning of 'In the fullness of time': if someone possessed the skill and the power to draw time and all that has happened in time during these six thousand years or will happen before the end of time, into the Now of the present, then that would be the 'fullness of time'. This is the Now of eternity in which the soul knows all things new and fresh and present in God with the same delight which I have in those things that are present to me now. I recently read in a book (who can fathom this?) that God is creating the world even now as he did on the first day when he created the world. Here God is rich, and here is God's kingdom. The soul which is to be born in God must fall away from time as time must fall away from her. She must rise up and must linger in contemplation of this wealth of God,[5] where there is length without length and breadth without breadth. There the soul knows all things and knows them in perfection.

What the masters tell us about the dimensions of the heavens beggars belief, and yet the least power in my soul is broader than the heavens, not to mention the intellect, in which there is breadth without breadth. In the head of the soul, in the intellect, I am as close to a point located a thousand miles beyond the sea as I am to the place where I am presently standing. In this expanse and wealth of God the soul attains knowing, nothing escapes her and she seeks nothing more.

'The angel was sent.' The masters say that the multitude of angels is a number beyond all numbers.[6] Their multitude is so great that it cannot be contained by a number: it cannot even be conceived of. But for someone who can conceive of distinction without number or quantity, even a hundred would be the same as one. If there were a hundred Persons in the Godhead, they would see only one God. Unbelievers and some uneducated Christians are astounded at this; even some priests know as little about it as a stone does, and take three in the sense of three cows or three stones. But whoever can conceive of distinction in God without number or quantity, knows that three Persons are a single God.

An angel is also so exalted that according to the best teachers, every angel is its own complete species.[7] It is just as if there were someone who possessed everything, all the strength and wisdom that everyone possesses now and shall possess in the future. That would be a miracle, and yet they would still be only human, since they would only possess everything which all other *people* have, and would be far from being an angel. Every angel therefore is its own species and is distinct from others as one kind of animal is from another. God is rich in this multitude of angels, and whoever knows this, knows the kingdom of God. It proclaims God's kingdom just as a king is proclaimed by the number of his knights. For this reason he is known as the 'Lord God of hosts'. But however exalted they may be, this whole host of angels must assist and cooperate with God if God is to be born in the soul. This means that they have delight, joy and bliss in the birth, although they do not bring it about. No creature can bring it about, for this is the work of God alone and the angels can only serve him in it. Everything which aids this therefore is a form of ministry.

The angel was called 'Gabriel'. And he acted according to his name. In fact, his name was no more Gabriel than it was Conrad. No one can know the angel's name. No master and no mind has ever penetrated to the place where the angel is known by name, and perhaps indeed it has no name. The soul too is nameless. It is no more possible to find a name for the soul than it is to find one for God, even though weighty tomes have been written about this. But in so far as she chooses to act, we give her a name. Consider a carpenter for instance. This is not so much his name as the name for what he does and of which he is master. 'Gabriel' took his name from the act which he proclaimed, since 'Gabriel' means 'power' (cf. Luke 1:35).[8] In this birth God acts powerfully or reveals his power. What end does the power of nature seek? Self-propagation. What end does all nature seek, which acts through generation? Self-propagation. The nature of my father wanted to reproduce a father according to its own father nature. Since it could not do this, it wished at least to produce something which was like itself in all ways. And since it lacked the power even to achieve this, it produced the most similar thing it could, which was a son. But when there is even less strength present, or when some mistake occurs, then it produces a human being which is even less like itself.[9] In God, however, there is perfect power, which is why in his birth he produces a perfect image of himself. God perfectly generates in the soul all that he is in terms of power, truth and wisdom.

St Augustine says: 'The soul becomes like that which it loves. If it loves earthly things, then it becomes earthly.' We might ask: if it loves God, does it then become God? If I said that, it would sound incredible to those whose understanding is too limited to grasp this. But Augustine says: 'I do not say it, but I refer you to Scripture, where we read: "I have said that you are gods!"' (Ps. 82:6).[10] Whoever possesses anything of that wealth of which I have just spoken, whether a glimpse, a hope or a confident expectation of it, will understand me well! Nothing has ever been as similar, as akin or as united to anything else through birth as in this birth the soul is to God. And if it happens that it is obstructed in anything so that it is not like God in all respects, then this is not God's fault. In so far as the soul's failings fall away from her, to that extent he makes her like himself. We cannot blame the carpenter for not being able to make a nice house from wood that is riddled with woodworm; the problem lies with his materials. It is the same with God's action in the soul. If the lowest angel could be reproduced or born in the soul, the whole world would be as nothing in comparison, for from the single spark of an angel there springs all that is green, leafy and bright in this world. But it is God himself who makes this birth happen, and the angel can do no more than assist him in it.

'Ave': that means 'without pain'.[11] Whoever has no creature in them, is 'without pain' and without hell, and whoever is a creature or possesses creatures the least, has the least pain. I said once that whoever possesses the world least, actually possesses it the most. No one owns the world as much as they who have given the whole world up. Do you know how God is God? God is God because there is nothing of the creature in him. He has never been named within time. Creatures, sin and death belong to time. In a certain sense they are all related, and since the soul has fallen away from time if she has fallen away from the world, there is neither pain nor suffering there. Indeed, even tribulation turns to joy for her there. If we were to compare everything which has ever been conceived of regarding delight and joy, bliss and pleasure, with the delight which belongs to this birth, then it would all be as nothing.

'Full of grace.' The least work of grace is more noble than all the angels according to their nature. St Augustine says that when God performs a work of grace (as when he converts a sinner and turns them into a good person), then this is greater than if he were to create a new world. It is as easy for God to invert heaven and earth as it is for me to turn an apple round in my hand. Where there is grace in the soul, it is so pure there, so like and so akin to God, and is without works, just as it is in the birth of which I have spoken. Grace does not perform works. St John 'never worked any signs' (cf. John 10:41). The work which the angel performs in God is so exalted that no master or mind can penetrate there and thus comprehend it. But from this work there falls a splinter (just as a splinter might fall from a length of wood that is being hewed), a flash, where the angel touches heaven with its lowest part, from which all that lives in this world receives its greenness, its flowering and its life.

I sometimes speak of two springs. Even if it seems strange, we must nevertheless speak from our own understanding. One spring, from which grace flows, is where the Father gives birth to his only-begotten Son; that same spring gives rise to grace and grace flows forth from it. The second spring is where creatures flow out from God, and this is as far removed from that other spring, where grace emerges, as heaven is from earth. Grace does not perform works. Where fire is in its own nature, it cannot harm anything or set it on fire. It is fire's heat which ignites things here on earth. And even heat, where it exists in the nature of fire, cannot burn or harm anything. Indeed, where heat exists in the nature of fire, it is as remote from the proper nature of fire as heaven is from earth. Grace does not perform any works; it is too subtle for that and is as far from performing works as heaven is from earth. An indwelling, an inhering and a union with God, that is what grace is and there 'God is with', for the words 'God is with you' immediately follow.[12] And that is where the birth occurs. No one should think that it is impossible to get this far. What difference does it make to me how difficult it is, if it is God who does the work? All his commandments are easily kept. Let him command me to do all that he will and I will be content, it will be only a small thing, as long as he grants me his grace as well. There are some who say that they do not have his grace. To these I reply: 'I am sorry. But do you ask for it?' – 'No.' 'Then I regret that even more.' Even if we cannot have grace, we can desire it. If we cannot desire it, then we can at least desire to have a desire for it. David says: 'I have desired a desire, Lord, for your justice' (cf. Ps. 119:20).

That this may be our desire, and that he may wish to be born in us, so help us God. Amen.

SERMON 3 (DW 28, W 17)

Ego elegi vos de mundo (John 15:16)

These words which I have spoken in Latin can be found in today's Gospel reading for the feast of a saint by the name of

Barnabas. Scripture tells us that he was an apostle, and our Lord says: 'I have chosen you, I have selected you from all the world, picked you out from the entire world and from all created things, that you should bring forth much fruit and that your fruit should remain' (cf. John 15:16). It is delightful when fruit is produced and remains, but fruit remains for those who themselves remain and dwell in love. At the end of this Gospel reading our Lord says, 'Love one another as I have loved you; and as my Father eternally loved me, so I have loved you. Keep my commandments, then you will remain in my love' (John 15:9, 10, 12).

All the commandments of God proceed from love and from the goodness of his nature for, if they did not come from love, then they could not be the commandment of God. God's commandment is the goodness of his nature, and his nature is the goodness in his commandment. Now whoever dwells in the goodness of his nature, dwells in God's love, but love has no Why. If I had a friend and loved him because of the benefits which this brought me and because of getting my own way, then it would not be my friend that I loved but myself. I should love my friend on account of his own goodness and virtues and on account of all that he is in himself. Only if I love my friend in this way do I love him properly. It is exactly the same with that person who stands in God's love, who does not pursue his or her own interests with respect to God, themselves or any other thing, but loves God purely for the sake of his goodness and for the goodness of his nature, loving him for the sake of all that is in him. That is real love. Love for the virtues is a flower and an ornament and the mother of all virtues, perfection and blessedness, for it is God, since God is the fruit of the virtues. God fructifies all virtues and is himself the fruit of virtue, and this is the fruit which 'remains' for us. If someone worked for a fruit which then remained, this would be a great delight for them. If someone were to give their vineyard or field to their servant so that he could work the land and keep the fruit, and if they were to give him also all that he needed to do this, then the servant would be delighted to have the fruit at no cost to himself. In the same way, those who dwell in the fruit of virtue know delight, for they have no worries or problems since they have taken leave of themselves and all things.

Now our Lord says: 'Whoever renounces anything for me and for my name's sake shall receive a hundredfold and eternal life' (cf. Matt. 19:29). But if you give it up for the sake of the hundredfold and of eternal life, then you have renounced nothing. Indeed, if you give it up for a thousandfold return, you have renounced nothing. You must give yourself up, and must do so completely, if you are really to renounce something. Once a man came to me – this happened quite recently – and told me that he had given away great amounts of land and possessions in order to save his soul. But I thought to myself: what small and insignificant things you have given away. To contemplate what you have renounced is blindness and stupidity. But if you have abandoned yourself, then you have really renounced something. Those who have taken leave of themselves are so pure that the world cannot endure them.

I once said on this point, quite recently, that whoever loves justice, takes possession of justice and is seized by justice and becomes justice. I once wrote in my book:[13] the just person is in service neither to God nor creatures, for such a person is free, and the closer they are to justice, the more they become freedom itself and the more they are freedom. For nothing created is free. As long as there is something above me which is not God, I am oppressed by it, however small it is or whatever it may be, even if it is reason and love. In so far as these are created and are not God, they oppress me, for they are not free. The unjust person is in service to truth, whether they like it or not, as they are to the whole world and to all creatures, and they are the slave of sin.

Once the thought entered my mind, not so long ago, that the fact I am human is something I have in common with everyone else. Cows, too, see and hear, eat and drink, but *what* I am belongs to no one other than myself, to no person, no angel or to God, except in so far as I am one with him. It is one purity and one unity. All that God works he works in the One which is identical with himself. God gives to all things equally, although they are not equal in their own works, and all things strive to effect in their works that which is the same as their own being. Nature performed in my father the work of nature. It was nature's purpose that I should become a father, just as he was a father. My father performs all his work for the sake of something that is the same as he is, for the sake of his own image, so that he is the result of his own work. The intention is always to produce a male. A female is born only when nature is diverted or obstructed, so that its work lacks full strength.[14] But where the work of nature comes to an end, God takes over and begins to create, for if there were no women there would be no men either. When the child is conceived in the womb, it has body, shape and form, which is nature's work. There it remains for forty days and forty nights until, on the fortieth day, God creates the soul in less than an instant so that the soul will be form and life for the body. Now the work of nature comes to an end, together with all that nature can effect in terms of shape, body and form. The work of nature ceases but, as it does so, it is fully restored in the activity of the rational soul. Now this is both a work of nature and a creation of God.

In created things, as I have often said before, there is no truth. But there is something which is above the created being of the soul and which is untouched by any createdness, by any nothingness. Even the angels do not have this, whose clear being is pure and deep; even that does not touch it. It is like the divine nature; in itself it is one and has nothing in common with anything. And it is with regard to this that many teachers go wrong. It is a strange land, a wilderness, being more nameless than with name, more unknown than known. If you could do away with yourself for a moment, even for less than a moment, then you would possess all that this possesses in itself. But as long as you have any regard for yourself in any way or for anything, then you will not know what God is. As my mouth knows what colour is and my eye what taste is: that is how little you will know what God is.

Now at this point we hear Plato, the great priest, speaking to us of great things.[15] He speaks of a purity which is not in the world. It is neither in the world nor outside the world; it is neither in time nor in eternity; it has neither an exterior nor an interior dimension. But from this God, the eternal Father, drives forth the abundance and the depths of his whole Godhead. To this he gives birth in his only begotten Son and makes us the same Son. But his giving birth is at the same time a remaining within, and his remaining within is his giving birth. The One always remains, which wells forth within itself. 'Ego', the Latin word for 'I', can be used properly by God alone in his unity. 'Vos', which means 'you', says that you should be one in this unity. This means that 'ego' and 'vos', 'I' and 'you', refer to unity.

That we may become this unity and may remain within it, so help us God. Amen.

SERMON 4 (DW 30, W 18)

Praedica verbum, vigila, in omnibus labora (2 Tim. 4:2, 5)

We shall read a passage today and tomorrow which concerns St Dominic and which St Paul wrote in his epistle. In our language it reads as follows: 'Speak the word, spread it abroad, bring it forth and propagate it.'

It is an amazing fact that something should flow out and yet remain within. That the word flows out and yet remains within is astonishing; that all creatures flow out and yet remain within is also astonishing. What God has given and has promised to give is astonishing, incredible and beyond belief. But this is as it should be, for if it were comprehensible and easy to believe, then that would not be right. God is in all things. The more he is in things, the more he is outside them: the more in, the more out and the more out, the more in. I have already said on a number of occasions that God created the whole world perfectly and entirely in the Now. God still creates now everything he made six thousand years ago or more, when he created the world. God is in all things, but in so far as God is divine and in so far as God is rational, he exists more properly in the soul and in angels, that is in the innermost and highest part of the soul, than he does anywhere else. And when I say the innermost, then I mean the highest, and when I say the highest, I mean the innermost part of the soul. And when I say the innermost and highest part of the soul together, then I mean both as if they were one. In that place, to which neither time nor the light of any image ever penetrated, in the highest and innermost part of the soul, God creates the whole of this world. Everything which God created six thousand years ago, when he made the world, and everything which he shall create over the next thousand years, if the world lasts that long, he creates in the innermost and highest part of the soul. Everything which is past, and everything which is present, and everything which is in the future God creates in the innermost part of the soul. Everything which God has ever worked in all the saints, he works in the innermost part of the soul. The Father gives birth to the Son in the innermost part of the soul, and he gives birth to you too together with his only begotten Son, and no less. If I wish to be a son of God, I must be a son in the same nature that his Son is Son, and nowhere else. If I wish to be a man or woman, I cannot be one in the nature of an animal, but must be one in the nature of a human being. But if I wish to be this particular person, then I must be in the particular nature of this person. St John says: 'You are the children of God' (1 John 3:1).

'Speak the word, proclaim it, bring it forth and propagate it.' Proclaim it. That which is spoken into us from without is coarse, but this word is pronounced within. 'Proclaim it' – that means: become aware of what is in you. The prophet says: 'God spoke one thing, but I heard two.' That is true: God has only ever uttered one thing. His speech is single. In this one utterance, he speaks his Son forth, the Holy Spirit and all creatures, and yet there is only one utterance in God. But the prophet says: 'I heard two things', which means God and creatures. There where God speaks creatures, creatures are God, but here on earth they are creatures.[16] People think that God became human only in the Incarnation, but this is not the case, for God has become human just as surely here and now as he did then, and has become human in order that he might give birth to you as his only begotten Son, and no less.

As I was sitting somewhere yesterday, I repeated a phrase taken from the Our Father: 'May your will be done' (Matt. 6:10). But it would have been better to say: 'May will itself be yours'[17] – that my will may be his will and that I may be him. This is what the Our Father means. And this phrase has a double meaning. The first is 'Be asleep with respect to all things!', which is to say that you should know nothing of time, creatures or images. The masters say: if someone who is soundly asleep were to slumber for a hundred years, then they would have no knowledge of any creature, of time or images. And then you could become aware of what God is doing within you. That is why the soul says in the

Book of Love: 'I am asleep but my heart is awake' (S. of S. 5:2). Therefore, if all creatures are asleep in you, you can see how God is at work in you.

The phrase 'labour in all things' also has three meanings. It means 'make the best of everything!', which is to say 'receive God in all things!'. For God is in all things. St Augustine says: 'God did not make all things and then go his own way, thus abandoning them, but he remained within them.'[18] People think that they have more when they have both things and God than when they have God without things. But this is wrong, for having all things as well as God is nothing other than having God alone, and if someone who has the Son as well as the Father thinks they have more than if they had the Son without the Father, then this would be wrong. For the Father with the Son is no more than the Son alone, just as the Son with the Father is no more than the Father alone. Therefore, receive God in all things, and that will be a sign that he has given birth to you as his only begotten Son, no less.

The second meaning of this phrase is: 'make the best of everything', which means 'love God above all and your neighbour as yourself' (Luke 10:27). This is a commandment from God. But I say that it is not only a commandment but that God has given us this as a gift and has promised to give us it. If you love a thousand marks which are in your rather than someone else's possession, then this is not right. If you prefer one person to another, then this is not right. If you love your father and mother and yourself more than you do someone else, then this too is not right. And if you prefer blessedness in yourself to blessedness in another, that is not right either. 'God forbid! What are you saying there? Should I love blessedness in someone else more than I do in myself?' There are many learned individuals who do not understand this, and it seems very hard to them. But it is not difficult; it is quite simple. And I will show you why it is not difficult. See how nature has a twofold purpose for every member of our body. The first function which it performs is to serve the whole body of which it is a part and then to serve each other individual member no less than itself, and it considers its own interests in its action no more than it does those of any other member. Now this should be far more the case in the world of grace. God should be the rule and the foundation of your love. The first intention of your love should be directed solely towards God first and then towards your neighbour and yourself, but your neighbour no less than yourself. If you love blessedness in yourself more than in another, this is wrong, for if you love blessedness in yourself more than in another, then you love yourself, and where you love yourself, God is not your sole love, and that is wrong. For if you love the blessedness in St Paul and St Peter as you do in yourself, then you possess the same blessedness which they have. And if you love the blessedness in the angels as in yourself, and the blessedness in Our Lady, then you truly enjoy the same blessedness in yourself as they do. It is yours as much as it is theirs. Therefore we read in the Book of Wisdom: 'He made him like his saints' (Si. 45:2).

The third meaning of 'make the best of everything' is: 'love God equally in all things'. This means to say that we should love him just as willingly in poverty as in wealth, in sickness as in health. We should love him just as much when we are living through a time of trial as when we are not, when we suffer as when we do not. Indeed, the greater the suffering, the less we suffer, as with two buckets. The heavier one bucket is, the lighter the other, and the more we give, the easier giving becomes. For someone who loves God, it would be just as easy to give up the whole world as it would be to give up an egg. The more we give, the easier it is to do so, as was the case with the apostles. The greater the suffering which befell them, the easier it was for them to endure.

'Labour in all things.' This means: where you find yourself dependent on multiple things and not on pure, naked and simple being, there you should exert yourself and 'labour in all things' 'in the performing of your service' (2 Tim. 4:5). That is tantamount to 'lift your head up!', which has two meanings. The first is 'shed everything which is yours and take possession of God, then God will belong to you as he belongs to himself, and he will be your God as he is his own God, no less'. What is mine comes to me from no one. But if I have it from someone else, then it is not mine but rather it is that person's from whom I have it. The second meaning is 'lift your head up!', which is 'dedicate all your works to God'. There are many people who do not understand this, which does not surprise me at all, since in order to understand this someone would have to be very detached and raised above all the things of this world.

That we may come to this perfection, so help us God. Amen.

SERMON 5 (DW 53, W 22)

Misit dominus manum suam et tetigit os meum et dixit mihi, etc.
Ecce constitui te super gentes et regna (Jer. 1:9, 10)

'The Lord stretched out his hand and touched my mouth and spoke to me.'

When I preach, I am accustomed to talk about detachment, saying that we should become free of ourselves and of all things. Secondly, I say that we should be in-formed back into the simple goodness, which is God. Thirdly, I say that we should be mindful of the great nobility which God has given the soul in order that we should become wonderfully united with him.

Fourthly, I speak of the purity of the divine nature, and of the radiance within it which is ineffable. God is a word: an unspoken word.

Augustine says: 'the whole of Scripture is in vain. If it is said that God is a word, then he is spoken, but if it is said that God is unspoken, then he is ineffable.'[19] But God is something, yet who can speak this word? No one can but he who is the word. God is a word which speaks itself. Wherever he is, he speaks this word, and where he is not, he does not speak it. God is both spoken and unspoken. The Father is speaking work, and the Son is working speech. What is in me, goes out of me: if I think something, then my speech reveals it and yet it remains within. In the same way the Father speaks the Son who remains unspoken and remains in him. I have said this repeatedly: God's going out is his coming in. The closer I am to God, the more he speaks himself in me. The more we rational creatures go out of ourselves in our works, the more we enter into ourselves. This is not the case with physical creatures:[20] the more they act, the more they go out of themselves. All creatures wish to speak God in all their works. They all speak as well as they can, but they cannot speak him. Whether they wish to or not, like it or not, even though they all want to speak God, he remains unspoken.

David says: 'The Lord is his name' (Ps. 68:4). 'Lord' means the setting up of a supremacy here, while 'servant' is a form of subjection. Certain names are proper to God, such as 'God', and are detached from all other things. 'God' is his truest name, just as 'human being' is our name. We are always human, whether we are foolish or wise. Seneca says: 'That man or woman is wretched who does not transcend their humanity.'[21] Certain names signify properties which are attributed to God, such as 'son' or 'father'. When we think of a father, we think simultaneously of a son. There cannot be a father without a son, nor a son without a father; but both contain within themselves an eternal essence which is beyond time. Thirdly, certain names signify both a looking up to God and a turning towards time. God has many names in Scripture. But I say that if someone perceives something in God and gives it a name, then that is not God. God is above names and nature. We read of a good man who turned to God in his prayer and wished to give him a name. Then a brother said to him, 'Be silent! You are dishonouring God!' There is no name we can devise for God. But some names are permitted to us, with which the saints have addressed him and which God has so consecrated in their hearts and bathed in a divine light. And here we should learn first of all how we should approach God. We should say: 'Lord, with the same names which you have so consecrated in the hearts of your saints and bathed in your light, we approach you and praise you.' Secondly, we should learn that there is no name we can give God so that it might seem that we have praised and honoured him enough, since God is 'above names' and is ineffable.

The Father speaks the Son with the whole of his power and speaks all things in him. All creatures are the utterance of God. If my mouth speaks and declares God, so too does the being of a stone, and we understand more by works than by words. Lower nature cannot comprehend the work which the highest nature performs by its most exalted power. If it could perform this itself, then it would itself be the highest nature. All creatures wish to echo God in all their works, but they can reveal him only a little. Even the way that the highest angels rise up and touch God is as different from what is in God as black is from white. The totality of what each and every creature has received is also quite different from what is in God, even though they all desire to declare the nearest approximation to it that they can. The prophet says: 'God spoke one thing but I heard two.' When God speaks in the soul, then he and the soul are one, but as soon as this state of oneness falls away, division ensues. The higher we ascend with our knowledge, the more we are one in him.

Therefore the Father always speaks the Son in unity and pours forth all creatures in him. They all clamour to return to that place from which they emerged. Their whole life and being is a clamouring and a hastening back to him from whom they were born.

The prophet says: 'The Lord has stretched forth his hand' (Jer. 1:9) and refers with these words to the Holy Spirit. Now he says: 'He has touched my mouth', and then: 'He has spoken to me' (Jer. 1:9). The 'mouth' of the soul is the soul's highest part, which is what is meant here, and the soul says: 'He has placed his word in my mouth' (Jer. 1:9). This is the kiss of the soul, when mouth is joined to mouth, when the Father gives birth to the Son in the soul and the soul is 'spoken to'. Now he says: 'Take heed. Today I have chosen you and have raised you above nations and kingdoms' (Jer. 1:10). In a 'today' God promises to choose us, where there is nothing and where, nevertheless, there is a 'today' in eternity. 'And I have raised you above nations', which means over the whole world, which you must be free of, and 'over kingdoms', which means that everything which is more than the One is too much, for you must die to all things and must be in-formed into the heights where we dwell in the Holy Spirit.

So help us God, the Holy Spirit. Amen.

SERMON 6 (DW 58, W 44)

Qui mihi ministrat, me sequatur, et ubi ego sum, illic et minister meus erit
(Joh. 12:26)

Our Lord Jesus Christ spoke these words: 'Whoever serves me should follow me, and wherever I am, there should my servant be also.' These words tell us three things. The first is that we should follow and serve our Lord when he says: 'whoever serves me should follow me'. Therefore these words apply well to St

Secundus, whose name means 'he who follows God', for he gave up his possessions, his life and all things for God's sake. In the same way those who wish to follow God should abandon whatever might hinder them. Chrysostom says: These are challenging words for those who have embraced this world and material things, which are sweet to possess but difficult and bitter to part with.[22] This shows us how demanding it is for certain people, who know nothing of spiritual things, to turn from the things of the world. As I have said often before: why does the ear not enjoy the taste of sweet things as does the mouth? Because it is not equipped to do so. For the same reason someone who lives in the flesh cannot perceive spiritual things. On the other hand, it is easy for an insightful person who understands the things of the spirit to free themselves from material things. St Denys says that God offers his heaven for sale;[23] but nothing is as cheap as heaven, when it is for sale, and nothing is as exalted and as delightful to possess when it has been earned. Heaven is cheap because it is on sale to everyone at the price they can afford. Therefore we should give all that we have for heaven, especially our own self-will. As long as we still cling to our self-will, we have not yet earned heaven. But for those who abandon themselves and their self-will it is easy to part from material things. I have often told you the story of how a master instructed his disciple on how to perceive spiritual things. The disciple said: 'I am raised up by your teaching and understand that all material things are like a small ship which is thrown about by the waves, or like a bird tossed on the wind.' For all spiritual things are higher than material ones, and the higher they are, the more they encompass the material.[24] Therefore material things are small with respect to spiritual ones, and the higher the spiritual ones are, the greater they are, and the more potent they are in works, the purer they are in their being. I have often said the following, which is a sure truth, that if someone were famished to the point of death and were then offered the finest food, they would prefer to die before tasting or enjoying the food, if God's likeness were not in it. And if someone were freezing to death, they could not touch or put on any kind of clothing unless God's likeness were in it. This proceeds from the first point: how we should part from all things and follow God.

The second point is this: how we should serve our Lord. St Augustine says: 'That person is a true servant who seeks nothing but God's glory in all their works.'[25] David too says: 'God is my Lord, him shall I serve', since he has served me and in all his service he needed me only for my own good. Therefore I should serve him too and seek only his glory. Other lords do not do this, but in their service they seek only what is good for them and they serve us only in order to exploit us. Therefore we are not bound to great service to them, since the reward should be measured according to the extent and the value of the service.

The third point is this: we should take note of the reward and of our Lord's words: 'wherever I am, there should my servant be also'. Where is the dwelling of our Lord Jesus Christ? It is in oneness with the Father. This is far too great a reward, that all who serve him should dwell in oneness with the Father, and so, when Christ spoke of his Father, St Philip said: 'Lord, show us your Father, and we shall be satisfied' (John 14:8), as if meaning that merely to see him would have been enough. But there is a far greater delight for us in *dwelling* with him. When our Lord was transfigured on Mount Tabor, offering us a glimpse of the glory which is in heaven, St Peter too asked our Lord to remain there for ever. We should feel an immense desire for union with our Lord and God. And these are the signs of union with our Lord and God: just as God is threefold in the Persons, he is one in his essence. This is also how we should understand the union of our Lord Jesus Christ with his Father and with the soul. In the same way that black and white are distinct (the one cannot tolerate the other, since white is not black), so too something and nothing are distinct. Nothingness is that which can receive nothing from anything, while something is that which can receive something from something. It is precisely the same in God: whatever is something is perfectly in God and is perfect in him. When the soul is united with God, then it perfectly possesses in him all that is something. The soul forgets itself there, as it is in itself, and all things, knowing itself in God as divine, in so far as God is in it. Thus far it possesses a divine self-love and is inseparably united with God so that it enjoys nothing but him and delights only in him. What more could we desire or know, if we are so blessedly united with God? Our Lord created us for just such a union with himself. When Lord Adam broke the commandment, he was driven out of Paradise, and our Lord set two guards before its doors. The first was an angel and the second a flaming and double-edged sword. This refers to the two ways in which we can attain heaven again, which we have lost. The first way is by the angelic nature. St Denys says that 'the angelic nature signifies the revelation of divine light'.[26] With the angels, through the angels and with the divine light the soul should strive back towards God until it returns to the first cause. The second is by the flaming sword, which means that the soul should return through good and godly works which are performed in fiery love for God and our fellow men and women.

That this should be our end, so help us God. Amen.

SERMON 7 (DW 48, W 60)

A master says: all things which are alike love each other and unite with each other, while all dissimilar things flee and hate each other.[27] Now one master says that there is no dissimilarity as great as that between heaven and earth.[28] The earth perceives within itself that it is remote and different from heaven, which is why it has fled from heaven to the lowest point and is immovable, so that it cannot approach heaven. But heaven has perceived within itself that earth has fled from it and has taken up the lowest position. Therefore it pours the whole of itself into the earth to make it fertile, to the extent that the masters consider that the wide span of heaven retains not so much as a pin-prick of its breadth but rather gives the whole of itself to the earth and makes it fertile. Therefore the earth is the most fertile of all temporal things.

I say the same of those who have destroyed themselves as they exist in themselves, in God and in all creatures. Such people have taken up the lowest position, and God must pour the whole of himself into them – or he would not be God. I declare the good, eternal and everlasting Truth that God must pour himself according to the whole of his capacity into all those who have abandoned themselves to the very ground of their being, and he must do so so completely that he can hold nothing back of all his life, all his being and nature, even of his divinity, which he must pour fully and in a fructifying way into those who have abandoned themselves for God and have taken up the lowest position.

As I made my way here today, I wondered how I might preach to you in such a way that you would be able to understand me. Then I thought of an analogy, and if you were able to understand it, you would understand both my meaning and the ground of all the sermons I have for so long been preaching. The analogy concerns my eye and a piece of wood. When my eye is open, it is an eye, but if it is closed, it is still the same eye. Nor does a block of wood decrease or increase in size by being looked at. Now listen carefully. If it now happens that my eye, which is one and simple in itself, is opened and directed towards the piece of wood in the act of seeing, then both remain what they are and yet both are so united through the act of seeing that we can truly say: 'eye-wood', the wood is my eye. But if the wood had no material form and was as immaterial as the seeing of my eye, then we could truly say that the piece of wood and my eye share a single being in the act of seeing. If this is the case with material things, then how much more so with spiritual ones! And you should also know that my eye has far more in common with the eye of a sheep which exists beyond the sea and which I have never seen, than it does with my own ears with which it actually coexists. This stems from the fact that the eye of a sheep exercises the same function as my own eye, and therefore I say that these have more in common with each other than my eyes do with my ears, which are distinct in their functions.

I have occasionally spoken of a light in the soul which is uncreated and uncreatable. I constantly return in my sermons to this light, which apprehends God without medium, without concealment and nakedly, just as he is in himself. Indeed, it apprehends him in the act of begetting. I can again say truthfully that this light has more unity with God than it does with any of the soul's faculties, although it coexists with these. For you should know that this light is not nobler in the being of my soul than the lowest or most basic faculty, such as hearing or sight or some other of the senses which fall victim to hunger or thirst, cold or heat. This is so because of the homogeneous nature of being. In so far as we take the soul's faculties in their being, they are all one and are equally noble. But if we take them according to their function, then one is far nobler and more elevated than another.

Therefore I say that when we turn away from ourselves and from all created things, to that extent we are united and sanctified in the soul's spark, which is untouched by either space or time. This spark is opposed to all creatures and desires nothing but God, naked, just as he is in himself. He is not satisfied with the Father, the Son or the Holy Spirit, nor with the three Persons together, as far as each exists in their particularity. I say truly that this light is not satisfied with the unity of the fertility of the divine nature. Indeed, I will say something that sounds even more astonishing: I declare by the good and eternal Truth that this light is not satisfied with the simple, still and divine being which neither gives nor takes, but rather it desires to know from where this being comes. It wants to penetrate to the simple ground, to the still desert, into which distinction never peeped, neither Father, Son nor Holy Spirit. There, in that most inward place, where everyone is a stranger, the light is satisfied and there it is more inward than it is in itself, for this ground is a simple stillness which is immovable in itself. But all things are moved by this immovability and all the forms of life are conceived by it which, since they possess the light of reason, live of themselves.

That we too may lead lives illumined by reason, may the eternal Truth, of which I have spoken, help us. Amen.

SERMON 8 (DW 50, W 93)

Eratis enim aliquando in tenebrae (Eph. 5:8)

St Paul says: 'Once you were in darkness, but now a light in the Lord.' The prophets who walked in light, recognized and found the hidden truth under the influence of the Holy Spirit. Sometimes they were moved to turn outside themselves and to speak of things that they knew would sanctify us, teaching us to know God. But then they were struck dumb and could not speak. This happened for three reasons.

Firstly, the goodness that they saw and recognized in God was so great and mysterious that their minds could not retain its image, for the images in their minds were all wholly unlike what they saw in God and were such a travesty of the truth that they preferred silence to lies. The second reason is that all they saw in God was so great and sublime that they could derive neither an image nor a form from it in order to speak of it. The third reason why they fell silent was that they looked into the hidden truth and saw there the mystery of God, without being able to put it into words. But occasionally it happened that they turned outside themselves and spoke, but then they lapsed into gross matter and wanted to teach us to know God through lowly creaturely things, since there was nothing that could adequately capture that truth.

Now Paul says: 'Once you were in darkness, but now a light in the Lord.' If we explore the Latin word *aliquando* fully, then we see that it means 'once' and refers to time, which is what keeps us from the light. For nothing is as opposed to God as time. Not only time is opposed to God, but even clinging to time, not only clinging to time but even having contact with time, not even having contact with time but even the smell or scent of time – just as a certain smell hangs in the air where an apple has lain: this is what is meant by contact with time. Our best teachers say that the firmament, the sun and the stars have no more than occasional contact with time.[29] In my opinion the soul is far higher than the heavens since in its highest and purest part it has nothing whatsoever to do with time. I have said on many occasions before that the Holy Spirit flowers from the work in God, from the birth in which the Father generates his only begotten Son and from this outflowing in such a way that it proceeds from them both and the soul flows forth in this procession. The image of the Godhead is impressed on the soul, and in the flowing out and flowing together of the three Persons the soul flows back and is formed back into its own first imageless image.[30]

This is what Paul means when he says: '*now* a light in the Lord'. He does not say: 'You are a light', but '*now* a light'. He means what I have often said, namely that to know things is to know them in their first cause. The masters say that where things are suspended at the point of their origin they have the clearest view of being for, where the Father generates the Son, there is an eternal present-time or Now. In the eternal birth of the Son, the soul flowed into being and received God's image imprinted upon it.

Once there was a discussion in the schools, and it was the opinion of some of the masters that God imprinted the image in the soul like one who paints a picture on the wall, which is not permanent. This view was opposed. Other masters put it better when they said that God imprinted his image permanently on the soul, like one of the ideas which permanently remain in it, such as 'Today I have a particular intention and tomorrow I shall have the same thought and I shall keep this thought alive by concentrating consciously upon it'. Therefore they said that God's works are perfect. For, if the carpenter were perfect in his work, then he would not require his materials; as soon as he conceived of a house, it would in that same moment be built. It is the same with God's works: as soon as he conceives them, they are perfectly realized in an eternal present-time. But then the fifth master came and put it best of all when he said that there is no process of becoming in God, but only a present moment, that is a becoming without becoming, a becoming-new without renewal and that this becoming is God's being. There is in God something so subtle that no renewal can enter there. There is something subtle in the soul too that is so pure and fine that no renewal can enter it either, for all that is in God is an eternal present-time without renewal.

There were four things I wanted to discuss: the subtlety of God and the subtlety of the soul, the activity in God and the activity in the soul. But I shall not speak of these now.

SERMON 9 (DW 41, W 43)

Qui sequitur iustitiam, diligetur a domino (Prov. 15:9) *Beati, qui esuriunt, et sitiunt iustitiam: quoniam ipsi saturabuntur* (Matt. 5:6)

I have taken a text from today's epistle for two saints, and another from the Gospel.[31] King Solomon says in the epistle, 'God loves those who pursue justice', and St Matthew says, 'Blessed are they who hunger and thirst for justice, for they shall be filled.'

Now notice the phrase 'God loves'. It would be a great blessing for me, indeed too great a blessing, if we desired that God should love *me*, as I have often said. What does God love? God loves nothing but himself and what is like him in so far as he finds this in me and finds me in him. In the Book of Wisdom we read: 'God loves only those who dwell in wisdom' (Wisd. 7:28). Another passage is even better: 'God loves those who pursue justice' 'in wisdom' (cf. Prov. 15:9). All the masters are agreed that God's wisdom is his only begotten Son. The text says 'who pursue justice' 'in wisdom', and therefore God loves those who pursue him, for he loves nothing in us except in so far as we are in him. There is a great difference between God's love and our love. We only love something in so far as we find God in it. Even if I had sworn to do otherwise, I could love nothing but goodness. But God loves to the extent that he is good (and it is not as if he could find anything in us to love other than his own goodness) and loves us in so far as we are in him and in his love. This is his gift: it is the gift of his love that we are in him and dwell 'in wisdom'.

St Paul says: 'We are transformed in love.' Now note this phrase 'God loves'. A miracle! What is God's love? His essence and his being – that is his love. If God were to be deprived of loving us, he would be deprived of his own being and divinity, for his being depends on his loving us. Thus the Holy Spirit flows forth. God bless us – what a miracle this is! If God loves me with the whole of his nature (which depends upon it), then God loves me as if his becoming and his being depended upon it. God has only one love, and with the selfsame love that the Father loves his only begotten Son, he also loves me.

Now there is another meaning. Take note: there is no problem with the text if we are prepared to explore it. It reads: 'who pursue justice' 'in wisdom'. The just person has such a need for justice that they can love nothing but justice, and if God were not just, they would take no notice of him, as I have often said. Wisdom and justice are one in God, and whoever loves wisdom in him, loves justice too. If the Devil were just, then they would love him, in so far as he is just, and not a fraction more. The just person loves neither this nor that in God, and if God were to give them the whole of his wisdom together with everything which he can give other than himself, they would pay no attention to it and it would not please them. For such people desire nothing and seek nothing, knowing no Why to justify their actions, just as God acts without a Why and knows no Why. The just person acts precisely as God acts, without a Why, and so as life lives for its own sake, seeking no Why to justify itself, in the same way the just person knows no Why to justify what they do.

Now take note of the following passage, where it says: 'they hunger and thirst for justice'. Our Lord says: 'They who eat me will hunger for more; they who drink me will thirst for more' (Ecclus. 24:21). How should we understand this? This is certainly not the case with physical things: the more we eat of them, the more we are filled. But with spiritual things we are never filled, for the more we have of them, the more we desire them. And therefore the text reads: 'They will thirst the more who drink me and hunger the more who eat me.' These people hunger so much for the will of God, and it gives them such delight, that they are so content with whatever God sends them that they cannot desire or will anything else. As long as we are hungry, the food tastes good, and the greater the hunger, the more satisfying it is to eat. This is true too of those who hunger for the will of God. His will is so pleasing to them, and they are so content with all that he wills and all that he sends them, that even if God wished to spare them something, they would not wish him to do so, since they are so content with what he originally willed for them. If I wished to make someone love me, and be especially pleasing to them, then I would prefer everything that is pleasing to them, and through which I become agreeable to them, to anything else. If it were the case that they preferred me to wear simple clothes rather than velvet, then there is no doubt that I would wear simple clothes rather than anything else. It is the same for someone who delights in God's will. Everything that befalls them, whether illness or poverty or whatever, is preferable to them to anything else. It pleases them better than anything else precisely because it is God's will.

Now I hear you ask: 'How do I know that it is God's will?' My answer is that if it were not God's will even for a moment, then it would not exist. Whatever is must be his will. If God's will is pleasing to you, then whatever happens to you, or does not happen to you, will be heaven. Those who desire something other than God's will get their just reward, for they are always in trouble and misery. They constantly have to endure violence and injustice, and suffering is their perpetual lot. And this is rightly so since they act as if they were betraying God for money, as Judas did. They love God for the sake of something else which is not God. And when they get what they want, they have no further concern with God. God is nothing created, neither devotion nor delight nor whatever you may care for. Scripture says: 'the world was made through him, yet the world knew him not' (John 1:10). If you think that by adding a thousand worlds to God you would somehow increase him, then you do not know God and do not have the least idea what he is, and you are a fool. Therefore we should have no concern for anything besides God. Whoever seeks something from God, as you have often heard me say, does not know what they are looking for.

This is how the Son is born in us – when we live without a Why and are born again into the Son. Origen writes sublimely of this (and had I written it, it would seem unbelievable to you): 'We are not only born in the Son, but are born also from him and again into him, being born anew and immediately in the Son. I say – and it is true – that in every good thought, intention or work we are always born anew in God.'[32] Therefore, as I have recently told you, the Father has only one Son and the less we turn our intention and attention to things other than God and the more we turn to nothing external, all the more shall we be transformed in the Son and all the more shall the Son be born in us and we be born in the Son and become one Son. Our Lord Jesus Christ is the sole Son of the Father, and he alone is both human and divine. But there is only a single Son in a single being, which is divine being. Thus we become one in him when he is the one object of our attention. God always wishes to be alone. This is a necessary truth, and it must always be the case that we should have only God in our thoughts.

God must have poured pleasure and delight into his creatures, although he kept the root of pleasure and the essence of all delight within himself. Let me give you an analogy. Fire sends its root into water together with its heat since, when we remove the fire, the heat remains for a while in the water as it does in the wood. The length of time the heat remains, and its intensity, is determined by how long and how intense the fire was while it was present. The sun, on the other hand, illumines the air and shines through it, but it does not send its root into it, for when the sun disappears there is no more light. It is the same with God and creatures: he casts the light of his pleasure upon creatures, but keeps the root of all pleasure in himself, since he wants us purely for himself and for no one else. God makes himself beautiful for the soul and offers himself to it and has tried with the whole of his Godhead to make himself attractive to the soul, for God wishes to be the only one who is pleasing to the soul and he will tolerate no rival. God does not allow himself to be restricted in any way, and it is his desire also that we should not strive for or desire anything other than himself.

Now some people are of the opinion that they are altogether holy and perfect, and go around the place with big deeds and big words, and yet they strive for and desire so many things, they wish to possess so much and are so concerned both with themselves and with this thing and that. They assert that they are seeking great piety and devotion, and yet they cannot accept a single word of reproval without answering back. Be certain of this: they are far from God and are not in union with him. The prophet says: 'I have poured my soul forth in myself' (cf. Ps. 42:4). But St Augustine puts it better when he says: 'I have poured my soul forth over myself.' It is necessary for the soul to transcend herself if she is to become one in the Son, and the more she goes beyond herself, the more she becomes one with the Son. St Paul says: 'We shall be transformed into the same image that he himself is' (cf. 2 Cor. 3:18).

It says in one text that virtue is never virtue unless it comes from God or through God or in God; one of these three must always apply. If this is not the case, then it cannot be virtue since anything we seek without reference to God is nothing. Virtue is God, or it exists in him without mediation. But I shall not tell you now what the best thing is. Though perhaps you will say: 'Tell us, sir, what is this? How can we be directly in God, neither striving nor seeking for anything other than him, and how can we be so poor and give up everything? It is hard counsel that we should not desire any reward.' Now be certain of this: God never ceases to give us everything. Even if he had sworn not to, he still could not help giving us things. It is far more important to him to give than it is for us to receive, but we should not focus upon this, for the less we strive for it, the more God will give us. God intends thereby only that we should become yet more rich and be all the more capable of receiving things from him.

Sometimes it is my custom, when I pray, to say these words: 'Lord, what we ask you for is so small. If someone asked me for it, then I would do it for them, and yet it is a hundred times easier for you to do than it is for me, and your desire to do it is greater too. And if we were to ask you for something greater, it would still be easy for you to give it. The greater the gift, the more willingly you give it.' God is ready to give us great things if only we can renounce everything in justice.

That we may 'pursue justice' 'in wisdom' and 'hunger and thirst' for it, and that we may 'be filled', so help us God. Amen.

SERMON 10 (DW 39, W 59)

Iustus in perpetuum vivet et apud dominum est merces eius (Wisd. 5:16)

In today's Epistle we read these words spoken by 'the wise man': 'the just person lives in eternity'. I have upon occasion explained what a just person is, but now I give it another meaning: a just person is someone who is established in justice and who is transformed into justice. The just man or woman lives in God and God lives in them, for God is born in the just as they are in him, since every one of the just person's virtues gives birth to

God and brings him joy. And not only every virtue of the just, but also every good work, however small it may be, which is done through the just person and in justice, gives God joy, filling him with joy, for nothing remains in its ground which is not thrilled through and through with joy. Those who are slow of understanding should simply accept this, while those who are enlightened should know it.

The just person seeks nothing through their works, for those whose works are aimed at a particular end or who act with a particular Why in view, are servants and hirelings. If you wish to be formed and transformed into justice then, do not intend anything particular by your works and do not embrace any particular Why, neither in time nor in eternity, neither reward nor blessedness, neither this nor that; such works in truth are dead. Indeed, even if you make God your goal, all the works you perform for his sake will be dead, and you will only spoil those works which are genuinely good. Not only will you spoil your good works, but you will also commit sins, for you will be behaving like a gardener who is supposed to plant a garden but who pulls out all the trees instead and then demands his wages. That is how you will spoil your good works. And so, if you wish to live and wish your works to live too, then you must be dead to all things and be reduced to nothing. It is a property of creatures to make one thing from another, but it is a property of God to make something from nothing. And so if God is to make something of you or in you, then you must first yourself become nothingness. Enter your own inner ground therefore and act from there, and all your works shall be living works. That is why 'the wise man' says that 'the just person lives in eternity' since it is because they are just that such a person acts, and all their works are living works.

Now 'the wise man' says 'his reward is with the Lord'. Let me say something about this. When he says 'with', this means that the reward of the just is wherever God is, for the blessedness of the just and the blessedness of God are one, since the just person is blessed where God is blessed. St John says: 'The Word was with God' (John 1:1). He too says 'with' and therefore the just person is like God, for God is justice. And it follows that whoever is in justice, is in God and is God.

Now let us discuss the word 'just' further. He does not say in Latin 'the just person', or 'the just angel', but only 'the just'. The Father begets his Son as the just and the just as his Son, for all the virtue of the just and of every work that comes from the virtue of the just is nothing other than the birth of the Son from the Father. That is why the Father never rests, but is always striving and urging that his Son should be born in me, as it says in Scripture: 'I will not hold my peace for Zion's sake and for Jerusalem I will not rest till the just is revealed and shines forth like lightning' (Is. 62:1). 'Zion' is the height of life and 'Jerusalem' the height of peace. Indeed, God rests neither for the sake of the height of life or of peace, but rather he urges and strives that the just should become manifest. Nothing should act but God alone in the one who is just. For truly, in so far as it is something external that prompts you to act, to that extent your works are dead, and even if it is God who prompts you to act from outside, then such works too are dead. If your works are to be living works, then God must spur you to action from within, from your innermost part, if they really are to be alive. For that is where your own life is, and that is the sole place where you are truly alive. I tell you that if you imagine one virtue to be greater than another, and if you value one more highly than another, then you do not love it as it is in justice and God does not work in you. For as long as you value one virtue more than another, to that extent you do not take the virtues as they are in justice, and you are yourself not just. For the just man or woman loves and practises all virtues in justice, since these are themselves justice.

Scripture says: 'Before the created world, I am' (cf. Ecclus. 24:14). It says: 'Before ... I am', which means that when we are raised above time into eternity, we perform a single work with God. Some people ask how it is that we can perform those works which God did a thousand years ago and which he will do a thousand years hence: this they do not understand. But in eternity there is no before and after, and what happened a thousand years ago and what will happen in another thousand years is one in eternity. Therefore what God did, what he created a thousand years ago, what he will do in a thousand years' time and what he is doing now are all one. And so whoever has been raised above time into eternity, acts with God both in what he did a thousand years ago and in what he will do a thousand years hence. This too is something that wise people should know and those with less understanding should believe.

St Paul says: 'We are eternally chosen in the Son' (Eph. 1:4). Therefore we should never rest until we become what we have always been in him (cf. Rom. 8:29), for the Father urges and strives that we should be born in the Son and become what the Son is. The Father gives birth to the Son and derives such peace and delight from this birth that the whole of his nature is consumed within it. For whatever is in God, moves him to give birth; the Father is driven to give birth by his ground, his essence and his being.

Sometimes a light becomes manifest in the soul, and it seems to us that this is the Son, even though it is only a light. For where the Son becomes manifest in the soul, there too is the love of the Holy Spirit. Therefore I say that it is the nature of the Father to give birth to the Son, and it is the nature of the Son that I should be born in him and in his image. It is the nature of the Holy Spirit that I should be consumed in him, dissolved in him, and transformed wholly into love. Whoever is in love and is wholly love, feels that God loves nobody other than themselves, and they know of no one who loves or indeed of anyone but themselves.[33]

Some teachers believe that the Spirit derives its blessedness from love, others that it derives it from the contemplation of God. But I say that it comes neither from love nor from knowledge nor from the contemplation of God. Now you could ask: does the Spirit therefore not contemplate God in its eternal life? Yes and no. In so far as it is born, it neither sees nor contemplates God. But in so far as it is actually being born, it does have a vision of God. Therefore the Spirit's blessedness resides where it is in the process of being born, for it lives where the Father lives, which is to say in the simplicity and nakedness of being. Turn away from everything therefore and exist in your naked being, for whatever is outside being is 'accidence' and all forms of 'accidence' create a Why.[34]

That we may 'live in eternity', so help us God. Amen.

SERMON II (DW 40, W 63)

Manete in me (John 15:4)
Beatus vir qui in sapientia morabitur (Ecclus. 14:22)[35]

Our Lord Jesus Christ says in the Gospel: 'Remain in me!' (John 15:4), and in the Epistle it says: 'Blessed is the man who dwells in wisdom' (Ecclus. 14:22). These two phrases mean the same thing: the one from the Gospel and the other from the Epistle.

Now take note of what we must have if we are to dwell in him, that is in God. There are three things we must have. The first is that we should take leave of ourselves and of all things and be attached to nothing external which acts upon the senses within, and also that we should not remain in any creature which is either in time or in eternity. The second is that we should not love this or that good thing but rather goodness as such from which all good things flow, for things are only desirable and delightful in so far as God is in them. Therefore we should not love any good thing more than the extent to which we love God in it, nor should we love God for the sake of his heavenly kingdom nor for the sake of anything else, but should love him for his goodness which he is in himself. For whoever loves him for anything else, does not dwell in him but dwells in that for the sake of which they love him. Therefore, if you wish to dwell in him, you must love him for his sake alone. The third is that we should not take God as he is good or just, but should take him in the pure and clear substance in which he possesses himself. For goodness and justice are a garment of God, since they enfold him. Strip away from God therefore everything which clothes him and take him in his dressing room where he is naked and bare in himself. Thus you will remain in him.

Whoever remains in him in this way will possess five things. The first is this, that between that person and God there is no distinction, and they are one. The angels are beyond number, since they do not have any particular number, and are without number on account of their great simplicity. Although the three Persons in God are three without number, they do possess multiplicity.[36] Between such a person and God, however, not only is there no distinction, but there is also no multiplicity, since there is only One. The second point is this, that such a person derives their blessedness from that purity from which God derives his own blessedness and maintains himself. The third point is this, that their knowing is one with God's knowing, their activity with God's activity and their understanding with God's understanding. The fourth is that God is always being born in them. But how is this so? Take note of this: when we uncover and expose the divine light that God has naturally created in us, then the image of God in us is revealed. For the birth of God means here the revelation of God since to say that the Son is *born* of the Father is to say that the Father paternally reveals his mystery to him. Therefore, the more and the more clearly we uncover the image of God in us, the more clearly God is born in us. And thus the continuous birth of God is to be understood as the way that God reveals his image and shines forth in it. The fifth thing is this, that such a person is continuously being born in God. But how again is this so? Take note of this: the revealing of God's image within us makes us like God, for through this image we are like God's image, which God is according to his naked essence. Therefore the more we reveal ourselves, the more we are like God, and the more we are like God, the more we are united with him. And so our continuous birth into God is to be seen in the extent to which we shine forth with our image into God's image, which God is according to his naked essence, and with which we are one. The union of God with this person is to be seen in the identity of these two images, for it is this image that makes us like God. Therefore, if it is said that someone is one with God and is God on the grounds of this unity, then this is based on that part of the image in which they are like him and not upon the created part. For when we consider someone as God, we do not consider them according to their creatureliness, but when we consider them as God, we are not denying their creatureliness in such a way as to negate it, rather this is to be seen as an affirmation of God which denies creatureliness in *him*. For when we consider Christ, who is both divine and human, according to his humanity, we are passing over his divinity, though not in such a way that we are denying it. It is simply a matter of what we are concentrating on at the time.[37] This is how St Augustine is to be understood when he said: 'We are what we love. If we love a stone, then we are a stone, if we love a person, then we are that person, if we love God – I hesitate to go on, for if I said that we would then be God, you might want to stone me. But let me refer you to the Scriptures.'[38] And so when someone wholly conforms themselves to God through love, they are stripped of images and are in-formed and transformed into the divine uniformity in which they are one with God. All this they possess by remaining within. Now observe the fruit which this produces. That is, if such a person is one with God, then they bring forth all creatures with God and, in so far as they are one with him, they bestow blessedness on all creatures.

Now the other passage, from the Epistle, reads as follows: 'Blessed is the man who dwells in wisdom.' He says 'in wisdom'. 'Wisdom' is a maternal name, for a maternal name suggests passivity since in God there is both activity and passivity. The Father is active, and the Son is passive, which comes from the fact that the latter undergoes the process of being born. Since the Son is the eternally begotten wisdom, in which all things are contained in diversity, he says: 'Blessed is the man who dwells in wisdom.'

Now it says: 'Blessed is the *man*'. I have often said that there are two powers in the soul: one is the man and the other the woman. Now it says: 'Blessed is the man'. The power in the soul which is called the man is the soul's highest faculty, in which God shines forth and is revealed. For only God can enter this faculty, and it always remains in God. Therefore if we considered all things in this faculty, we would take them not as *things* but rather as they exist in God. And so we should always dwell in this faculty, for all things are as one in it. Then we would dwell in all things in the same way and would receive them as they are all one in God, and we would then possess all things. We would have stripped away the grossest part from all things and would receive them as they are delightful and desirable. That is how we possess them there, for it is God's own nature to pour forth all that he has created and even his very self into that place. And therefore we are blessed if we constantly live in this faculty, for then we shall always live in God.

That we may ever live in God, so help us our dear Lord Jesus Christ. Amen.

SERMON 12 (DW 1, W 6)

Intravit Jesus in templum et coepit eicere vendentes et ementes (Matt. 21:12)

In today's Gospel we read that our Lord entered the temple and drove out those who were buying and selling there, saying to others who were offering doves for sale and the like: 'Take these things away; remove them at once' (John 2:16). Why did Jesus eject those who were buying and selling, ordering those who sold doves to remove them? He wanted the temple to be empty and it was as if he had said: 'This temple is mine by right and I wish to have it to myself and to have command of it.' What does this mean? This temple, in which God wants to hold sway according to his will, is the human soul, which he formed and created in his own likeness, as we know from his words 'let us make man in our image and likeness' (Gen. 1:26). And this is what he did. He made the human soul so similar to himself that neither in heaven nor on earth among all the glorious creatures which God so marvellously created is there one which is as like him as the human soul. That is why God wishes the temple to be empty, so that there shall be nothing there but himself. And this is the case because the temple is so pleasing to him, since it is so like himself, and he feels so much at home in the temple, whenever he is alone in it.

Now take note! Who were the people who were buying and selling, and who are they now? Listen carefully. I wish to speak only of good people in this sermon, but I shall just indicate who these traders were and are, these people who were buying and selling just as they do today, and who our Lord drove out. And our Lord still does drive out all those who buy and sell in his temple, not allowing a single one to remain. Now see, those people are all traders who refrain from serious sin, who wish to be good people and who do good works for the glory of God such as fasting, keeping vigil, praying and the like, all good works, and yet they do them in order that our Lord should give them something in return or do something for them which they desire: in other words these people are all merchants. This must be understood in a general sense in that they want to give one thing in exchange for another and thus want to engage in a process of bartering with our Lord. But they deceive themselves in their trade. For if they gave up for God's sake all that they have or all that they are capable of doing, if they expended themselves entirely for God, then God would in no way be obliged to give them anything at all or do anything for them, unless he freely chooses to do so. For they are what they are on account of God, and what they have comes to them from God and not from themselves. Therefore God does not owe them anything for their good works and their giving, unless he freely chooses to grant them something through grace and not on account of their works or gifts, since they do not give from what is theirs, nor do they act from themselves, as Christ himself says: 'Without me you can do nothing' (John 15:5). These are very foolish people, who wish to barter with God, and they know little or nothing of the truth. That is why our Lord drove them out of the temple. The light and the darkness cannot exist together in the same place. God is truth and light in himself. So when God enters the temple, he banishes ignorance, which is darkness, and reveals himself with light and with truth. When the truth is known, the merchants vanish, for truth does not desire any kind of trade-off. God does not seek his own interests[39] but in all his works he is untrammelled and free and acts from pure love. The same is true of that person who is united with God. They too are unfettered and free in all their works, performing them for God alone, not seeking their own interests; and God works in them.

I say further: so long as we seek something from God in any of our good works, we are like these merchants. But if you wish to be entirely free of this bartering, so that God will let you be in this temple, then all you do in your works should be done solely for the praise of God, and you should remain as free as nothingness is free, which is neither here nor there. You should desire nothing at all in return for it. And if you act in this way, your works will be spiritual and divine, all the merchants shall have been driven from the temple and God alone will dwell there; for such a person intends only God. See, this is how the temple can be free of merchants. See, that person who thinks neither of themselves nor of anything other than God and the glory of God, is truly simple and free of any veniality in all their works, and does not seek to serve their own interests just as God is simple and free in all his works without seeking to serve his own interests.

I have mentioned too that our Lord said to those who were offering doves for sale: 'Take these things away; remove them at once.' He did not drive them out nor did he berate them severely but said quite gently: 'Take these things away', as if he wished to say: 'These are not evil in themselves but nevertheless they stand in the way of the purest truth.' These are all good people who do their works solely for God's sake, not seeking to serve their own interests thereby, but still linking them to the self, to time and number, to a before and an after. In their works they are impeded in the attainment of the best truth of all, namely that they should be simple and free, as our Lord Jesus Christ is simple and free, who is ceaselessly conceived anew at a point beyond time by his heavenly Father and in that same eternal now is perfectly and ceaselessly born into his Father's majesty, with thanks and praise, in equal honour. Exactly the same should be true of us who wish to become receptive to the highest truth and to live in it with neither a before nor an after, unhindered by our works and by any of the images we have ever known, simple and free, receiving anew the divine gift in this eternal now and freely bearing it back into our Lord Jesus Christ in this same light with thankful praise. This is how the doves can be removed, which means to say the obstacles and self-attachment of all those works which are otherwise good, since we do not seek to serve our own interests in them. That is why our Lord said gently: 'Take these things away; remove them at once', as if he meant that although they were good, they were also an obstacle.

When the temple becomes free of hindrances, that is from attachment to self and ignorance, then it is so radiantly clear and shines so beautifully above all that God has made and through all that God has made that no one can match its radiance but the uncreated God alone. And in truth, the temple is like no one and nothing else but the uncreated God. Nothing below the angels is like this temple. Even the highest angels have only an imperfect likeness to this temple of the noble soul. Their partial likeness to the soul lies in their knowledge and love. But a limit has been set above them beyond which they cannot go. The soul, on the other hand, can do so. If a soul – the soul of someone still bound to time – were on the same level as the highest angel, that person would still be capable of advancing infinitely beyond the angel, new in every moment, without number or mode, that is beyond the mode of the angels and of all created intelligences. God alone is free and uncreated, and thus he alone is like the soul as far as freedom, though not uncreatedness, is concerned, since the soul herself is created. When the soul enters the light that is pure, she falls so far from her own created somethingness into her nothingness that in this nothingness she can no longer return to that created somethingness by her own power. But God places himself[40] with his uncreatedness beneath her nothingness and contains the soul in his somethingness. The soul has dared to become nothing and cannot return to herself by her own power – so far has she gone out of herself before God catches her. And this must necessarily be the case. For, as I said before: 'Jesus entered the temple and drove out those who were buying and selling there, saying to others who were offering doves for sale and the like: "Take these things away".'

And so we come to the phrase 'Jesus entered and began saying "Take these things away"', which they did. Now there was no one in the temple but Jesus, and he began to speak in the temple. You should know that if someone else wishes to speak in the temple, then Jesus must be silent, as if he were not at home, and indeed he is not at home in the soul for there are strangers there with whom the soul speaks. If Jesus is to speak in the soul, then she must be alone and must herself be silent if she is to hear Jesus. Now then, in he comes and begins to speak. What does he say? He utters that which he is. What is he then? He is a word of the Father. And in this Word the Father speaks himself together with the whole of his divine nature and everything that God is as he knows it, and he knows it as it is. Since he is perfect in knowledge and power, he is perfect too in his speaking. By speaking the Word, he speaks himself and all things in another Person, imparting to him his own nature, and he utters forth in the same Word all intelligent beings as creatures who are akin to that Word according to the *image* in so far as the image dwells within and does not shine forth, as it does when each has its own separate being, although the images that shine forth have received the possibility of attaining a likeness to the Word by the grace of the Word itself. The Father has wholly uttered that same Word, as it is in itself: the Word and everything in the Word.

Now since the Father has uttered this, what then does Jesus say in the soul? As I have told you, the Father speaks the Word and speaks in the Word and not otherwise, while Jesus speaks in the soul. The manner of his speaking is that he reveals himself and all that the Father has uttered in him according to the receptiveness of the spirit. He reveals the sovereignty of the Father in the spirit with equal and immeasurable power. When the spirit receives this power in the Son and through the Son, then it too becomes powerful in all it does so that it becomes equal and powerful in all virtues and in perfect purity so that neither joy nor grief, nor anything which God has created in time, can destroy us, but rather we are powerfully established in this as in a divine power, in comparison with which all things are powerless and small.

Secondly, Jesus reveals himself in the soul in an infinite wisdom which he himself is, in which wisdom the Father knows himself with all his sovereignty, as well as that same Word, which is itself wisdom and everything it contains, as it is one. When this wisdom is united with the soul, all doubt, all falsehood and all darkness is removed from her and she is placed in a pure, clear light which is God himself, as the prophet says: 'Lord, in your light we will see light' (Ps. 36:10). Thus God is known with God in the soul; then she knows herself with this wisdom and all things, and this same wisdom knows her with itself, and with the same wisdom she knows the Father's sovereignty in fertile generative power, and essential is-ness in simple unity without distinction.

Jesus reveals himself thirdly with an infinite sweetness and abundance, which rises from the power of the Holy Spirit, spilling over and flooding into all receptive hearts with a wealth of abundance and sweetness. When Jesus reveals himself with this abundance and sweetness and unites himself with the soul, then with this same abundance and sweetness the soul floods into herself, forth from herself, beyond herself and beyond all things and, by grace, she flows powerfully back into her own primal origin without mediation. Then the outer self is utterly obedient to the self within, and shall remain always in constant peace in the service of God.

That Jesus may enter us too, driving out all obstacles and making us one, as he is one God with the Father and the Holy Spirit, so that we may be one with him and may eternally remain so, so help us God. Amen.

SERMON 13 (DW 2, W 8)

Intravit Jesus in quoddam castellum et mulier quaedam, Martha nomine,
excepit illum in domum suam (Luke 10:38)

I have quoted a passage, first in Latin, which is taken from the Gospel and which means in our language: 'Our Lord Jesus Christ entered a citadel and was received by a virgin who was a wife.'[41]

Now note the fact that it has to be a 'virgin' who receives him. 'Virgin' means someone who is free of all alien images, as free in fact as that person was before he or she existed. We might ask how it is possible for someone who has been born and who has reached the age of reason to be as free of images as they were before they existed, even though they know many things, all of which are necessarily images: how then can such a person be free of them? Now take note of the following point. If I possessed such great intelligence that all the images that anyone had ever conceived, together with all those which are in God himself, existed in my mind, but in such a way that I was free of an ego-attachment to them in what I did or in what I refrained from doing, neither with a 'before' or an 'after', but rather I remained free and empty in this present moment for the most precious will of God, constantly ready to fulfil it, then I would be a virgin unburdened by any images, just as certainly as I was before I existed.[42]

I say further that the fact that someone is a virgin does not take anything away from the works they have done but rather leaves them free and virginal, unhindered with respect to the highest truth, just as Jesus is empty and free and virginal in himself. We too must be virgins if we are to receive the virginal Jesus, since, in the view of the learned, the foundation of union is the meeting of like and like.

Now take note of this and listen carefully! If we were only ever a virgin, we would produce no fruit. If we are to be fruitful, then we must be a 'wife'. 'Wife' is the noblest name that can be applied to the soul and it is more excellent than 'virgin'. It is good that we should receive God into ourselves, and in this receptivity we are virgins. But it is far better that God should be fruitful in us, for only the fruitfulness of the gift shows gratitude for the gift and there the spirit is 'wife' in reproductive thankfulness, as it gives birth to Jesus back into the heart of God the Father.

Many good gifts are received in virginity, but they are not born back into God in wifely fertility with gratitude and praise. These gifts corrupt and turn to nothing so that they can never serve to improve us or to give us joy. Thus our virginity is useless since we do not then become a wife with full fertility. That is the problem. Therefore I have said: 'Jesus entered a citadel and was received by a virgin who was a wife.' This must necessarily be the case, as I have explained to you.

Married couples hardly produce more than a single child a

year. But it is a different kind of 'married couple' that I mean now: all those whose ego is bound up with prayer, fasting, holding vigil, and all kinds of external observances and ascetical practices. By a 'year' I mean every kind of ego-attachment to any work, which removes our freedom to be at God's disposal in this present moment and to follow him alone in that light with which he prompts us to do certain things and not to do others, free and new in every moment, as if we neither could nor wished to do anything else. By a 'year' I mean any form of ego-attachment or any regimented work which takes from us this freedom, ever new; for their soul will produce no fruit unless they have first completed the work which they began with ego-attachment, and they shall lack trust both in themselves and in God unless they have first completed the work to which their ego is attached, and without which they shall have no peace. Therefore they produce no fruit, unless they have satisfactorily performed their work. This is what I call a 'year', and yet the fruit is slight since it is the product of a work performed with ego-attachment and not in freedom. I call such people 'married couples' since they have an attachment of the ego. They scarcely produce any fruit, and what they do bring forth is paltry enough.

A virgin, who is a 'wife', who is free and unhampered by any attachment of the ego, is always as close to God as she is to herself. She brings forth many fruits, which are substantial, for they are neither more nor less than God himself. This virgin, who is a wife, brings forth this fruit and this birth, and produces a hundred or a thousand fruit every day, an innumerable amount, becoming generative and fertile from the noblest ground of all, that is, she too generates from that same ground from which the Father bears his eternal Word. For Jesus, the light and reflection of the Father's heart – St Paul declares that he is the light and reflection of the Father's heart and shines powerfully through the heart of the Father (cf. Heb. 1:3) – this Jesus is united with her and she with him, and she shines and gleams with him as a single oneness, as a pure, clear light in the heart of the Father.

I have said often enough that there is a power in the soul which is untouched by either time or flesh. It flows from the spirit and remains within the spirit and is entirely spiritual by nature. Now God is green and flowering in this power in all the joy and all the honour which he is in himself. There is such great delight there and such inconceivably deep joy that no one can adequately describe it. For the eternal Father ceaselessly gives birth to his eternal Son in this power in such a way that this power also gives birth to the Son of the Father and to itself as the same Son in the sole power of the Father. If someone possessed an entire kingdom or all the goods of the earth, and if they gave it all up for the sake of God, becoming one of the poorest of the earth, and if God then gave that person as much suffering as he has ever given anyone, and if they had to endure this all their life long, and if God then allowed them to glimpse just once and for only a fraction of a second how he is in this power, their joy would be so great that all of this suffering and all of this poverty would be insignificant. Indeed, even if God did not grant them heaven after this, they would already have received too great a reward for all they had ever suffered; for God exists in this power as he does in the eternal Now. If the spirit were for ever united with God in this power, then we would never grow old, for the Now in which God created human beings and the Now in which the last member of the human race will pass away, and the Now in which I am presently speaking to you, are all the same in God and are nothing other than a single Now. See, this person exists in a single light with God, which is why there is neither passivity nor temporal succession in them but only an unchanging eternity. For such a person there are truly no more surprises, and all things exist in him or her essentially. Therefore neither future events nor the effects of chance can bring them anything new, since they live in a single now-time, ever new, without ceasing. There is such divine majesty in tnis power.

There is a further power, which also has nothing to do with the body.[43] It flows from the spirit and remains in the spirit and is entirely spiritual by nature. In this power God burns and glows ceaselessly with all his riches, with all his sweetness and with all his bliss. Truly, in this power there is so much joy and such great, immeasurable delight that no one can reveal it or give an adequate account of it. I say again: if there were someone who even for a moment could truly grasp with their intelligence the bliss and the joy which are in it – all the suffering that they could or have had to endure would seem insignificant to them, nothing at all. I go further and say that it would seem to them to be nothing but a joy and a comfort.

You can genuinely tell whether your suffering is your own or whether it is God's suffering in the following way. If you suffer for your own sake, in whatever way this may be, then this suffering causes you pain and is difficult to endure. But if you suffer for God's sake and for his sake alone, then this suffering causes you no pain and is not difficult for you to endure, since it is God who bears the burden. In truth, if there were someone who wished to suffer for God and only for his sake, and if all the suffering there has ever been and that exists now in all the world were to fall upon them, they would feel no pain and it would not be difficult for them to endure it, for God would bear the burden. If someone were to put a heavy load on my neck and someone else were to bear its weight for me, then I would be as happy to be laden with a hundred such loads as with one, since they would not be heavy for me and would cause me no pain. In brief, God makes light and sweet whatever it is that we endure for him and for his sake alone. And thus I began this sermon with the words: 'Our Lord Jesus Christ entered a citadel and was received by a virgin who was a wife.' But why was this so? It had to be the case that she was both a virgin and a wife. Now I have explained to you how Jesus was received, but I have not yet told you what that 'citadel' is, to which I shall now turn.

Sometimes I have said that there is a power in the soul that can alone be said to be free. Sometimes I have said that it is a refuge of the spirit and sometimes I have said that it is a light of the spirit. Sometimes I have said that it is a spark. But now I say that it is neither this nor that, and yet still it is a something which is as far above this or that as heaven is above earth. Therefore I shall now name it in a nobler manner than I have ever done before, and yet it mocks such reverence and the manner and is far above them. It is free of all names and is devoid of all forms, quite empty and free as God is empty and free in himself. It is so entirely one and simple, as God is one and simple, that no one can see inside it in a particular manner. This same power of which I have spoken, in which God flowers and is green with all his divinity, as the spirit in God, in this same power the Father bears his sole-begotten Son as truly as he does in himself, for he truly lives in this power, and together with the Father the spirit bears the same sole-begotten Son and itself as the same Son and is the same Son in this light and is the truth. If you could see this with my heart, then you would understand what it is I am saying: for it is true, and the truth itself tells it.

Now note this! So unified and simple is the 'citadel' in the soul, of which I speak and to which I am referring, above all manners and modes, that that noble power of which I have spoken is not worthy to peep into this citadel even once, for a split second. Even that other power, of which I spoke, and in which God glows and burns with all his wealth and with all his bliss, never dares to peer in there. So entirely one and simple is this citadel, and so far above all particular manner and all powers is this single oneness, that no power or manner can ever look into it, not even God himself. In full truth and as truly as God lives:

God himself will never look in there even for a moment, nor has he ever done so in so far as he exists in the manner and individual nature of his Persons. This is easy to understand since this single oneness possesses neither a particular mode of being nor an individual nature. Therefore, if God is ever to look in there, it must cost him all his divine names and the individual nature of his Persons. All this must be left outside, if he is to peep in. He must be simple oneness, without mode or individual nature, in which he is neither Father nor Son nor Holy Spirit 'in this sense and yet is still something which is neither this nor that.

See, as he is one and simple, that is how he can enter this oneness, which I call a citadel in the soul, and in no other way can he enter in, but only in this way can he enter and be within. In that part the soul is like God, and in no other. What I have told you is true, as truth itself is my witness, and I pledge my soul on it.

That we may be just such a 'citadel' which Jesus may enter and be received, remaining eternally in us in the way I have described, so help us God. Amen.

SERMON 14 (DW 8, W 82)

In occisione gladii mortui sunt (Hebr. 11:37)

Of the martyrs we read that they 'died by the sword'. Our Lord said to his disciples: 'Blessed are you when you suffer for my name's sake' (Matt. 5:11, 10:22).[44]

We read 'they died'. This means in the first place that whatever we suffer in this world and in this life will have an end. St Augustine says all suffering and endeavour has an end, but the reward that God gives us is eternal. Secondly, we should be constantly aware of the fact that this life is mortal and that we should not fear any suffering or want that may befall us, since it will all have an end. Thirdly, we should behave as if we were already dead, untouched by good things or bad. There is a master who says that nothing can touch the heavens, which means that that person is heavenly for whom things count so little that they cannot touch him or her.[45] Another master says that since all creatures are so insignificant, how is it that they can so easily make us turn from God, when the soul in her least part is more precious than heaven and all creatures? He replies that this is the result of our caring so little for God. If we cared more for God, as we should, then it would be almost impossible for us to fall. And it is good advice that we should behave in this world as if we were dead. St Gregory says that only those who are entirely dead to the world can possess God in full measure.[46]

But the fourth point is the best one. He says that they are dead. It is death that gives them being. One master says that nature destroys nothing without creating something better in its place. When air becomes fire, then that is something better, but when air becomes water, this is degradation and error.[47] If this is true of nature, then it is even more so of God: he never destroys anything without replacing it with something better. The martyrs are dead and have lost their *life* but have received *being*. A master says that the noblest thing is being, life and knowing. Knowing is higher than life or being since, in knowing, it must already possess life and being. On the other hand, life is nobler than being or knowing, as the tree, which lives, is nobler than the stone, which only possesses being. But if we take being in its purity, as it is in itself, then being is higher than knowing or living, for by possessing being, it also possesses knowing and living.

They have lost their lives but have found being. One master

says that nothing is so like God as being: in so far as something has being, it is like God.[48] Another says that being is so pure and so exalted that all God is, is being. God sees nothing but being, he knows nothing but being, being is his circumference. God loves nothing but his being, he thinks of nothing but his being. I tell you: all creatures are being.[49] One master says that certain creatures are so close to God and bear the imprint of so much divine light within themselves that they can bestow being on other creatures too. This is not true, for being is so exalted and so pure and so akin to God that no one can bestow being but God alone in himself. Being is the particular property of God. A master says that one creature can bestow *life* upon another.[50] But for this reason, everything that is something dwells in being. Being is the first name.[51] Everything that is deficient, is descent from being. The whole of our life should be being. As far as our life is being, thus far it is in God.[52] As far as our life is enclosed in God, thus far it is akin to God. Any life, however small, which is taken in so far as it is being, will be nobler than anything that was ever given life. Of this I am sure: if the soul knew even the very least thing that has being, then she would never turn from it again, even for a moment. In so far as it possesses being in God, the very least thing that we see in God – even a flower – is nobler than the whole world put together. To know the very least thing, as it exists in God, in so far as it has being, is better than knowing an angel.

If the angel turned to the knowledge of creatures, night would fall. St Augustine says that when angels know creatures without God, then that is like the evening light, but when they know creatures in God, that is like the morning light. But if they know God, as he is in himself pure being, then that is like the midday sun.[53] I say we should know and recognize the nobility of being. No creature is so small that it does not desire being. When caterpillars fall from trees, they climb back up the wall so that they can preserve their being. That is how noble being is. We praise dying in God whereby he removes us to a being which is better than life: a being in which our life lives, and in which our life becomes being. We should pass willingly into death in order to receive a being that is better.

I have occasionally said that wood is better than gold, which is very strange. A stone would be nobler, in so far as it possesses being, than God and his divinity without being, if it were possible to deprive him of being. Life must be very intense if dead things are to become alive in it, death itself turning to life. For God nothing dies; all things are alive in him. 'They are dead', Scripture says of the martyrs, and they have been transported to an eternal life, to that life in which life is being. We should be wholly dead so that we are untouched by good things or bad. We should see the things we know in their primal cause. It is impossible to know something properly if you do not know it in its primal cause. And it can never be true knowledge when something is not known in its productive cause. In the same way life can never be perfected unless it is returned to its productive cause, where life is being, which the soul receives when she dies down to her depths, so that we may live in that life where life is being. What stops us from achieving this constantly, according to one master, is that we have contact with time. Whatever is touched by time, is mortal. Another master says that the course of the heavens is eternal, and that time derives from this but only as a descent from it. The heavens are eternal in their course, knowing nothing of time, which indicates that the soul should be transported to pure being. The second obstacle is the existence of contradiction. What is a contradiction? Sorrow and joy, black and white, stand in opposition to each other and have no endurance in being.

There is a master who says that the soul is given to the body in order to be purified.[54] The soul, when she is cut off from the body, has neither reason nor will: she is one and cannot return to

God by her own strength. She possesses reason and will in her own ground as in their root but not in their action.[55] The soul is purified in the body so that she can gather what has been divided and dispersed. When that which the five senses have dispersed returns to the soul, then she has a power in which it all becomes one. The soul is purified also in the performance of the virtues, which means to say when the soul climbs up to a life which is unified. This is where the purity of the soul lies, in which she is purified from a life which is divided and enters a life which is unified. Everything which is divided in lower things becomes united when the soul climbs up to a life in which there is no contradiction. When the soul enters the light of reason, then she knows nothing of contradiction. But that which falls away from this light, falls into mortality and dies. Thirdly, the purity of the soul is shown also when she inclines to nothing at all. Whatever inclines towards something else, must die and cannot endure in being.

We ask God, our dear Lord, to help us move from a life which is divided to a life which is one. So help us God. Amen.

SERMON 15 (DW 10, W 66)

In diebus suis placuit deo et inventus est iustus (cf. Eccles. 44:16–17)[56]

The passage which I have just quoted to you in Latin is written in the Epistle and can be used of a holy confessor. The translation is as follows: 'In his days he was found just within; he pleased God in his days.'[57] He found justice from within. My body is more in my soul than my soul is in my body. My body and my soul are more in God than they are in themselves, and justice is this: the origin of all things in truth. As St Augustine says: 'God is closer to the soul than she is to herself.'[58] The proximity of the soul to God allows of no distinction between them in truth. That same act of knowledge in which God knows himself is the knowing of every detached spirit and no other. The soul takes its being directly from God; therefore God is closer to the soul than she is to herself and therefore God is present in the soul with the whole of his divinity.

Now a master asks whether the divine light flows into the faculties of the soul just as purely as it exists in the being of the soul since the soul has her being directly from God and the faculties flow immediately from the being of the soul. But the divine light is too exalted to have anything in common with the faculties; for God is distant and alien to everything which comes into contact with anything else. Therefore, since the faculties do come into contact with other things, they lose their virginity. Divine light cannot shine through them, although they can become receptive to it by practice and purification. With regard to this another master says that the faculties are given another light which is similar to the inner one. It is similar to it but not identical with it. They receive an impression from this light so that they become responsive to the other light. Another master says that all the faculties of the soul which act within the body, shall die with the body, with the exception of knowledge and will. Only these will remain for the soul. But if the faculties which act in the body die with the body, they nevertheless remain in their root.[59]

St Philip says: 'Lord, show us the Father and we shall be satisfied' (John 14:8). Now no one comes to the Father except through the Son (John 14:6). Whoever sees the Father sees the Son (John 14:9), and the Holy Spirit is their mutual love. The soul is so simple in herself that she can only ever perceive one image in the present. When she perceives the image of a stone, she does not perceive that of an angel, and if she perceives the image of an angel, she does not perceive any other image. But she must love in that moment whatever image she perceives. If she perceives a thousand angels, then this would be as many as two angels and yet she would not perceive more than one angel. Now we should unite ourselves as oneness. St Paul says: 'Now that you have been set free from sin, you have become the servants of God' (Rom. 6:22). The sole-begotten Son has freed us from our sins. But now, more to the point than Paul, our Lord says: 'I have not called you servants but have called you friends', 'the servant does not know his master's will' (but the friend knows all that his friend knows), and 'all that I have heard from my Father, I have made known to you' (John 15:15). All that my Father knows I know, and all that I know, you know; for I and my Father have a single spirit. They who know all that God knows, know God. He or she grasps God in his own being, in his own unity, in his own present and in his own truth; with such a person all is well. But they who are unaccustomed to inward things do not know what God is. Like someone who has wine in their cellar but who has never tasted it, they do not know that he is good. The same is true of those who live in ignorance: they do not know what God is and yet they believe that they are alive. But this conviction does not come from God. We must have a pure, clear knowledge of divine truth. When someone has a right intention in all their works, then God is the origin of that intention, God himself and the divine nature is its realization, and its completion is in the divine nature, that is in God himself.

Now one master says that there is no one who is so foolish that they do not strive for wisdom.[60] But why then do we not become wise? There is much to be said about this. The most important factor is to break through and beyond all things and the origin of all things, and it is this process that weighs us down. That is why we remain trapped in ourselves. If I am wealthy, then I am not necessarily wise too, but if I am in-formed by the essence of wisdom and its nature and am myself wisdom, then I am wise.

I once said in a convent that the true image of the soul is found where nothing is in-formed or out-formed but that which is God himself. The soul has two eyes: an inner and an outer eye.[61] The inner eye of the soul is the one which perceives being and receives its own being directly from God: this is the activity which is particular to itself. The outer eye of the soul is that which is directed towards all creatures and which perceives them in the manner of an image and the function of a faculty. But they who are turned within themselves so that they know God according to their own taste and in their own being, are freed from all created things and are secure in themselves in a very fortress of truth. Just as I once said that on Easter Day our Lord came to his disciples through locked doors, so too God does not enter those who are freed from all otherness and all createdness: rather he already exists in an essential manner within them.

'He pleased God in his days.' We are concerned here with more than just one day since it is said 'in his days', which means the soul's day and God's day. The last six or seven days and those days which existed six thousand years ago are as close to the present day as yesterday is. Why? Because there time exists in a perpetual Now. Since the heavens revolve, day comes with the first revolution of the heavens. There the day of the soul occurs in a Now, and in her natural light, in which all things are, there is a whole day: there day and night are one. But God's day is where the soul stands in the day of eternity in an essential Now, and the Father gives birth to his sole-begotten Son in a perpetual present and the soul is herself born again into God. Every time this birth takes place, the sole-begotten Son is born. Therefore there are far more sons born to virgins than are born to married women, for the former give birth above time in eternity. However many sons there may be to which the soul gives birth in eternity, there is still no more than a single Son since this happens above time in the day of eternity.

Now all is well with that person who lives in virtues, for I said a week ago that the virtues are in the heart of God. Whoever lives in virtue and acts in virtue, all is well with them. Whoever does not seek their own interest in anything, neither in God nor in creatures, lives in God and God lives in them. Such a person delights in abandoning all things and spurning them, and it is their joy to bring all things to their highest perfection. St John says: 'Deus caritas est', which means 'God is love', and love is God, 'and whoever dwells in love, dwells in God and God dwells in them' (1 John 4:16). They who dwell in God have a good residence and are an heir of God, and they in whom God dwells share a house with noble companions. Now one master says that God gives the soul a gift which moves the soul to inner things. Another maintains that the soul is touched without means by the Holy Spirit for in that love in which God loves himself, in that same love he loves me, and the soul loves God in the same love in which he loves himself, and if this love did not exist, in which God loves the soul, then neither would the Holy Spirit exist. The soul loves God in the warmth and the burgeoning of the Holy Spirit.[62]

Now one evangelist writes: 'This is my beloved Son in whom I am well pleased' (Mark 1:11). Another writes: 'This is my beloved Son in whom all things please me' (cf. Luke 3:22). And a third: 'This is my beloved Son in whom I am pleasing to myself' (cf. Matt. 3:17). All that is pleasing to God, is pleasing to him in his sole-begotten Son; and all that he loves, he loves in his sole-begotten Son. Now we should live in such a way that we are one with the sole-begotten Son and are the sole-begotten Son. Between the sole-begotten Son and the soul there is no distinction. There can never be an equal love between servant and master. As long as I am a servant, I shall be both distant and distinct from the sole-begotten Son. And if I were to see God with the same eyes with which I perceive colour, then that would be quite wrong, since it would be temporal and all that is temporal is remote from God and alien to him. If we consider time, even in its smallest part, in the Now, still it is time and exists in itself. As long as we have time and space, number, multiplicity and quantity, all is not well with us and God is far away. Therefore our Lord says: 'Whoever wishes to follow me must forsake themselves' (Luke 9:23); no one can understand my words or my teaching unless they have first forsaken themselves. All creatures in themselves are nothingness. Therefore I have said: take leave of nothingness and grasp perfect being, in which there is a right will. Whoever has abandoned the whole of their will, will appreciate my teaching and will understand my words. Now there is a master who says that all creatures have received their being directly from God; that is why creatures love God by nature more than they do their own selves. If the spirit were to know its own pure state of detachment, then it would not be able to incline to any thing but would remain in its own detached state. Therefore it is said: 'he pleased God in his days'.

The day of the soul and the day of God are different. Where the soul is in her natural day, she knows all things above time and space; nothing is either close to her or distant from her. Therefore I have said that all things are equally noble in this day. I once said that God is creating the world *now* and that all things are equally noble in this day. If we said that God created the world yesterday or that he would do so tomorrow, then we would be foolish. God creates the world and all things in an eternal present, and the time which passed a thousand years ago is just as present to God now and just as close to him as present time. The Father bears his sole-begotten Son into that soul which stands in a perpetual Now, in which same birth the soul is born again into God. It is a single birth: as often as the soul is born back into

God, that is how often the Father gives birth to his sole-begotten Son in her.

I have spoken of a power in the soul. It does not grasp God where it first emerges in so far as he is good, nor does it grasp God in so far as he is truth: it delves deep, ceaselessly seeking, and grasps God in his unity and his desert. It grasps God in his wilderness and in his own ground. Therefore it does not rest content with anything, but seeks further to discover what God is in his Godhead and in the singularity of his own nature. Now it is said that there is no greater unity than that of the three Persons as one God. Then it is said that there is no greater unity than that between God and the soul. When the soul receives a kiss from the Godhead, she stands in absolute perfection and blessedness, embraced by unity. In the first touch in which God has and still does touch the soul as being uncreated and uncreatable, there, by the touch of God, the soul is as noble as God himself. God touches the soul as he does his own self. I once preached in the Latin language, on the Feast of the Holy Trinity, and said that distinction, which is to say distinction within the Trinity, comes from its unity. The unity is the distinction, and the distinction is the unity. The greater the distinction, the greater the unity, since this is the distinction without distinction. If there were a thousand Persons, there would still be only unity. When God sees a creature, he bestows being upon it, and when a creature sees God, it receives its being from him. The soul's being is intellective and cognitive, and so wherever God is, the soul is, and wherever the soul is, there too is God.

Now it is said: 'He is found within.' That is within, which is to say in the ground of the soul, in the innermost part of the soul, in the intellect, not going out and not looking at any thing. There all the powers of the soul are equally noble; it is here that 'he is found just within'. Being 'just' means remaining the same in suffering and joy, in bitterness and sweetness, and not allowing anything to hinder us in any way from finding ourselves unified in justice. The just person is one with God. Likeness is loved. Love always loves what is the same as itself. Therefore God loves the just man or woman as he loves himself.

That we may find ourselves within in the day and in the season of the intellect, in the day of justice and in the day of blessedness, so help us Father, Son and Holy Spirit. Amen.

SERMON 16 (DW 12, W 57)

Qui audit me non confundetur (Ecclus. 24:30)

The words which I have quoted in Latin are uttered by the eternal Wisdom of the Father and mean: 'Whoever hears me shall not be ashamed.' If they are ashamed of anything, it is of the fact that they are ashamed. 'Whoever works in me does not sin. Whoever reveals me and radiates me shall have eternal life.' Any of these three sentences I have quoted would be enough for a sermon. Firstly, I shall discuss the words of eternal Wisdom: 'Whoever hears me shall not be ashamed.' They who are to hear the eternal Wisdom of the Father must be within and must be at home and must be one if they are to hear the eternal Wisdom of the Father.

There are three things that prevent us from hearing the eternal Word. The first is corporality, the second is multiplicity and the third is temporality. If only we could transcend these three, we would dwell in eternity, in the Spirit, in unity and in the desert, and there we would hear the eternal Word. Now our Lord says: 'No one hears my word or my teaching unless they have first abandoned their self' (cf. Luke 14:26). For if we are to hear God's word, we must be wholly detached. The hearer is the same as the heard in the eternal Word. The whole of the eternal Father's teaching is his being, his nature and his whole divinity, which he reveals to us in his only begotten Son, teaching us to become like his Son. Someone who has gone out of themselves to the extent of becoming his only begotten Son comes into the possession of what the Son possesses. All that God does and all that he teaches, he does and teaches in his Son. All that God does he does in order that we may become his only begotten Son. When God sees that we are his only begotten Son, then God presses so urgently upon us and hastens towards us and acts as if his divine being were about to collapse and become nothing in itself so that he can reveal to us the whole abyss of his Godhead, the abundance of his being and his nature. God urgently desires that this should become ours just as it is his. Such a person is established in God's knowledge and in God's love and is nothing other than what God is.

If you love yourself, then you love everyone as much as yourself. But as long as there is anyone whom you do not love as much as yourself, then you have never properly loved yourself – unless you love everyone as yourself, loving all in one person, in someone who is both human and divine. Such a person, who loves themselves and everyone as much as themselves, is doing the right thing. Now some people say: I love my friend, who is a source of good things in my life, more than I do someone else. This is not right; it is imperfect. But we must accept it, just as some people cross the sea with a slack wind and still reach the other side. It is the same with those who love one person more than another, although this is natural. But if I loved him or her as much as I love myself, I would be just as happy that whatever happens to them, whether joy or pain, death or life, should happen instead to me, and this would be true friendship.[63]

Therefore St Paul says: 'I would be willing to be eternally

separated from God for the sake of my friend and for God's sake' (Rom. 9:3). To be separated from God for a moment is to be separated from him for ever, and to be cut off from God is the pain of Hell. So what does St Paul mean when he says these words? The masters ask the question whether St Paul was still on the way to perfection or whether he had already attained it. I say that he was already wholly perfect, or he could not have said these words. Let me now clarify St Paul's comment that he wished to be separated from God.

Taking leave of God for the sake of God is the greatest act of renunciation that someone can make. Now St Paul renounced God for the sake of God: he left all that he could get from God and he left all that God could give him and all that he could receive from God. When he took leave of these things, he renounced God for the sake of God, and yet God remained with him, as God exists in himself, not according to the manner in which he is gained or received but according to the being which he himself is. He never gave anything to God, nor did he ever receive anything from God; rather there is a single oneness here, a pure union. Here the person is truly human and can no more experience suffering than the divine essence can. As I have often said, there is something in the soul which is so close to God that it becomes one with him and not united. It is one, and has nothing in common with anything else, nor does anything created have anything in common with it. All created things are nothingness, but this is remote from and alien to all createdness. If we were wholly composed of this, we would be entirely uncreated and uncreatable. If everything that is material and flawed were included in this oneness, then it would be nothing other than what the oneness is in itself. If I were to find myself even momentarily in this state of being, then I would take as little notice of myself as I would of a dung-worm.

God gives to all things equally and so, as they flow forth from

God, all things are equal and alike.⁶⁴ Angels, men and women and all creatures are equal where they first emerge from God. Whoever takes things in their first emergence from God, takes all things as equal. Now if they are equal as they exist in time, they are even more so where they exist eternally in God. If we take a fly as it exists in God, then it is nobler in God than the highest angel is in itself. Now all things are equal and alike in God and are God. And this likeness is so delightful to God that his whole nature and being floods through himself in this likeness.⁶⁵ This is as delightful for him as when you let a horse run free in a green meadow which is completely flat and even. It is the horse's nature to expend its energy in springing and bucking on the meadow: this is his delight and accords with his nature. In the same way it is delightful for God to find likeness. It is a pleasure for him to pour out his nature and his being into this likeness, since likeness is what he himself is.

Now the question arises with respect to the angels as to whether those angels who dwell with us, serving us and protecting us, possess a lesser degree of likeness in their joy than do those who are in eternity, or whether they have been somehow reduced by becoming active through protecting and serving us. I say: no, not at all! Their joy and their likeness is none the less on this account, for the work of angels is the will of God and the will of God is the work of angels, which is why they are not impeded in their joy, their likeness or their work. If God commanded an angel to go to a tree and to remove caterpillars from it, then the angel would be willing to remove the caterpillars, and this would be his joy, and would be the will of God.

That man or woman who is thus rooted in the will of God desires nothing other than what God is and what he wills. If they are ill, they would not desire to be well. All suffering is a joy for them, and all multiplicity is simplicity and unity in so far as they are in God's will. Indeed, even if it meant the pains of hell, it would be joy and blessedness for them. They are bare and have gone out of themselves and such a person must be bare of all that can be given them from without. If my eye is to perceive colour, it must be free of all colours. If I see the colour blue or white, then the seeing of my eye, which perceives the colour, is exactly the same as what it sees, as what is seen by the eye. The eye with which I see God is exactly the same eye with which God sees me. My eye and God's eye are one eye, one seeing, one knowledge and one love.

That person who is thus rooted in God's love must be dead to themselves and to all created things so that they are no more concerned with themselves than they are with someone who is over a thousand miles away. Such a person remains in likeness and in unity and is always the same. No unlikeness enters them. This person must have abandoned themselves and the whole world. If there were a person to whom the whole of this world belonged and they gave it up for God's sake as simply as they received it, our Lord would return the whole world to them together with eternal life. And if someone else, who possessed nothing but their own good will, thought: Lord, if this world were mine and if I had another world and then another (making three of them), and if they desired: Lord, I will give this one up and myself as simply as when I received them from you, then God would give that person just as much as if they had actually given everything away with their own hand. But someone else, who has nothing physical or mental to give away, would renounce the most. Whoever entirely renounces themselves even for a moment would be given all things. But if someone had abandoned themselves for twenty years and then took themselves back for a moment, then it would be as if they had never renounced themselves at all. That person who *has* detached themselves from everything and who *is* detached, never glancing even for a moment at what they have given up, who remains steadfast, unmoved in themselves and immutable – such a person alone has truly attained detachment.

That we may remain steadfast and immutable, like our eternal Father, so help us God and eternal Wisdom. Amen.

SERMON 17 (DW 21, W 97)

Unus deus et pater omnium (Eph. 4:6)

I have read a passage in Latin from the Epistle where St Paul writes: 'One God and Father of all, who is blessed above all and through all and in us all'. I shall take another text from the Gospel, where our Lord says: 'Friend, climb up higher, draw higher' (Luke 14:10).

In the former text, where Paul says 'One God and Father of all', he omits one little word which signifies change.[66] When he says 'one God', he means that God is one in himself and is distinct from all things. God belongs to no one, and no one belongs to him: God is one. Boethius says that God is one and does not change.[67] Everything which God ever made, he made subject to change, and all created things bear the marks of changeability upon their backs.

This means that we should be at one within ourselves and distinct from all things, and should be unshakeably at one with God. Outside God there is only nothingness. Therefore it is impossible that there could be any change or instability. Whatever seeks a place beyond itself, undergoes change. But God contains all things in himself in fullness; therefore God seeks nothing beyond himself but seeks something only in the fullness in which it already exists within himself. And no creature can comprehend anything as it exists in God.

Further teaching is to be found in the words: 'Father of all, who is blessed'. Now this passage contains change within itself. When it says 'Father', we too are meant. If he is our Father, then we are his children, and so both honour and any disrespect he is shown affect us too. When a child sees how much its father loves it, then it realizes that it must live a pure and innocent life for his sake. For this reason we too should live in purity since God himself says: 'Blessed are the pure in heart, for they shall see God' (Matt. 5:8). What is purity of heart? Purity of heart is being detached and removed from all physical things, gathered and enclosed in oneself, and then springing forth from purity into God and being united there. David says that those works are pure and innocent which emerge and are perfected in the light of the soul; but those works are even more innocent which remain within, in the spirit, and do not emerge at all. 'One God and Father of all.'

Now we come to the other passage: 'Friend, climb up higher, draw higher.' I shall combine these two. When he says 'Friend, climb up higher, draw higher', then this is a dialogue between the soul and God in which the soul receives the answer: 'One God and Father of all'. A master says that friendship resides in the will. In so far as friendship lies in the will, it cannot unite. I too have put it this way: love does not unite. Although love unites with respect to action, it does not do so with respect to being.[68] This is why it is said 'one God' and 'climb up higher, draw higher'. Only pure Godhead can enter the ground of the soul. Even the highest angel, although he is so close and akin to God and there is so much of God in him (his action is always in God, he is united with God in being and not in action, he indwells God and is always with him, and he is noble to a wonderful degree), nevertheless even he cannot enter the soul. There is a master who says that all creatures who possess distinction are not worthy that God should act in them. The soul in herself, where she exists above the body, is so pure and so fine that she absorbs nothing but pure Godhead. Yet even God cannot penetrate within unless all that has been added to him is first stripped away. That is why you were given the answer: 'one God'.

St Paul says: 'one God'. Oneness is purer than goodness and truth. Although goodness and truth add nothing, they do nevertheless add something in the mind: when they are thought, something is added. But oneness adds nothing, where God exists in himself, before he flows out into the Son and the Holy Spirit.[69] Therefore he said: 'Friend, climb up higher'. A master says: oneness is a negation of negation.[70] If I say that God is good, then I am adding something to him. Oneness on the other hand is a negation of negation and a denial of denial. What does 'one' mean? One is that to which nothing has been added. The soul takes the Godhead where it is purified in itself, where nothing has been added to it, where nothing has been thought. One is the negation of negation. All creatures contain a negation within themselves: one creature denies that it is another. One particular angel denies that he is another. But with God there is a negation of negation: he is one and negates all else, since there is nothing outside God. All creatures are in God and are his own Godhead, which signifies the fulness of which I spoke above. He is one Father of the whole Godhead. I speak therefore of one Godhead, since nothing yet flows forth there, nothing is moved or thought. By denying something of God – if I were to deny goodness of God for instance (though I can in truth deny nothing of God) – by denying something of God, I grasp something which he is not. It is precisely this which must be got rid of. God is one; he is the negation of negation. That is why he said: 'One God, Father of all' and 'Friend, climb up higher'.[71]

A master says the nature of an angel has neither power nor action, since it knows nothing but God. It knows nothing of anything else.[72] Certain of the soul's powers absorb from outside, like the eye. However fine that which it takes in may be, stripped of its coarseness, it is still absorbing something from outside which is connected with the here and now. But knowledge and the intellect strip everything away and assimilate what entirely lacks the element of a here and now. To this extent the intellect is akin to the angelic nature.[73] And yet it still receives from the senses: the intellect assimilates what is conveyed by the senses from outside. The will does not do this, and in this respect the will is nobler than the intellect. The will only receives anything in pure knowledge, where there is neither here nor now. What God means to say is that however exalted or pure the will may be, it must become yet more so. And so God replies by saying: 'Friend, climb up higher, and you will receive honour' (Luke 14:10).

The will desires blessedness. I was asked what the difference is between grace and blessedness. Grace, as we experience it in this life, and blessedness, which we shall later possess in eternal life, are to each other as flower to the fruit. When the soul is entirely filled with grace, and there remains nothing more in her which is not moved by grace and perfected by it, still not everything (as it is in the soul) which the soul has to do is performed so that she can be perfected by grace. I have already said that grace does not effect a work but rather pours all adornments into the soul. This is the wealth in the kingdom of the soul. I say that grace does not unite the soul with God but is rather a fulfilment. This is its work: to lead the soul back to God. There she receives the fruit from the flower. As regards the will, in so far as it desires blessedness and in so far as it wishes to be with God and is accordingly raised up, God enters it in purity, and in so far as our intellect apprehends God purely, as he is truth, to that extent God enters our intellect. But as he descends into the will, this must rise up. Therefore he says: 'One God', and 'Friend, climb up higher'.

'One God': in the oneness of God the divinity of God is perfected. I say this, that God could never give birth to his sole-begotten Son if he were not one. All that God works in creatures and in his divinity God derives from his oneness. I say further:

God alone possesses oneness. That is the defining characteristic of his being, and it is on account of this that God is God. Everything which is multiple depends upon the One, but the One depends upon nothing. The wealth and wisdom and truth of God are entirely one in God; and not just one but also oneness. All that God possesses is in the One, and it is one in him. The masters say that the firmament revolves so that it makes all things one, which is why it revolves so swiftly.[74] God possesses all his wealth as one, upon which his nature depends, and it is the soul's blessedness that God is one: it is her adornment and her glory. He said: 'Friend, climb higher and glory will be yours.' It is the glory and adornment of the soul that God is one. And God acts as if he were only one in order to please the soul and as if he adorned himself only in order to make the soul fall in love with him. Therefore we want first one thing and then another. Now we practise wisdom and now some art or other. It is because the soul does not possess the One that she will never find rest until all things are one in God. God is one; this is the blessedness of the soul, her adornment and her peace. A master says that God in all his works has all things in mind. The soul is all things.[75] God pours into the soul whatever is noblest, purest and highest beneath her. God is all and is one.

That we may become one with God, so help us 'one God, Father of all'. Amen.

SERMON 18 (DW 42, W 80)

Adolescens, tibi dico: surge (Luke 7:14)

In the Gospel according to St Luke we read of a 'young man who was dead. Then our Lord came by and took pity on him and touched him, saying: "Young man, I tell you and command you, rise up!'"

Now know this: in all good people God is wholly present, and there is a something within the soul in which God lives and in which the soul lives in God. But when the soul turns outwards to external things, she dies as God too dies to the soul. But in no way does God die to himself; rather he lives on in himself. When the soul parts from the body, the body is dead while the soul lives on in herself. God too is dead to that soul, but he lives on in himself. Now know this: there is a power in the soul which extends further than the heavens, which are wide beyond belief and are wider than language can express, but that other power in the soul is greater by far.[76]

Now listen carefully! The heavenly Father speaks in that noble power to his only begotten Son: 'Young man, rise up.' The union of God with the soul is so great that it is beyond belief, and God is in himself so exalted that he is beyond the reach of either knowledge or desire. Desire extends further than anything that can be grasped by knowledge. It is wider than the whole of the heavens, than all angels, even though everything that lives on earth is contained in the spark of a single angel. Desire is wide, immeasurably so. But nothing that knowledge can grasp or desire can want, is God. Where knowledge and desire end, there is darkness, and there God shines.

Now our Lord says: 'Young man, I tell you, rise up!' If I am to hear the voice of God in me, then I must be as wholly removed from all that is mine as I am from what lies on the other side of the sea, especially with respect to time. The soul is as young in herself as she was when she was created, and the particular age she is given holds only for the body in which she, the soul, is active in the senses. A master says that if an old person had young eyes, they would see as well as young people do. Yesterday I said something as I sat which sounds quite incredible. I said that

Jerusalem is just as close to my soul as the place where I am now standing. In truth, whatever is a thousand miles further away than Jerusalem is as close to my soul as my own body. I am as sure of this as I am that I am a man, and this is not difficult for learned priests to understand. Know this: my soul is as young today as when she was first created. Indeed, she is far younger! And know this too: I shall be ashamed if she is not younger tomorrow than she is today.[77]

The soul has two powers which have nothing in common with the body, namely reason and the will. These act above time. If only the eyes of the soul were opened so that her intelligence could grasp the truth clearly! Now know this: such a person would find it as easy to take leave of everything as they do to give up a pea or a lentil or nothing at all. Indeed, upon my soul, all things would be as nothing to them. Now there are certain people who turn from things out of love, but who still have great regard for what they have left. But those who understand in truth that even when they have given themselves up and have abandoned all things, this is still absolutely nothing – those who live in this way, truly possess all things.

There is in the soul a power which finds all things equally pleasing. In fact, the very worst and the very best thing are exactly the same for this power, which receives everything from a position above the here and now. 'Now' is time and 'here' is place, the place where I am presently standing. But if I had gone out of myself and were entirely free of myself, then the Father would give birth to his only begotten Son so purely in my spirit that the spirit would give birth to him in return. Truly, if my soul were as ready as that of my Lord Jesus Christ, then the Father would act in me as purely as he does in his only begotten Son and no less so, for he loves me with the same love with which he loves himself. St John says: 'In the beginning was the Word, and the Word was with God and the Word was God' (John 1:1). Now, whoever wishes to hear this passage in the Father, where it is quite still, must themselves become wholly still and detached from all images and from all forms. Indeed, we should cleave so faithfully to God that nothing can cause us either joy or grief. Rather, we should accept all things in God, just as they are in him.

Now he says: 'Young man, I tell you, rise up.' He wishes to perform the work himself. If someone orders me to carry a stone, then they might as well tell me to carry a thousand stones as one, if they actually intend to carry the stones themselves. Or if one person orders another to carry a hundredweight, they might as well say a thousand as one, if they intend to do the work themselves. For God wishes to perform this work himself and we need only follow him, without offering resistance. If only the soul remained within, she would find all things present there. There is a power in the soul, which is not merely a power but is rather being, and not just being, but rather something that liberates from being.[78] It is so pure, exalted and sublime in itself that no creature can enter into it, but only God, who dwells within it. In truth, God himself cannot enter in there in so far as he has a particular manner, in so far as he is wise or good or rich. Indeed, God cannot enter there with any particular manner of being but rather only with his naked and divine nature.

Now take note of the words that he uses: 'Young man, I tell you . . .' What is this 'telling' of God?[79] It is the work of God, and this work is so noble and so exalted that God alone performs it. Now know this: all our perfection and all our blessedness depends upon our breaking through, passing beyond all createdness, all temporality and all being and entering into the ground that is without ground.

We beseech God, our precious Lord, that we may become one, dwelling within, and may God help us to enter this ground. Amen.

SERMON 19 (DW 5a, W 13a)

In hoc apparuit caritas dei in nobis, quoniam filium suum unigenitium misit deus in mundum ut vivamus per eum (1 John 4:9)

St John says: 'God's love was revealed to us in this, that he sent his Son into the world that we should live through him', and our human nature has been immeasurably ennobled by the fact that the All-Highest came down and assumed the nature of a human being.

There is a teacher who says: when I consider that our nature has been raised above that of creatures and that it is placed above the angels and is adored by them, I must rejoice from the bottom of my heart, for Jesus Christ, my precious Lord, has given me everything that he possesses in himself. And he says too: in all those things he imparted to his Son, Jesus Christ, the Father had me in mind, loving me more than him and imparting these things to me rather than to him. How can this be? God gave them to his Son on my account, for I was needy. Therefore, whatever he gave his Son, he meant for me and truly gave them to me as well as to him. And I exclude neither the unity nor the sanctity of the Godhead, nor anything else. Nothing that he gave him in human nature is more alien or distant to me than it is to him, for God cannot give only in part. He must either give everything or not at all. His gift is irreducible and indivisible and belongs not to time but to eternity. And, as I live, you should know that if we are to receive from him in this way, then we must be established in eternity, raised above time. In eternity all things are present. What is above me is as close and as present to me as that which is at my side. There we shall receive from God what we are to have from him. God knows nothing but himself: his eye is directed only at himself. What he sees, he sees in himself. Therefore God does not see us when we sin. And so God knows us only in so far as we exist in him: that is, in so far as we are without sin. And all the works which our Lord performed, he has given me so that they are no less meritorious for me than my own works are. But since the whole of his nobility is as much our possession and is as close to us, to me as it is to him, why then do we not receive as much as he does? This is something you must understand! Whoever wants to attain this gift, the gift of universal human nature that is equally available to all, then just as there is nothing in human nature which is either more distinct from, closer to or further away from any one person than another, so too you must make no distinctions in the way you relate to people, being no closer to yourself than you are to anyone else. You should love, respect and regard all others as yourself; and you should feel that whatever happens to someone else, whether good things or bad, is happening to you.[80]

Now this is the second meaning: 'he sent him into the world'. Here we must understand that great world into which the angels peer. And us? We should be there with all our love and desire, as St Augustine says: 'through love we become what we love. Now should we say that if we love God, we become God?'[81] That sounds like paganism. The love that someone gives contains not two but one and oneness, and when I love I am more God than I am in myself. The prophet says: 'I have said you are gods and children of the most high' (Ps. 82:6). It may sound strange to say that we can become God in such a way in love, and yet this is true in the eternal truth. Our Lord Jesus Christ proves it.

'He sent him into the world.' One meaning of the Latin word *mundum* is 'pure'. Now take note! There is no place more suited to God than a pure heart and a pure soul: there the Father gives birth to his Son, just as he gives birth to him in eternity, no more and no less. What is a pure heart? That heart is pure which is detached from all creatures, for all creatures cause impurity since they are nothingness and nothingness is a deficiency which sullies the soul. All creatures are a pure nothingness; neither angels nor creatures can be said to be something. They cause impurity since they are made of nothingness; nothingness is what they are. They touch all things[82] and cause impurity, since they are made of nothingness. They are and were nothingness. Nothingness is what is counter to all creatures and displeasing to them. If I placed a piece of red-hot coal in my hand, then that would cause me pain. This comes solely from 'nothingness', and were we free of nothingness, we would not be impure.

And now 'we live in him', with him. There is nothing we desire so much as life. What is my life? That which is self-moving from within. But that which is moved from without is not alive. If we live with him then, we must also act with him from within so that we do not act from without. Rather we should be moved by that from which we live, that is by him. We can and must act from our own inner self. And so if we are to live in him or through him, then he must become our own inner self and we must act from our own inner self. Just as God effects all things from his own inner self and through himself, in the same way we too must act from our own inner self, which is him in us. He is wholly our own, and all things are our own in him. All that is in the possession of the angels, the saints and Our Lady, is mine in him and is neither more distant nor alien to me than what is in my own possession. All things are equally my own in him. And if we are to come to this very own, so that all things are our own, then we must apprehend him equally in all things, no more in one than another, for he is in all things alike.

There are people who savour God in one way but not in another, and they want to possess God according to one manner of devotion and not another. I can tolerate this, but it is quite wrong. If we are to take God correctly, then we must take him equally in all things: in tribulation as in prosperity, in tears as in joy. He should always be the same for you. If you believe, without having committed a mortal sin, that you lack both devotion and serious intent and that, not having devotion or serious intent, you do not have God, and if you then grieve over this, this itself becomes your devotion and serious intent. Therefore you should not confine yourself to just one manner of devotion, since God is to be found in no particular way, neither this one nor that. That is why they do him wrong who take God just in one particular way. They take the way rather than God. Remember this then: intend God alone and seek him only. Then whatever kinds of devotional practice come to you, be content with those. For your intention should be directed at God alone and at nothing else. Then what you like or dislike is all right, and you should know that to do it differently is to do it wrongly. They who desire so many ways of devotion push God under a bench. Whether it is the gift of tears or sighings or the like – none of this is God. If these come to you, all well and good. If they do not come to you, that too is all right and you should receive what God wishes to give you in that moment, remaining always in humility and absence of self, and always considering that you are unworthy of any good which God might give you if that is his wish. Thus the passage is explained which St John wrote: 'God's love was revealed to us in this'. If we were like this, then this good would be revealed in us too. The fact that it is concealed is entirely our own fault. We are the cause of all our obstacles. Guard yourself against yourself, and you have good protection. And even if we do not wish to accept his love, he has nevertheless chosen us for this. If we do not accept it therefore, we shall regret it and shall be sorely punished. That we do not arrive at the place where this good is received is not his fault but ours.[83]

SERMON 20 (DW 16a, W 14a)

A master says that if every medium were removed between myself and a wall, then I would be at the wall but not in it. But this is not the case with spiritual things, for with them one thing is always in another. That which receives is the same as that which is received, for it receives nothing other than itself. This is difficult. Whoever understands it has been preached to enough. But now just a little about the image of the soul.[84]

There are many teachers who are of the opinion that this image is born from the will and from knowledge, but this is not the case. Rather I say that this image is a product of itself with neither will nor knowledge. Let me give you an analogy. Imagine that a mirror is held up to my face – whether I wish to or not, with neither will nor knowledge of myself, my image is formed in the mirror. This image does not derive from the mirror, nor from itself. Rather this image is grounded in the one who gives it its being and its nature. When the mirror is removed from me, then I am no longer imaged in it, for I am myself this image.

Another analogy. When a branch grows from a tree, it bears both the name and the nature of the tree. What grows out is the same as what remains within, and what remains within is the same as what grows out. Thus the branch is an expression of itself.

The same is true for the image of the soul: what goes out is the same as what remains within and what remains within is the same as what goes out. This image is the Son of the Father and I myself am this image[85] and this image is wisdom. Therefore God be praised now and for evermore. Amen. May those who do not understand this, not be troubled.

SERMON 21 (DW 86, W 9)

Intravit Iesus in quoddam castellum, et mulier quaedam, Martha nomine,
excepit illum (Luke 10:38)[86]

St Luke writes in his gospel that our Lord entered a small town where he was received by a woman called Martha. She had a sister, whose name was Mary. Mary sat at the feet of our Lord and listened to his words, while Martha moved about and waited on our Lord.

Now there are three things which caused Mary to sit at the feet of our Lord. The first was that the goodness of God had seized her soul. The second was an inexpressible desire: she was filled with longing, but did not know what for. She was filled with desire, but did not know why. The third thing was the sweet consolation and the bliss which came to her from the eternal words which flowed from the mouth of Christ.

There were three things too which caused Martha to move about and to serve her beloved Christ. The first was her maturity and the ground of her being which she had trained to the greatest extent and which, she believed, qualified her best of all to undertake these tasks. The second was wise understanding which knew how to perform those works perfectly that love commands. And the third was the particular honour of her precious guest.[87]

The masters say that God is prepared to satisfy the desires of every person both with respect to the pleasures of the mind and the senses. We can discern how God satisfies both our mind and senses in the precious friends of God. Satisfying our senses means that God gives us consolation, bliss and contentment, and the precious friends of God cannot be spoilt in this respect in the domain of their lower senses.[88] But mental pleasure, on the other hand, is pleasure in the spirit. By mental pleasure I mean those occasions when the crown or highest part of the soul is not pulled down by all our bliss, and is not submerged therefore in feelings of delight, but rather remains upright, sovereignly above such things. Only then do we find ourselves in a state of mental pleasure, when neither the joys nor griefs of creatures can pull the tip of the soul downwards. And by creatures here I mean all those things which we perceive below God.

Now Martha says: 'Lord, tell her to help me.' This was not said grudgingly but rather she was obliged to say it from a loving good-will. We must call it either loving good-will or affectionate teasing. But why? Pay attention. She saw that Mary was bathed in joy, her soul filled with pleasure. Martha knew Mary better than Mary knew Martha, for she had already lived long and well, and it is life that gives the best knowledge. Better than joy or light, life knows everything that we can strive for in this life except God, and in a certain sense it does so more purely than even the light of eternity can.[89] The eternal light teaches us to know ourselves as well as God, and not ourselves without God. When life sees only itself, then the distinction between what is the same and what is different emerges more clearly. St Paul attests to this, as do the pagan masters. In his ecstatic vision St Paul saw God and himself in a spiritual manner in God but he could not clearly distinguish one virtue from another there, which was a consequence of the fact that he had not practised them in his own life. The pagan masters on the other hand achieved such great knowledge through the practice of virtues that they perceived every virtue more clearly than Paul or any other saint did in their first ecstasy.

This was also the case with Martha. That is why she said: 'Lord, tell her to help me', as if she meant to say that her sister seemed to think that she could do whatever she wished simply by sitting at the Lord's feet and enjoying his consolation. 'Let her see now whether this is really the case, and tell her to stand up and go away.' This was said frankly but out of affectionate love. Mary was so filled with longing that she yearned without knowing what for, and desired without knowing what it was she desired. And we cannot escape the suspicion that by sitting where she was, dear Mary was more concerned with her feelings of pleasure than with spiritual gain. That is why Martha said: 'Lord, tell her to help me', since she was afraid that Mary might get caught up in her reverie and fail to advance any further. Christ answered her by saying: 'Martha, Martha, you are worried, you are concerned with many things. Mary has chosen the better part which shall never be taken from her' (Luke 10:41–42). Christ did not say this to Martha reprovingly but rather indicated to her that Mary would indeed become as she wished her to be.

But why did Christ say 'Martha, Martha', thus naming her twice? Isidore says there is no doubt that neither prior to nor after his birth in human form did God ever call anyone by name who was subsequently lost, but the case is more doubtful for those whom he did not call by name.[90] By Christ's naming of people I understand his eternal knowledge: being inscribed indelibly and from eternity in the living book which is Father, Son and Holy Spirit, prior to the creation of all creatures. None of those who were named in it, whom Christ actually called by name, were lost. Moses is proof of this, to whom God himself said, 'I have called you by name' (Ex. 33:12), and Nathaniel, to whom our beloved Christ said, 'I knew you when you lay beneath the fig tree' (John 1:50). The fig tree signifies God, in whom Nathaniel's name was written from eternity. Thus it is shown that none of those individuals were lost, or ever shall be lost, whom Christ addressed by name with his human tongue from the eternal Word.

But why did he call Martha twice by name? He wished to show that Martha was wholly in possession of all that is good and all that a creature can possess, whether temporal or eternal. With the first 'Martha' he was referring to her perfection in temporal works. With the second, he showed that she lacked nothing that is necessary for eternal blessedness. Therefore he said 'you are careful', meaning: 'you are in the midst of things, but things are not in you'. They who are careful are unhindered in their actions.[91] They are unhindered whose works conform to the eternal light. Such people are among things but not in them. They are very close to them but possess them no less than if they, the people, were up above in the circle of eternity. 'Very close', I say, for all creatures serve as a means to something else. There are two kinds of means. The first is that without which I cannot attain God: works and actions within time, which do not detract from our eternal blessedness. We perform works when we act virtuously from outside, and *actions* when we act from within with intelligent understanding. But the second means is precisely the abandoning of the first. For that is the reason why we exist in time at all, in order to come closer to God, becoming more like him, by rational 'actions' in time. This is also what St Paul means when he says: 'Redeem the time, the days are evil' (Eph. 5:16). 'Redeeming the time' means ceaselessly rising up to God through reason and not in the distinctions of sensory images but rather in living and rational truth. And in 'the days are evil', 'day' is to be taken as suggesting 'night' since, if there were no night, there would be no day and we would not speak of it at all for all would be a single light. It is this to which St Paul refers, for an illuminated life is too slight in which darkness still exists, concealing and obscuring eternal blessedness from the noble spirit. This was also Christ's meaning when he said, 'Go on while you have the light' (John 12:35). For whoever acts in the light, rises up to God, free and unencumbered by any means: their light is their 'actions' and their 'actions' are their light.

This was how it was for Martha. Therefore he said to her: 'Only one thing is necessary', and not two. You and I, once enfolded by the eternal light, are one. But this 'two-one' is a burning spirit which exists above all things and yet is below God in the circle of eternity. This is two, since it does not see God without means. Its knowledge and its being, or its knowledge and the cognitive image, never become one. It is only possible to see God where God is seen spiritually, with no image at all. There one becomes two, two is one: light and spirit, both are one in the embrace of the eternal light.

Now take note of what the 'circle of eternity' is. The soul has three ways to God. The first is to seek God in all creatures with many and varied actions with burning love. This is what King Solomon was referring to when he said: 'I have sought rest in all things' (Ecclus. 24:7).

The second is a pathless way, which is free and yet fixed, in which we are raised and exalted above ourselves and all things, with neither will nor images, although not yet in substantial being. Christ was referring to this when he said: 'You are blessed, Peter. Flesh and blood have not illumined you, but being caught up in the higher mind. When you call me God, my heavenly Father has revealed it to you' (Matt. 16:17). But even St Peter did not see God as he is, although he was raised up to the 'circle of eternity' beyond all created understanding by the power of his heavenly Father. I tell you, without his knowledge he was violently seized by the heavenly Father in a loving embrace and raised up in spirit into the power of the heavenly Father beyond all comprehension. There, from above, St Peter heard the sound of a sweet creaturely voice, which was nevertheless free of all sensual pleasure, in the simple truth of the unity of God and humanity in the person of the heavenly Father-Son. I dare even to say this: if St Peter had seen directly into the nature of God, as he did later, and as St Paul did when he was transported to the third heaven, then the speech of even the highest angel would have seemed coarse to him. But still he spoke a few sweet words, which beloved Jesus did not require, since he sees into the ground of the heart and spirit – he who stands immediately before God the Father in the freedom of true unity. This is what St Paul meant when he said: 'a man was caught up and heard such words as may not be uttered by men' (2 Cor. 12:2–4). From that you should understand that St Peter had reached the 'circle of eternity' but did not in unity gaze upon God in his own being.

Although the third way is called a 'way', it is also a kind of 'being at home'. It is seeing God directly in his own being. Now our beloved Christ says: 'I am the way, the truth and the life' (John 14:6): one Christ in the Person, one in the Father, one in the Spirit as three – 'way, truth and life', and one as precious Jesus in whom all this is. All creatures circle this way, and function as a means. But in this way they are led to God the Father by the light of his Word and are embraced by the love of the Holy Spirit which is of them both. This transcends anything that can be said in words. Listen to this miracle! How astonishing: to be without and within, to grasp and be grasped, to see and be ourselves seen, to hold and be ourselves held – that is the goal, where the spirit dwells in peace, united with precious eternity.

Let us return to our explanation of how dear Martha, and all God's friends, can be said to be 'with concern' and not 'in concern'. Here action in time is just as noble as any uniting of the self with God, for it is as profitable to us as anything that we can encounter, with the sole exception of the vision of God in his own essence. Therefore Christ says: 'You stand with things and with concern', meaning thereby that she was exposed to troubles and depression with her lower faculties since she was not swamped by the enticements of the Spirit. She was with things and not in them . . .[92]

Three things are essential to the works we perform. These are that we should act with orderliness, insight and perspicacity. By orderliness I mean that which corresponds to the highest in all its aspects, and by insight I mean that than which for the time being we know nothing better. And finally by perspicacity I mean sensing in good works the joyful presence of the living truth. Where all three of these things coincide, they draw us as close to God and are as beneficial for us as all the raptures of Mary Magdalene in the desert.[93]

Now Christ says: 'you are concerned with many things' and not with the one thing. This means that when she stands upright on the circle of eternity, simple, pure and without any actions, she is troubled by any form of 'means' which prevents her from remaining there in delight. Such a person is 'worried' by this, and is anxious and depressed. But Martha was securely established in mature virtue and had an unencumbered mind, free of any impediment. Accordingly she wished that her sister might be in the same state for she saw that she, her sister, was not yet *essentially* there. It was from the mature ground of her soul that she wished that her sister too should possess all that belongs to eternal blessedness. That is why Christ says: 'Only one thing is necessary'. But what is this one thing? It is God. This is what all creatures need, for if God took back what is his, all creatures would fall into nothingness. If God removed what is his from the soul of Christ, where his spirit is united with the eternal Person, then Christ too would be no more than a creature. Therefore we have a great need of the one thing. Martha feared that her sister would remain trapped in her pleasant feelings and in the sweetness, and she wished that her sister might become as she herself was. Therefore Christ said: Be at peace, Martha. She 'has chosen the better part'. But this shall pass. The very highest thing that a creature can possess will be hers, and she will become blessed as you are blessed.

Now understand this concerning the virtues. Virtuous life depends upon three things which concern the will. The first is giving the will up for God, since it is absolutely necessary to completely fulfil what we shall know then, whether by the process of letting go or acquiring. There are three kinds of will. The first is a 'sensual' will, the second a 'rational' will and the third an 'eternal' will. The sensual will demands instruction and motivates us to listen to authentic teachers. The rational will consists in planting our feet in all the deeds of Christ and the saints, which means to say that we direct our works, our way of life and all our actions towards the highest end. When all this has been fulfilled, then God causes something else to descend into the soul's ground: the eternal will together with the loving command of the Holy Spirit. Then the soul says: 'Lord, give me what your eternal will is!' When she has satisfied the condition we have just explained, thus pleasing God, the beloved Father speaks his eternal Word into the soul.

Now good people say that we should become so perfect that no occasion of joy can ever touch us again and we are as immovable in joy as we are in sorrow. This is wrong. I tell you that there can never be a saint who is so great that they cannot be moved in this way. I say rather that it may be given to a saint in this life that nothing can distract them from God. You claim that as long as words can move you to joy and sorrow you are imperfect! This is not the case! And it was not true even for Christ himself, as he revealed when he said: 'My soul grieves even unto death' (Matt. 26:38). Christ was so hurt by words that if a single creature were to suffer the griefs of all, this would not be so terrible as the suffering of Christ. This was the consequence of the nobility of his nature and the holy union of human and divine nature in him. Therefore I say that there has never been nor shall there ever be a saint who has not felt the pain of suffering and the delight of joy. It may be the case that every once in a while there is someone who, through the love and grace and miracle of God, is unmoved by either suffering or joy when their faith or something else is under attack and they are flooded with grace. And again, perhaps there are saints who cannot be distracted from God by anything so that, although the heart suffers while they are not in a state of grace, their will dwells simply in God and says: 'Lord, I am yours and you are mine!' And whatever happens in such a person, it cannot harm their eternal blessedness as long as it does not touch the highest tip of the spirit where they are one with God's most precious will.

Now Christ says: 'You are concerned with many things.' Martha was so formed in essence that her actions did not obstruct her. Both her works and actions led her to eternal blessedness. Although in her case this was mediated, a noble nature, constant perseverance and virtue in the above sense are greatly beneficial. Mary too began as Martha before maturing to be Mary, for as she still sat at the feet of our Lord, she had not yet truly become Mary – although Mary by name she had not yet become Mary in her being, since she was still in the grasp of sweet and pleasant feelings and was still under instruction, learning how to live.[94] But Martha was already formed in essence. That is why she said: 'Lord, tell her to get up', as if she meant: 'Lord, I wish that she would not sit there enjoying her pleasurable feelings. I wish that she would learn how to live so that she might possess life essentially. Tell her to get up so that she may become perfect.' Mary was not her name as she sat at the feet of our Lord. Mary is the name rather of one who has a well-disciplined body which is obedient to instruction. And obedience is when the will is satisfied with what understanding dictates.

Now some good people maintain that they have progressed so far that the presence of physical objects no longer affects their senses. But this is not the case. I shall never reach the point where a hideous noise is as pleasing to my ears as sweetly sounding strings. But this much is possible – that a rational, God-conformed will may be free of all natural pleasures and, upon hearing such a noise, commands the sensual will not to be concerned with it so that the latter replies: 'I gladly agree!' Then conflict will turn to joy, for what we must strive for with great effort becomes our heart's delight, and only then does it bear fruit.

Now some people want to maintain they have advanced so far that they are free even of good works. But I say again that this cannot be. It was after receiving the Holy Spirit that the disciples first began to practise virtues. 'Mary sat at the feet of our Lord and listened to his words', and she learned, for she was still under instruction and learning how to live. But later, when she had learned and Christ had ascended into heaven and she had received the Holy Spirit, only then did she begin to serve, travelling across the sea, preaching, instructing and becoming a servant and washer-woman to the disciples. It is when the saints become saints that they begin to perform good works and that is when they first begin to gather the treasure of eternal blessedness. All that they did before paid the debt of guilt and averted punishment. Christ himself is a witness to this: from the very beginning when God became human and humanity became God, he began to work for our blessedness up to the point of dying on the cross. There was not a single part of his body that had not practised particular good works.

That we may follow him faithfully in the practice of true virtues, so help us God. Amen.

SERMON 22 (DW 52, W 87)

Beati pauperes spiritu, quoniam ipsorum est regnum caelorum (Matt. 5:3)

Blessedness spoke to Wisdom and said: 'Blessed are the poor in spirit, for theirs is the kingdom of heaven.'[95]

All the angels, all the saints and everything that was ever born must be silent when the Wisdom of God speaks, for all the wisdom of the angels and all creatures is a pure nothingness before the unfathomable Wisdom of God. And this Wisdom has said that the poor are blessed.

Now there are two kinds of poverty: external poverty, which is good and very praiseworthy in those who willingly practise it for love of Our Lord Jesus Christ, since this is what he did when he was on earth. But I do not wish to speak further of this poverty, for there is another kind of poverty, which is internal, and which is referred to by Our Lord when he says: 'Blessed are the poor in spirit'.

Now, I ask you to be poor enough to understand what it is that I am saying to you, for I declare by Eternal Wisdom that if you do not yourself become the same as that Wisdom of which we wish to speak, then my words will mean nothing to you.

Some people have asked me what poverty is in itself and what it means to be a poor man or woman.

Bishop Albrecht says that a poor person is someone who takes no pleasure in anything which God has created – and this was well said.[96] But we can improve on this and offer a more profound definition of poverty by saying that a poor person is someone who desires nothing, knows nothing and possesses nothing. It is of these three things that we wish to speak, and I beseech you for the love of God to understand me if you can. But if you do not understand, then do not worry, for I shall be speaking of a particular kind of truth which only a few good people can grasp.

In the first place we say that a poor person is someone who desires nothing. Some people do not understand this point correctly. I mean those who cling to their own egos in their penances and external devotions, which such people regard as being of great importance. God have mercy on them, for they know little of the divine truth! These people are called holy because of what they are seen to do, but inside they are asses, for they do not know the real meaning of divine truth. Although such people are happy to say that a poor person is one who desires nothing, they interpret this as meaning that we must live in such a way that we never perform our own will in anything but that we should desire rather to carry out God's most precious will. These people are all right, for they mean well and that is why they deserve our praise. May God in his mercy grant them heaven! But I tell you by the divine truth that such people are not truly poor nor are they like those who are poor. They are greatly esteemed by people who know no better. But I tell you that they are asses, who understand nothing of God's truth. May they attain heaven because of their good intent, but of that poverty, of which we now wish to speak, they know nothing.

If someone were now to ask me what it means to be a poor person who desires nothing, then I would say that as long as it is someone's will to carry out the most precious will of God, such a person does not have that poverty of which we wish to speak. For this person still has a will with which they wish to please God, and this is not true poverty. If we are to have true poverty, then we must be so free of our own created will as we were before we were created. I tell you by the eternal truth that as long as you have the will to perform God's will, and a desire for eternity and for God, you are not yet poor. They alone are poor who will nothing and desire nothing.

When I existed in my first cause, I had no God and I was my own cause. I willed nothing and desired nothing, for I was naked being and I knew myself by the savour of truth. Then I desired myself and nothing else. What I desired, that was myself, and I was myself what I desired, and I was free both of God and of all things. But when I emerged by free choice and received my created being,[97] I came into the possession of a God for, until creatures came into existence, God was not 'God', but was rather what he was. Then, when creatures emerged and received their created being, God was not 'God' in himself but in creatures.[98]

Now we say that God, in so far as he is this 'God', is not the supreme goal of creatures, for even the least creature possesses this much in God. And if it were the case that a fly had reason and, through reason, was able to seek the eternal abyss of divine being from which it had emerged, then we would say that God, together with all that he is as 'God', could not satisfy the longing even of this fly. Therefore we ask God to free us from 'God' so that we may be able to grasp and eternally enjoy truth where the highest angels, the fly and the human soul are all one – in that place where I desired what I was and was what I desired. And so we say: if we are to be poor in will, then we must will and desire as little as we willed and desired before we came into being. It is in this way that someone is poor who *wills* nothing.

Secondly, they are poor who *know* nothing. From time to time we have said that we should live as if we did not live, either for ourselves, for truth or for God. But now we put it differently, going further, and say that they who are to have this poverty must live in such a way that they do not know that they do not live either for themselves, for truth or for God. They must rather be free of the knowledge that they do not know, understand or sense that God lives in them. More even than this: they must be free of all the knowledge that lives in them. For when we were contained in the eternal essence of God, there was nothing other than God in us, but what was in us was ourselves. Therefore we say that we should be as free of self-knowledge as we were before we were created, that we should allow God to do what he will and that we should be entirely free of all things.

Everything which ever emerged from God is programmed to act. Loving and knowing are the two forms of activity which belong to humanity. Now there is a debate as to which of these is the place where blessedness is to be found. Some masters have taught that it lies in knowledge, others that it lies in love, while others still consider that it lies in both knowledge and love. These are closer to the truth. But we say that it lies neither in knowledge nor in love, but rather there is a something in the soul which is the source of both knowledge and love, although it does not itself know or love, as do the soul's faculties. Whoever comes to know this discovers where blessedness lies. It has neither a past nor a future, and it is not something to which anything can be added, for it cannot become larger or smaller. Therefore it does not possess any knowledge of the fact that God acts in it, rather it is itself that which delights in itself just as God delights in himself. We too should be so solitary and unencumbered that we do not know that it is God who acts in us. Thus we will have poverty. The masters say that God is being, rational being, who knows all things. But we say that God is neither being, nor rational being, nor does he know either this or that. Therefore God is free of all things, which is why he *is* all things. Now they who wish to be poor in spirit, must be poor in all their knowing so that they have no knowledge of anything, neither of God, nor of creature, nor of themselves. This is why it is necessary that we should desire to know or perceive nothing of God's works. In this way we can become poor in knowing.

Thirdly, a poor person is someone who *possesses* nothing. Many have said that not possessing the material things of the earth is perfection, and this is certainly true when it is voluntary. But this is not the sense that I have in mind.

I said before that a poor person is someone who does not even *will* to perform God's will, but who lives in such a way that he or she is as free both of their own will and of God's will as they were before they were created. Of this we say that it is the highest poverty. Further, we have stated that a poor person is someone who knows nothing of the action of God within them. And this again is the purest poverty when someone is so free of knowledge and perception. But the third kind of poverty of which I shall now speak is the ultimate one, and this is the poverty of someone who possesses nothing.

Now listen carefully! I have often said, as great masters have said, that we should be so free of all things and all works, both inner and outer, that we become the place where God can act. But now we put it differently. If it is the case that someone is free of all creatures, of God and of themselves, if God finds a place to act in them, then we say: as long as this exists in someone, they have not yet reached the ultimate poverty. For God does not intend there to be a place in someone where he can act, but if there is to be true poverty of spirit, someone must be so free of God and all his works that if God wishes to act in the soul he must himself be the place in which he can act, and this he is certainly willing to be. For if God finds us *this* poor, then God performs his own active work and we passively receive God in ourselves and God becomes the place of his work in us since God works within himself. In this poverty, we attain again the eternal being which we once enjoyed, which is ours now and shall be for ever.

There is a passage in St Paul which says: 'All that I am I am by the grace of God' (1 Cor. 15:10). But now my words seem to be above grace, above being, above knowledge and will, above all desire, and so how can St Paul's words be true? It was necessary that God's grace should be in him, since it was this that made perfect in him what was imperfect.[99] When the grace came to an end and completed its work, then Paul remained what he was.

And so we say that we should be so poor that we neither are nor possess a place in which God can act. If we still have such a place within us, then we still have multiplicity. Therefore I ask God to make me free of 'God', for my most essential being is above 'God' in so far as we conceive of God as the origin of creatures. And so in that essence, where God is above all existence and all multiplicity: I myself was there, there I desired myself and knew myself to make this man. Therefore I am my own self cause according to my essence, which is eternal, and not according to my becoming, which is in time. There I am unborn, and according to the manner of my unbornness, shall never die. According to the manner of my unborn nature, I have been eternal, as I am now and ever shall be. But what I am according to my nature which was born into the world, that shall die and turn to nothing, for it is mortal. Therefore it must decay with time. In my birth,[100] all things were born, and I was the cause of my own self and of all things. Had I wished that I should not exist, then neither would anything else have existed. And if I did not exist, then neither would God have existed as 'God'. I am the cause of God's existence as 'God'. But it is not necessary for you to know this.[101]

One great master says that breaking through is better than flowing out, and this is true. When I flowed forth from God, all things said: God is. But this cannot make me blessed, for I know myself as creature in this. But in the breakthrough, where I am free of my own will and of God's will and of all his works and am free of God himself, there I am above all creatures and am neither 'God' nor creature, but I am rather what I once was and what I shall remain now and for evermore. There I receive an impulse which shall raise me above the angels. In this flight I receive such great wealth that God, with all that he has as 'God' and with all his divine works, cannot satisfy me, for the consequence of this breakthrough is that God and I become one. Then I am what I have once been, and I neither increase nor decrease, but am an immovable cause which moves all things. God can find no place in us then, for with this poverty we attain that which we have eternally been and shall for ever remain. Here God is one with our spirit, and this is poverty in its ultimate form.

Whoever does not understand these words, should not be

troubled. For as long as someone is not themselves akin to this truth, they will not understand my words, since this is an unconcealed truth which has come directly from the heart of God.

That we may live in such a way that we have eternal knowledge of this, so help us God. Amen.

SERMON 23 (DW 69, W 42)

Modicum et iam non videbitis me (John 16:16)

I have read out a passage in Latin, which St John wrote in his gospel and which we read on this Sunday. These are the words of Jesus to his apostles: 'A little, a short while, and you shall no longer see me.'[102]

If anything, however small, adheres to the soul, we cannot see God. St Augustine posed the question what is eternal life and this was his answer: 'If you ask me what eternal life is, then you should ask eternal life itself and listen to what it has to say.' No one knows better what heat is than someone who is hot. No one knows better what wisdom is than someone who is wise, and no one knows better what eternal life is than eternal life itself. Now eternal life, which is our Lord Jesus Christ, says: 'That is eternal life, that we know you alone as the true God' (John 17:3). If someone were to glimpse God from afar, as if through a medium or in a cloud, they would not separate themselves from God even for a moment for anything in the world. How overwhelming is it then, do you think, when we see God directly? Now our Lord says: 'In a little while you shall no longer see me.' All the creatures that God ever has created or ever could create if he wished are 'a little' compared with God. Heaven is so vast and so wide that you would not believe me if I told you. If you were to take a needle and were to prick heaven with its point, then that pin-prick of heaven would be greater with respect to both heaven and this world than this world and heaven are with respect to God. Therefore it is aptly said: 'A little, a short while, and you shall no longer see me.' As long as there is still something of the creature in you, however small it may be, you shall not see God. That is why in the Book of Love the soul says: 'I have run around and sought him whom my soul loves, and have not found him' (cf. S. of S. 3:2). She found angels and much else but not him whom she loved. She said: 'After that, when I had leapt over a little or a small space, I found him that my soul loved' (cf. S. of S. 3:4), just as if she had said: 'when I had tested all creatures (which are meant by "a little"), I found him whom my soul loves'. The soul which seeks God must leap over all creatures.

Now know that God loves the soul to a miraculous degree. If God could be prevented from loving the soul, then he would lose his life and his being. It would kill him, if it is possible to say such a thing, for that same love with which God loves the soul is his life, and in that same love the Holy Spirit burgeons and this same love is the Holy Spirit. Now since God loves the soul so much, the soul must herself be something great.

In the book *On the Soul* a master says: 'If there were nothing in between, then the eye could discern an ant or a midge in heaven', and he spoke well, for he meant the fire and the air and other things which exist between heaven and the eye. But another master says: 'If there were no medium, then my eye would not be able to see anything at all.'[103] Both are right.

The former says that 'If there were nothing in between, then the eye could discern an ant or a midge in heaven', and he is right. For if there were nothing between God and the soul, then she could indeed see God since God neither knows nor tolerates any intermediary. If the soul were denuded, stripped of all intermediaries, then God too would be stripped bare for her and would give himself to her fully. As long as the soul is not denuded and stripped of all intermediaries, however small these may be, she shall not see God. If there existed anything between the body and the soul, even a hair's breadth, then they would never have been truly united. If this is the case with physical things, it is even more true in the spiritual realm. Boethius says: 'If you wish to know the truth in its purity, lay aside joy and suffering, fear, anticipation and hope.'[104] Joy and pain, fear and anticipation – all these serve as intermediaries. As long as you regard them and they regard you, you shall not see God.

The other master says: 'If there were no medium, then my eye would not be able to see anything at all.' If I place my hand on my eye, I cannot see my hand. But if I hold it before my face, I see it straight away. This is a consequence of the coarse materiality of my hand, which must be purified and refined in the air and the light if it is to enter my eye as an 'image'. You can see how this happens with a mirror. If you hold it up to your face, you can see your image in it. The eye and the soul are like this mirror, so that everything which is presented to them appears in them. Therefore I see neither the hand nor the stone in themselves, but rather I see the image of the stone. But I do not see this image in another image or in another medium but rather I see it directly and without an image since the image is itself the means and no other. This results from the fact that an image has no image, just as motion does not move – it causes entities to move – and greatness itself is without size but is the cause whereby certain objects are big. Thus the image is itself imageless, for it cannot be seen in another image. The eternal Word is both the medium and the image itself, which exists without mediation and without image so that the soul can comprehend God in the eternal Word, knowing him directly without an image.

There is a power in the soul which is the intellect. From the point of its origin and as soon as it becomes aware of God and savours him, it possesses five characteristics. Firstly, it is detached from the here and now. Secondly, it bears no likeness to anything else. Thirdly, it is pure and unmixed with anything else. Fourthly, it is active or exploratory in itself. Fifthly, it is an 'image'.

Firstly, it is detached from the here and now. 'Here' and 'now' stand for space and time. 'Now' is the very least period of time. It is neither a piece of time nor is it a portion of time, but rather it is a taste of time, the sharp point of time and an end of time. And yet, however small it may be, it must be removed. Everything that touches time or smacks of time must be removed. Now for the being detached from 'here'. 'Here' stands for space. The space in which I am now standing is very small. And yet, however small it may be, it must still be removed, if I am to see God.

Secondly, that this power is like nothing else. A master says: 'God is a being that nothing is like and nothing can be like.' Now John says: 'We shall be called children of God' (1 John 3:1). If we are to be his children, we must be like him. But then how can a master say that there is nothing like him? We must understand this in the following way. This power in the soul is like God precisely because it is not like anything at all. Just as there is nothing like God, neither is there anything like this power. Of course, it is the nature of all creatures to work and to strive to become like God. The heavens would never revolve if they did not seek and strive for God or God's likeness. If God were not in all things, nature would neither effect nor desire anything for, whether you like it or not, whether you are aware of it or not, nature secretly seeks and strives for God in its innermost part. No man or woman has ever felt such a thirst that they would not still have refused a drink, were it offered them, unless there were something of God in it. Nature does not demand either food or drink, clothing or comfort or anything in anything if God is not in it. Secretly nature always seeks and strives to find God in things.

Thirdly, that this power is pure and unmixed with anything else. The nature of God is such that he cannot endure being mixed or combined with anything. Neither is this power mixed or combined. There is nothing alien in it, and nothing alien can enter it. If I said of a beautiful person that they are both blond and dark, then I would be doing them an injustice. The soul must be completely unmixed with anything. If anything were to be attached to my hood or placed upon it, then whoever were to pull at my hood would pull this too. If I were to leave this place, all that is attached to me would go too. If someone pulls away that which the spirit rests upon or is attached to, they will also remove the spirit. But someone who does not rest upon anything or is attached to anything will remain unmoved even if heaven and earth were to turn upside down, since he or she is attached to nothing and nothing is attached to them.

Fourthly, that it is always inwardly seeking. God is a being who always dwells in the innermost place. That is why the intellect always seeks within. The will, on the other hand, is directed outside, to what it loves. If for example my friend comes to visit me, then my will with its love turns wholly towards him and finds in this its pleasure. Now St Paul says: 'We shall know God as we are known by him' (1 Cor. 13:12). St John says: 'We shall know God as he is' (1 John 3:2). If I am to be coloured, then I must have in myself what belongs to colour. I can never be coloured without taking the nature of colour into myself. I can never see God except in that in which God sees himself. Therefore St Paul says: 'God dwells in an unapproachable light' (1 Tim. 6:16). But let no one give up on this account! We are on the way or are approaching the goal, and that is good, although it is far from the truth for it is not yet God.

Fifthly, that it is an 'image'. Now pay attention to this point since it contains the whole of the sermon. One image is so wholly united with another image that no distinction can be discerned between them. We can conceive of fire without heat and of heat without fire, and we can conceive of the sun without light and light without the sun, but still we cannot discern any distinction between one image and another.[105] I say further that even the all-powerful God can perceive no distinction there since both are born together and together they die. I do not die if my father dies. If he dies, then it is no longer possible to say 'he is his son' but rather 'he was his son'. If a wall is painted white, in so far as it is white it is like all whiteness. But if you then paint it black, it is dead to all whiteness. The same is true here: if the image is lost which is formed after God, then the image of God is also lost. Let me say something, one or two things, about this. Listen carefully. Intellect peers in and examines every corner of the Godhead; it takes the Son in the heart of the Father and in the divine ground and places him in its own ground. The intellect drives in and is satisfied neither with goodness nor wisdom nor with truth nor even with God himself. In truth, it is as little satisfied with God as it is with a stone or a tree. It never rests, but breaks into the divine ground, where goodness and truth originate. It takes the divine *in principio* at its point of origin, where goodness and wisdom begin, before the divine acquires a name, before it breaks forth: intellect takes it then in a far higher ground than that of either goodness or wisdom. But their sister, the will, is content with God in so far as he is good, while intellect strips all this away, breaking in and through to the root where the Son wells up and the Holy Spirit burgeons.

That we may understand this, becoming eternally blessed, so help us Father, Son and Holy Spirit. Amen.

SERMON 24 (W 2, PF 2, DP 58)

Ubi est qui natus est rex judaeorum? (Matt. 2:2)

'Where is he who is born King of the Jews?' Now note where this birth takes place: 'Where is he who is born . . .?' But I say, as I have often said, that this birth takes place in the soul just as it takes place in eternity, no more and no less. For there is only *one* birth, and this takes place in the essence and ground of the soul.

But this raises certain questions. Firstly, since God exists spiritually in all things and is by nature more inwardly present in things than they are in themselves, and since wherever God is he must act and know himself and speak his Word, we are bound to ask which are the particular characteristics of the soul that make it more responsive to this action of God than other rational creatures which God indwells in the same way. Now take note of the following answer!

God exists in all things essentially, actively and powerfully. But he is fertile in the soul alone. If all creatures are the vestige of God, then the soul alone is naturally made in his image.[106] The birth must serve to adorn and perfect this image. And the soul, alone of all creatures, is responsive to God's action and birth. Truly, whatever form of perfection enters the soul, whether divine, simple light or grace or blessedness, this must all enter the soul with this birth and in no other way. If you just wait for this birth to take place in you, you will find all that is good, all consolation, all bliss, all being and all truth. If you miss it, then you will miss all that is good and all blessedness. Whatever enters you in this birth, brings you pure being and enduring substance, but whatever you seek which is outside this birth shall perish – take it as and where you will, still it will all perish. Only this gives being, all else passes. But in this birth you will partake in the divine influx and all its gifts. Those creatures who are not in God's image are not receptive to this, for the soul's image belongs in a special way to this birth that takes place truly and particularly in the soul, being generated by the Father in the soul's ground and innermost part, into which no image nor any faculty have ever glanced.

The second question is this: since the work of this birth happens in the being and ground of the soul, then surely it takes place just as much in a sinner as it does in a good person? What grace or benefit does it hold for me therefore? If the ground of both their natures is the same, then does that mean that the nobility of nature of those, even of those who are in Hell, remains intact?

Observe the following teaching. It is the peculiar characteristic of this birth that it always brings new light. It constantly introduces a strong light into the soul since it is the nature of goodness to pour itself forth wherever it may be. In this birth God pours himself into the soul with light so much that the light gathers in the being and ground of the soul and spills over into the faculties and the outer self. This happened to Paul too when God bathed him in his light as he journeyed, and spoke to him. A likeness of the light became externally visible, so that even his companions saw it, and it enveloped Paul as it did the saints (Acts 9:3). The abundance of light in the ground of the soul flows over into the body, which is then filled with radiance. But sinners can receive nothing of this, nor are they worthy to do so, since they are filled with sin and evil, which are called 'darkness'. Therefore it is said: 'The darkness shall neither receive nor comprehend the light' (cf. John 1:5). The problem is that the paths which this light should take are blocked with falsehood and darkness. After all, light and darkness cannot coexist any more than God and creatures can. If God is to enter, then the creatures must leave. We are well aware of this light. Whenever we turn to

God, there is a light that shines and burns in us, guiding us as to what we should do and what we should not do, and giving us many other kinds of good instruction, of which we had no knowledge or understanding in the past.

'But how do you know all this?'

Now listen! Something often touches your heart so that it turns away from the world. How could that happen if not through this enlightenment? It happens with such gentleness and delight that you begin to find oppressive all that is not God or of God. You are drawn to God and you become aware of much good guidance without knowing where it comes from. But this inner movement originates neither from any creature nor from their promptings, for the stirrings and effects of creatures come from without. The ground of the soul, however, is touched only by this and the more you are free of yourself, the more you shall find light, truth and understanding. Therefore the only reason why anyone has ever erred in anything is that they have departed from this and have turned too much to external things. St Augustine says that there are many who have sought light and truth, but only without, where they are not to be found. Thus they finally go so far outside themselves that are never able to enter in again. That is why they have not found the truth, for the truth is within, in the ground, and not without. Whoever wishes to find light and understanding in all truth, must watch and observe this birth in themselves and in their ground, and then all their faculties shall be illumined as will their outer self. For, as soon as God touches the ground within with his truth, the light shines into the soul's powers so that such a person can do more than he or she could ever be taught to do. The prophet says: 'I have gained greater understanding than all those who ever taught me' (cf. Eccles. 1:16). Now note that it is impossible for this birth to happen in sinners since this light cannot burn and shine in them. This birth cannot coexist with the darkness of sins, even though it does not occur in the faculties of the soul but rather in her being and her ground.

Now a further question presents itself. Since God the Father is born only in the being and ground of the soul, of what concern is it to the faculties? In what way do they serve it if they just stand idly by? What is the point of this birth if it does not take place in the faculties? This is a good question. Now observe the answer.

The action of all creatures is directed towards a final end. The final end is always the first in intention but the last in execution. Thus God too intends a beatific final end in all his works, which means to say he intends himself and intends that he should draw the soul, with all her faculties, to this final end, that is, to himself. It is for this that God performs all his works, and the Father gives birth to the Son in the soul: so that all the faculties of the soul should arrive at this goal. He lies in wait for all that is in the soul and summons it all to this feast and celebration. But the soul has scattered herself abroad through her powers, in the activity of each one: the power of seeing in the eye, of hearing in the ear, of taste in the tongue. And thus the soul's inner activity is weakened. For being divided is an imperfection in every power. Therefore if the soul wishes to work effectively within, she must reunite all her powers, gathering them back from scattered things into internal action. St Augustine says that the soul is more present where she loves than where she gives life to the body. Let me give you an analogy. There was once a pagan master who was devoted to the science of calculation.[107] He had directed all his powers to this and, seated by the glowing embers of a fire, was calculating and exploring this art. Then someone approached him and drew a sword, not knowing that it was the master, and said: 'Tell me quickly who you are, or I shall kill you!' The master was so entirely immersed in his thoughts that he neither saw nor heard his enemy and could not answer him, not even by saying 'My name is such and such'. After the enemy had shouted for a long time without getting an answer, he struck the master's head off. Now this happened as the result of the pursuit of a natural science. How much more should we remove ourselves from all things, gathering our powers together, in order to see and to know the sole, immeasurable, uncreated and eternal truth? For this you should gather all your senses, all your faculties, the whole of your intellect and memory, drawing it all into the ground in which this treasure lies buried. If this is to happen, then know that you must strip yourself of all other works and must enter a state of unknowing, if you are to succeed in finding this.

But now another question arises. Would it not be better if each faculty retained its own activity, without hindering another in its work or indeed obstructing God in his action? Could there not be in me some kind of natural knowledge which would not serve to obstruct anything, just as God knows all things without impediment or as the saints do? This is a valuable question. Now listen to the following answer.

The saints see in God only a single image, and in this single image they know all things. Indeed, this is how God too sees himself and knows all things in himself. He does not need to turn from one thing to another, as we do. If it were the case for us in our earthly life that we always had a mirror before our face in which we could see all things in a single moment, knowing them in a single image, then neither action nor knowledge would be an obstacle for us. But since we must turn from one thing to another, we can never engage with the one without being hindered in this by the other. For the soul is bound so tightly to the faculties that she flows with them to wherever they go since the soul must be present with them in all their activity, and must be so with commitment, or the faculties cannot work at all. If her attention is dissipated in external works, she will necessarily be weakened with respect to inner works. For this birth to take place God requires a bare soul, untrammelled and free, in which nothing is but himself and which is filled with expectation for nothing other than himself. This was Christ's meaning when he said: 'Whoever loves anything but me, whoever loves father and mother or many other things is not worthy of me. I did not come upon earth to bring peace but a sword, to cut away all things, to part you from sister, brother, mother, child and friend that in truth are your enemies' (cf. Matt. 10:34–36). For what is familiar to you is in truth your enemy. If your eye is to see all things, your ear to hear all things and your heart to consider all things, then truly your soul must be divided and dissipated among all these things.

Therefore a master says: if someone is to perform an inner work, they must draw in all their powers as if in the corner of their soul, hiding from all images and forms, and then they shall be able to act. They must thus enter a forgetfulness and an unknowing. Where this word is to be heard, there must be stillness and silence. We cannot serve this word better than with stillness and silence; there it can be heard and properly understood, and there we are in a state of unknowing. Where we know nothing, there it reveals itself and makes itself known.

Now we come to a further question. You might say: sir, you are basing all our salvation on a form of unknowing. That sounds like a lack of something. God created humanity in order that we should *know*, as the prophet says: 'Lord, make them know'. Wherever there is unknowing, there is a lack and an absence. Such a person is no better than a beast, an ape, a fool, which is true for as long as he or she remains in unknowing. At this point we must come into a transformed knowing, an unknowing which comes not from ignorance but from knowledge. Then our knowing shall be divine knowledge, and our unknowing shall be ennobled and enriched with supernatural knowing. With respect to this, being passive shall make us more perfect than being active. Therefore one master says that the power of hearing is far nobler than the power of seeing, for we learn more wisdom through what we hear than through what we see, and it is through the former that we live more in wisdom. It is said of a pagan master that as he lay on his death-bed, his disciples talked in his presence of an exalted science. The master raised his head, listened and said: 'Let me learn this science so that I can rejoice in it for all eternity.' Hearing internalizes, while seeing, or at least the act of seeing, is more directed outwards. Therefore we shall be far more blessed in the life eternal by virtue of our hearing than on account of our seeing. For the process of the hearing of the eternal Word takes place within me, while the act of seeing proceeds from me, and in my hearing I play a passive role, while in my seeing I play an active one.

Our blessedness does not lie in our active doing, rather in our passive reception of God. God is far nobler than creatures, and that is how much nobler his action is than mine. Indeed, in his immeasurable love God has placed our blessedness in passive receptivity, for we are more passive than active, and we receive far more than we give. But every gift demands that we become receptive to a further, and greater, gift. Every divine gift increases our receptivity and our desire to receive what is great and noble. Therefore certain masters say it is in this that the soul is equal to God. For the infinity of the soul's receiving matches the infinity of God's giving.[108] As God is omnipotent in his action, the soul is unfathomable in her passivity, which is why she is transformed with God and in God. It is for God to act and the soul passively to receive. God should know and love himself in her while she should know with his knowledge and should love with his love. Therefore she is made far more blessed by what is his than by what is her own, and her blessedness is rooted in his action rather than in her own.

St Denys's disciples asked him why Timothy so excelled them all in perfection, to which Denys said that Timothy was a God-suffering man. Whoever can understand this would excel everyone in the world.

And so your unknowing is not a lack but rather your highest perfection, and passively to receive is your highest action. In this way you must cease being active and must draw all your powers to a point of stillness, if you truly desire to experience this birth within yourself. If you wish to find the new-born king, then you must ignore everything which you might otherwise find, and cast it aside.

That we may ignore and reject all that is unpleasing to this new-born king, so help us God, who became a son of man so that we may become the children of God. Amen.

SERMON 25 (W 4, PF 4, DP 59)

Et cum factus esset Jesus annorum duodecim (Luke 2:42)

We read in today's Gospel that when our Lord was twelve years old, he went with Mary and Joseph to Jerusalem, to the temple. When they returned again, Jesus remained in the temple, without their knowledge. When they arrived home and missed him, they sought him among their friends and relatives and among the crowd but could not find him. They had lost him among all the people. Therefore they had to go back again, to their starting point, and as they reached the temple, they found him.

This too is what you must do, truly, if you wish to find the noble birth, leaving the 'crowd' and returning to the source and ground from which you came. All the faculties and works of the soul constitute the 'crowd': memory, reason and will, which all serve to divide and diversify you. Therefore you must leave them all: the activity of the senses and imagination and everything in which you are present to yourself or to your intentions. Only then can you find this birth, and not otherwise, believe me. It was never discovered among 'friends', 'relatives' or 'acquaintances': rather, that is where it is lost.

Therefore the following question arises: whether we can find this birth through particular things which, while divine, are mediated to us from outside by the senses. Certain concepts concerning God are an example of this, including the idea that God is good, that he is wise, merciful or whatever it may be that reason can derive from itself and which is similarly divine. Can all this bring us the birth? Indeed not. For although it may all be good and of God, it is still all mediated by the senses from outside. But if this birth is to shine out in truth and purity, there must be a movement solely from within, from God. All your activity must be stilled, and all your powers must serve him and not yourself. If this work is to be perfect, then God alone must perform it and you must passively receive it. Where you truly go out of your will and your knowledge, God truly and willingly enters in with his knowledge and shines there with great brilliance. Where God is to know himself in this way, then your knowing can neither coexist with it nor serve its ends. You should not imagine that your reason can evolve to the extent of understanding God. Rather, if God is to shine divinely within you, your natural light cannot assist this process but must become a pure nothingness, going out of itself. Only then can God enter with his light, bringing back with him all that you have renounced and a thousand times more, including a new form which contains all things in itself.

The Gospel provides an analogy for this. When our Lord had spoken kindly to the heathen woman at the well (John 4:6ff.), she left her jug, ran to the town and proclaimed to all that the Messiah had come. But the people did not believe her, and they went out with her to look at him themselves. Then they said to her: 'Now we believe, not because of your words: we believe rather because we have seen him ourselves' (John 4:42). In the same way, truly, neither the skills of all creatures, nor your own wisdom nor the whole extent of your knowledge can bring you to the point that you have a divine knowledge of God. If you wish to know God in a divine manner, then your knowing must become a pure unknowing, a forgetting of yourself and of all creatures.

Now you could say: but sir, what is there left for my reason to do if it stands entirely bare and wholly inactive? Is this the best way, if I raise my mind to an unknowing knowing, which cannot ever exist? For, if I know something, then this is neither unknowing nor naked simplicity. Should I stand in complete darkness?

Yes indeed! You are never better placed than when you are in complete darkness and unknowing.

But sir, must it all be removed? Can there be no return?

No, truly. There can be no return.

What is this darkness? What is it called?

Its name means nothing other than a state of potential receptivity, which in no way lacks being, but is a potential receptivity in which you shall be perfected. That is why there is no return from this. But if you do go back, it cannot be on account of any truth but only on account of something else, such as the senses, the world or the devil. If you give way to this impulse, then you shall lapse into sin and may even fall into eternal damnation. Therefore there is no turning back but only a constant advance in order to realize this potentiality, which never rests until it is filled with being. And rightly so, just as matter does not rest until it is filled with all possible forms, or intellect does not rest until it is filled to its capacity.

With regard to this a pagan master says that nature has nothing which is swifter than the heavens: they outstrip everything as they follow their course. And yet, truly, the human mind goes even faster than this. If only it remained true to its potential, maintaining itself undefiled and undiminished by lower and coarse objects, then it would outstrip the highest heavens and would never rest until it reached the all-highest, there to be fed and nourished by the greatest good, which is God.

If you were to ask how beneficial it is to pursue this potentiality and to maintain ourselves in bareness and simplicity, holding only to this darkness and unknowing, without turning back, then I would say that it offers the sole possibility of gaining him who is all things. The more you are empty of self and are freed from the knowledge of objects, the closer you come to him. Concerning this desert, Jeremiah writes: 'I will lead my beloved into the wilderness and will speak to her in her heart' (Hos. 2:14). The true word of eternity is uttered only in solitude, where a man or woman is empty of self and multiplicity and is remote from them. The prophet hungered for this desolate self-abandonment when he said: 'Who will give me the wings of a dove that I may fly away and be at rest?' (Ps. 55:6). Where do we find peace and rest? Only in abandonment, in the desert and in isolation from all creatures. On this David says: 'I would rather be rejected and spurned in the house of my God than dwell with great honour and wealth in the tavern of sinners' (Ps. 84:10).

Now you could say: sir, if it is necessary that we should be stripped of all things and emptied of them, outside and within, the faculties together with their activity – if all this must be removed, then it is grievous if God allows us to remain without any support. 'Woe is me that my exile is prolonged' (Ps. 120:5), as the prophet says, if God prolongs my dereliction without casting his light upon me, speaking to me or working in me, as you are suggesting here. If we thus enter a state of pure nothingness, is it not better that we should do something in order to drive away the darkness and dereliction? Should we not pray or read or listen to a sermon or do something else that is virtuous in order to help ourselves?

No, certainly not! The very best thing you can do is to remain still for as long as possible. You cannot turn away from this state to other things without doing yourself harm, that much is sure. You wish to be prepared in part by yourself and in part by God, which cannot be. You cannot think about or desire this preparation more swiftly than God can carry it out. But supposing that it could be divided: the preparation would then be yours and the inpouring or action would be his, which is quite impossible. You should know that God *must* pour himself into you and act upon you where he finds you prepared. You should not think that God is like a carpenter on earth who works or does not work as he will and for whom it is a matter of choice as to whether he should do something or not, according to his inclination. This is not the case with God who must act and must pour himself into you wherever and whenever he finds you prepared, just as the sun must pour itself forth and cannot hold itself back when the air is pure and clean. Certainly, it would be a major failing if God did not perform great works in you, pouring great goodness into you, in so far as he finds you empty and bare.

This is also what the masters write when they maintain that at the very same moment that the matter of the child in the womb is fully prepared, God pours the living spirit into the body, which is the soul or the body's form. Both happen in a single moment: the being prepared and the inpouring of the soul. When nature has reached its highest point, God bestows his grace, and at the very same moment that the spirit is ready, God enters it, without hesitation or delay. In the Book of Mysteries it is written that our Lord said to the people: 'Behold I stand at the door, knocking and waiting. If anyone lets me in, I shall eat with him' (Rev. 3:20). You need to seek him neither here nor there, for he is no further than the door of your heart. There he stands, waiting for someone who is ready to open the door and to let him in. You do not need to call him from far away; he can hardly wait for you to let him in. He desires you a thousand times more urgently than you do him. The opening of the door and his entering in happen in exactly the same moment.

Now, you might say: how can this be? I cannot feel his presence in any way.

Listen to this. Sensing his presence is not in your power but in his. He will show himself when it suits him to do so, and he can also remain hidden if that is his wish. This is what Christ meant when he said to Nicodemus: 'The spirit breathes where it will: you hear its voice but do not know where it comes from, or where it is going' (John 3:8). He contradicted himself in what he said: 'you hear but do not know'. Is hearing not also knowing? Christ meant that it is by hearing that we receive the spirit or draw it into ourselves, as if he wished to say: 'you receive the spirit but know nothing of it'. Now know this! God can leave nothing empty; neither God nor nature can tolerate emptiness in anything. Therefore, if it seems to you at present that you cannot feel his presence and that you are entirely empty of him, then this is not in fact the case. For if there is something empty beneath heaven, whatever it may be – large or small – heaven will draw it up to itself, or heaven will have to descend to it and fill it with itself. God, who is the master of nature, cannot tolerate emptiness in anything. Therefore remain still and do not waver from this emptiness, for if you turn away from it at this point you shall never be able to find it again.

Now you might say: sir, you are always saying that this birth must take place in me, that the Son must be born in me. Well now, can you tell me please how I might recognize that this birth has actually happened?

Certainly! There are three ways, and I shall now tell you one of them. I am often asked if it is possible for someone to advance so far that neither time, multiplicity nor matter are obstacles to them any more. Yes, indeed! When this birth has truly taken place in you, then no creatures can hinder you any more. Rather they all point you to God and to this birth. Take lightning as an analogy. It immediately turns whatever it strikes, whether tree, beast or man, towards itself. Even if a man's back is turned, the lightning will immediately turn his face towards itself. If a tree had a thousand leaves, they would all turn their right side towards the flash. See, that is how it is for all those for whom this birth has already taken place. They are swiftly turned to this birth, in whatever may be happening to them at the time, however coarse it may be. What was previously an obstacle to you is now a great help. Your face is fully turned to this birth. Indeed, in everything that you see or hear, whatever it may be, in all things you can receive nothing but this birth. All things become pure God to you, for in all things you see nothing but God. Just as when someone looks for a long time into the sun: whatever they look at subsequently, the image of the sun shall always appear. Whenever you do not seek God and do not see him in each and every thing, then you do not have this birth.

Now you may ask: does someone who has advanced so far still need to practise penances, or do they neglect something if they fail to do so?

Listen to this! All forms of penance – fasting, vigils, prayer, kneeling, self-flagellation, hair-shirts, sleeping on boards, or whatever – were created because the body and the flesh are always opposed to the spirit. The body is often too strong for it, and there is constant warfare between them, an eternal struggle. Here on earth the body is bold and strong, for it is in its own home. The world aids it, this earth is its homeland, and all its serving-maids support it: food, drink and physical comfort – all these work against the spirit. Here the soul is in exile; all her serving-maids and relatives are in heaven. There she is well connected, if she establishes herself there and makes herself at home. It is in order to assist the spirit here in its exile, and to weaken the flesh somewhat in this struggle so that it does not overwhelm the spirit, that we restrain it with penitential practices, curbing it so that the spirit can resist it. This is done in order to constrain the flesh, but if you lay upon it the bridle of love, then you will tame and control it in a way that is a thousand times better. It is with love that you can most swiftly overcome the flesh, and love will prove for it the heaviest burden. Therefore God intends nothing for us so much as love. For love is just the same as the fisherman's hook: the fisherman cannot lay hold of the fish unless it is attached to the hook. If it has swallowed the hook, the fisherman can be sure of his fish, whichever way it turns, this way or that, he knows he will get it. I say the same of love: they who are caught by it have the strongest bonds and the sweetest burden. Whoever has taken this sweet burden upon themselves, achieves more and advances further than they would with all the penances and chastisements that everyone in the world could all perform together. They can endure cheerfully all that befalls them and that God sends them, and they can cheerfully forgive all the evil that others do to them. Nothing brings you closer to God and gives you God so much as this sweet bond of love. Whoever has found this path does not leave it again. Whoever hangs on this hook is caught so fast that foot and hand, mouth, eye, heart and all that makes us what we are, must become God's possession. Therefore you can never overcome this enemy better, so that he does not harm you, than with love. And so it is written: 'Love is as strong as death and as hard as hell' (cf. S. of S. 8:6). Death separates the soul from the body, but love separates all things from the soul: she cannot tolerate whatever is not God or of God. Whoever is caught in this trap and walks this path, whatever they may do or not do is all entirely one. It makes no difference whether they do something or not. And yet the least act or devotional practice of such a person is more beneficial and fruitful for themselves and for everyone and is more pleasing to

God than the devotions of all those who have less love even though they are without mortal sin. Their rest is more beneficial than others' works. Watch out for this hook, therefore, so that you may be blessedly caught, and the more you are caught, the freer you shall be.

That we may be caught and freed in this way, may he help us who himself is love. Amen.

SERMON 26 (DW 85, W 85)

Puella, surge (Luke 8:54)

'Rise up!'[109]

Our Lord placed his hand on the girl and said: 'Rise up!' The 'hand of God' is the Holy Spirit. All works are performed by warmth, for if the fiery love of God grows cold in the soul, the soul will die, and if God is to act in the soul, then God must be united with her. If the soul is to be united with God, she must be separated from all things and must be as solitary as God is solitary. A work which God performs in an empty soul is more precious than heaven and earth. It is for this that God created the soul, that she should be united with him. One of the saints says that the soul is created from nothing, and that God created her himself, with no one else present.[110] Had anyone else been present, God would have been afraid that the soul might be drawn to them and not to himself. Therefore the soul must be alone, as God is alone.

Spiritual things and physical things cannot be united with each other. If divine perfection is to reign in the soul, then the soul must be spirit, as God is spirit. And if God wishes to bestow gifts on the soul in the soul, then he can only do so with restraint. Therefore it is in himself that he takes her into himself, and in this way she is united with him.[111] Let me give you an analogy. When fire and stone unite, both being material, the stone often remains cool on account of its inner density. The same is true of air and light: whatever you see in the air, you see in the sun. But since they are both material, there is more light in a whole mile than there is in a half, and more in half a mile than there is in a house. But the closest parallel that we can find is that of body and soul. These are so united with each other that the body cannot act without the soul nor the soul without the body. God is to the soul as the soul is to the body, and when the soul departs from the body, the body must die. So too must the soul die if God departs from her.

There are three obstacles which hinder the union of the soul with God. The first is that she is too scattered and is not unified in herself, since the soul is never unified when she inclines to creatures. The second is that she is mixed with temporal things. The third is that when she is turned to the body, she cannot be united with God.

On the other hand, there are three things which further the union of God with the soul. The first is that the soul is unified and undivided, for if she is to be united with God, she must be simple as God is simple in himself. The second is that she is raised above herself and all transient things and holds to God. The third is that she is separated from all material things and acts from her primal and original purity. Augustine says of the free soul: If you do not desire me, I desire you; if I desire you, then you do not desire me. When I seek you, you flee from me.[112] As they return, all pure spirits take the same path back to the purity of God.

SERMON 27 (W 56, DP 26)

Nolite timere eos, qui corpus occidunt, animam autem occidere non possunt
(Matt. 10:28)

'Do not fear those who would kill the body, for they cannot kill the soul.' Spirit gives the spirit life. Those who wish to kill you are flesh and blood, and what is flesh and blood, shall die. The noblest thing in us is blood, when we will what is good, and the very worst thing in us is blood, when we will what is evil. If the blood subdues the flesh, then we are humble, patient, chaste and possess all the virtues. But if the flesh overcomes the blood, we are proud, angry and lustful, and possess all the vices. Here we are praising St John. I cannot praise him any more than God has already done.

Now listen! I shall say something at this point that I have never said before. When God created heaven and earth and all creatures, God did not *act*. There was no work for him to do, and there was no action or work in him. Then God said: 'We will make a likeness' (Gen. 1:26). It is easy to create something: we do this as and when we will. But what I make, I make alone, with myself and in myself and I impress my own image fully upon it. 'We will make a likeness', not 'you, Father, or you, Son, or you, Holy Spirit' but 'we': the Holy Trinity together – 'we will make a likeness'. When God made humankind, he performed in the soul a work that was like himself, his active and enduring work. This work was so great that it was nothing other than the soul herself, and the soul was nothing other than the work of God. God's nature, his being, and his divinity depend upon his being active in the soul. Blessed, blessed be God! When God acts in the soul, then he loves his work. And wherever the soul may be in which God accomplishes his work, there the work is so great that it is nothing other than love. Love on the other hand is nothing other than God. God loves himself and his nature, his being and his divinity. But in the love in which God loves himself, he also loves all creatures – not as creatures, but creatures as God. In the love in which God loves himself therefore, he loves all things.

Now I shall say something that I have never said before. God delights in himself. In the delight in which God delights in himself, he delights also in all creatures. With the delight with which God delights in himself, with that delight he delights in all creatures – not as creatures but in creatures as God. In the delight in which God delights in himself, in that delight he delights in all things.

Now pay attention! All creatures tend towards the highest perfection. I ask you to listen to this by the eternal truth, by the everlasting truth and by my soul. I shall again say what I have never said before. God and Godhead are as far apart from each other as heaven and earth. I say further: the inner and the outer self are as far apart as heaven and earth. But with God the distance is many thousands of miles greater. That is, God *becomes* and *unbecomes*. Now I return to my original phrase: God delights in himself in all things. The sun casts its light upon all creatures, and whatever it illumines, the sun draws into itself. And yet it suffers no diminution in its own brightness. All creatures are prepared to lose their lives for the sake of their being. All creatures convey themselves into my mind in order that they should exist mentally within me. I alone prepare creatures for God. Just think of what you are all doing![113]

Now I come back to my 'inner and outer self'. I look at the lilies in the field, their brightness, their colour and all their petals, but I do not see their fragrance. Why not? Because their scent is in me. On the other hand, what I say is in me and I utter it forth from myself. All creatures have the flavour of creatures only for my outer self, like wine, bread and meat. But for my inner self nothing has the flavour of a creature but rather that of a gift from

God, though for my innermost self they smack not of a gift from God but of eternity.

I take a bowl of water, lay a mirror in it and place it in the light of the sun. Then the sun gives forth its light from its own circumference and from its own ground, but without exhausting itself. The reflection of the mirror lying in the sun is the sun but it is also what it is in itself. It is the same with God. God is in the soul with his essence, his being and his divinity, and yet he is not in the soul. The reflection of the soul is God in God, and yet she, the soul, is what she is in herself.

God 'becomes' God when all creatures speak God forth: there 'God' is born. When I was still in the ground, in the depths, in the flood and source of the Godhead, no one asked me where I wished to go or what I was doing. But as I flowed forth, all creatures uttered: 'God'. If someone were to ask me: 'Brother Eckhart, when did you leave your house?', then I was in there. This is how all creatures speak of God. And why do they not speak of the Godhead? All that is in the Godhead is One, and of this no one can speak. God acts, while the Godhead does not act. There is nothing for it to do, for there is no action in it. It has never sought to do anything. The difference between God and Godhead is that one acts and the other does not. If I return to 'God' but do not remain there, then my breakthrough is far better than my flowing-out. I alone free all creatures from their own *ratio* into my reason so that they may all be one in me.[114] But when I enter the ground, the bottom, the flood and the source of the Godhead, no one asks me where I come from or where I have been. There no one has missed me, and there God 'unbecomes'.

Whoever has understood this sermon, I wish them well. Had no one been here, I would still have had to preach it to this collecting-box. There are some poor folk who return home and say: 'I wish to sit down, to eat my bread and to serve God.' But I say by the eternal truth that these people shall remain in error and can never attain what those others attain who follow God in poverty and in exile. Amen.

SERMON 28 (DW 83, W 96)

Renovamini spiritu (Eph. 4:23)

'You shall be renewed in your spirit, which is called *mens*', that is 'mind'. Thus says St Paul.[115]

Now St Augustine says that together with the essence of the soul in her highest part, which is called *mens* in Latin or 'mind', God created a power which the masters call a container or shrine of spiritual forms or formal images. It is this power that makes the Father like the soul in the flowing-out of his divinity through which, in the distinction of the Persons, he has poured into the Son and the Holy Spirit the whole treasure of his divine being. In the same way the memory pours forth the treasure of its images into the powers of the soul. Now whenever the soul – with this power – sees anything that is imaged (whether the image of an angel or indeed her own image), then this is an imperfection in her. Even if she sees God, in so far as he is 'God' or in so far as he is something imaged or triune, this is an imperfection in her. But when all images are removed from the soul and she perceives the single Oneness, the pure being of the soul, resting in herself, receives the pure, formless being of divine unity which is being beyond being. O miracle of miracles! What a wonderful receptivity it is when the being of the soul can endure nothing but the pure unity of God.

Now St Paul says: 'You shall be renewed in spirit'. All creatures under God experience renewal, though God himself is not subject to renewal but only to eternity. What is eternity? Listen to this! It is a property of eternity that being and being young are the same in it, for eternity would not be eternal if it could *become* new and were not already forever new. But now I say that angels experience renewal in that they are given knowledge of things to come, for they know the future in so far as God reveals it to them. And the soul too experiences renewal in so far as she is called 'soul', for 'soul' signifies that she gives life to the body and is the form of the body. She experiences renewal also in so far as she is called 'spirit'. She is called 'spirit' because she is removed from all that is 'here' and 'now' and from all that belongs to nature. But where she is an image of God and is as nameless as God is without name, there she experiences no renewal but only eternity, as God does.

Now pay attention to this. God is nameless for no one can either speak of him or know him. Therefore a pagan master says that what we can know or say of the First Cause reflects ourselves more than it does the First Cause, for this transcends all speech and all understanding.[116] Accordingly, if I say that 'God is good', this is not true. I am good, but God is not good! In fact, I would rather say that I am better than God, for what is good can become better and what can become better can become the best! Now God is not good, and so he cannot become better. Since he cannot become better, he cannot become the best. These three are far from God: 'good', 'better', 'best', for he is wholly transcendent. If I say again that 'God is wise', then this too is not true. I am wiser than he is! Or if I say that 'God exists', this is also not true. He is being beyond being: he is a nothingness beyond being. Therefore St Augustine says: 'The finest thing that we can say of God is to be silent concerning him from the wisdom of inner riches.'[117] Be silent therefore, and do not chatter about God, for by chattering about him, you tell lies and commit a sin. If you wish to be perfect and without sin, then do not prattle about God. Also you should not wish to understand anything about God, for God is beyond all understanding. A master says: If I had a God that I could understand, I would not regard him as God.[118] If you understand anything about him, then he is not in it, and by understanding something of him, you fall into ignorance, and by falling into ignorance, you become like an animal since the animal part in creatures is that which is unknowing. If you do not wish to become like an animal therefore, do not pretend that you understand anything of the ineffable God.

'What then should I do?'

You should sink your 'being-you' into his 'being-him', and your 'you' and his 'him' should become a single 'me' so that with him you shall know in eternity his unbecome 'isness' and his unnameable 'nothingness'.

Now St Paul says: 'You shall be renewed in spirit'. If we wish to be 'renewed in spirit', then the six powers of the soul, the highest and the lowest, must each have a golden ring on their finger, all gilded with the gold of God's love. Now listen carefully! There are three lower powers. The first is called discrimination (*rationalis*). On this you should have the golden ring of 'enlightenment', which means that your powers of discrimination are always illumined outside time by the divine light. The second is called irascibility (*irascibilis*). On this you should have the ring of peace. But why? This is so because in so far as you are in peace, thus far you are in God, and in so far as you are outside peace, thus far you are outside God. The third power is concupiscence (*concupiscibilis*). On this you should have the ring of contentment, so that you are contented with all creatures below God. But of God you can never have a sufficiency. The more you have of God, the more you desire him. If you could ever have enough of God, so that you were contented with him, then God would not be God.

So too must you have a golden ring on all the higher powers of the soul. Of these there are also three. The first is called a retentive power (*memoria*). It is this power which is likened to the Father in the Trinity. On this you should have the golden ring of containment, whereby you contain within yourself all eternal things. The second power is called reason (*intellectus*). This power is likened to the Son. On this you should have the golden ring of knowledge, that you may know God always. But how? You should know him without image, unmediated and without likeness. But if I am to know God without mediation in such a way, then 'I' must become 'he', and 'he' must become 'I'. More precisely I say: God must become me and I must become God, so entirely one that this 'he' and this 'I' become one 'is' and act in this 'isness' as one, for this 'he' and this 'I', that is God and the soul, are very fruitful. But if thereby a single 'here' or 'now' enter in, then this 'I' can never become one in being and action with this 'he'. The third power is called the will (*voluntas*), which is likened to the Holy Spirit. On this you should have the golden ring of love so that you love God. You should love God without regard to the fact that he wins our love, for God does not win our love: he transcends love and the prompting of love.

'How then should I love God?'

You should love God non-mentally, that is to say the soul should become non-mental and stripped of her mental nature.[119] For as long as your soul is mental, she will possess images. As long as she has images, she will possess intermediaries, and as long as she has intermediaries, she will not have unity or simplicity. As long as she lacks simplicity, she does not truly love God, for true love depends upon simplicity. Therefore your soul should lose all her mental nature and should be left non-mental, for if you love God as 'God', as 'Spirit', as 'Person', as 'Image', then all this must be abandoned. You must love him as he is a non-God, a non-Spirit, a non-Person, a non-Image. Indeed, you must love him as he is One, pure, simple and transparent, far from all duality. And we should eternally sink into this One, thus passing from something into nothing.[120] So help us God. Amen.

SERMON 29 (J 46)

There is an uncreated Spirit and a created spirit which flows from the uncreated Spirit and which constitutes the angels on the one hand and the rational spirit that is the soul on the other. The uncreated spirit is eternal being. The Father turns the eye of his unfathomable heart towards his own being, which is his nature, and gazes upon himself. And when he sees himself, he sees in himself the whole world, all abundance, all excellence and all things altogether. In the same gaze with which he looks upon himself, he forms a Word and speaks himself in the Word, and all the world, all abundance and all things altogether. The Word speaks itself back into the Father in all the world and in all excellence. In this gaze, in which the Father sees himself so fruitfully and the Word in all the world sees the Father,[121] they have such great delight that all the joy and bliss that all the angels and all the saints ever won, even our Lady, is as nothing in comparison with the immeasurable delight which they receive in a revelation of the divine nature. Thus the third Person flows from them both, which is the Holy Spirit. And from them there also flows the way that God is himself in all things together with all that creatures possess.[122]

If we are to become worthy to receive the Holy Spirit, then we should act as the uncreated spirit of God acts. We should turn the eyes of our intellect into ourselves and should gaze upon the excellence of our spiritual being (as we are formed in the image of the Holy Trinity after which we were created), having been created in order to become united with the uncreated Spirit of God. As we then gaze upon the riches of our own self, as we are meant to be, we should delight in its wealth with the self, from which there should grow in us so great a desire and such great pleasure that we can never seek fullness or desire in any other place. Thus we should act as the uncreated Spirit of God acts.

But if we wish to receive the Holy Spirit worthily, we should also act in the same manner as the created spirit which is the angel. For the angels gaze unceasingly into the mirror of the Godhead and each receives the divine light according to the measure of their worthiness, as they are turned towards God. Each receives and passes it on to the others, and the others pass it on to those who are lower down.[123] Thus we too should always gaze into the mirror of the Godhead, and should pass on what is revealed to us to others, who do not receive it so quickly, although they are of the same nature as ourselves.

If we wish to receive the Holy Spirit, we should also act in the same manner as the third spirit, which is the spirit of reason. For the rational spirit maintains itself in the light of its own self-knowledge and sees the truth in all things as in the light of reason. This spirit too should be stripped completely bare, so that it transcends all rationality. You should know your own self-reflection inwardly,[124] so that you are not yourself in any thing but only in the highest good. We should see with reason and with knowledge. And so the seer, the creator and the image-maker must be stripped bare, as the hand of God is bare. What is the hand of God? It is the power of God that is active on account of his eternal work. Thus we should know God with invisible light and should abandon all that is not God.

That the uncreated Spirit may unite us in itself in all perfection, so help us God. Amen.

SERMON 30 (J 82)

The question arises whether there exists a form of attraction between God and creatures.[125] The answer is that while God is not drawn to creatures, since he sees only himself, creatures are indeed drawn to God since all that has ever emerged from God looks back to him. Let us consider this in the highest image. At the very moment the highest image peers out of God, it looks back in again, its countenance uncovered, in order to comprehend the divine being but without any means from the work by which it received the whole of its own being. This image is God in his activity, and thus it is called an image of God. In its break-out it is a creature, and then it is called an image of the soul.

Now noble soul, consider yourself and the nobility that is in you, for you have been honoured in that you have received the image of God beyond all other creatures.[126] Do not pursue mean things since you have been created for greatness. This is how we should understand the soul to be the kingdom of God.

'Seek first the kingdom of God' (Luke 12:31). This should be the whole of our desire and our endeavour, in order to come to know the nobility of God and the nobility of the soul. Now take note of how we should set about seeking the kingdom of God. In the Song of Songs it is written: 'Do you not know yourself, most beautiful of women? Go out then and follow in the footsteps of your lord' (cf. S. of S. 1:8). These words concern the soul, for she is the most beautiful of all creatures. And if she knows her own beauty, then she should go out. Now observe the three ways in which the soul 'goes out' from her own threefold being. The first form of her being is that of createdness. The second is that of her existence in the personal Word of the Trinity.[127] Her third type of being is the one she possesses in the outflowing nature that is active in the Father, who is the origin of all creatures.

With regard to the first form of going-out, note that the soul must go out from her createdness! Christ says: 'Whoever wishes to follow me must take up their cross, deny themselves and follow me' (Matt. 16:24). Now know this as surely as you know that God lives: as long as we fail to be as empty of ourselves as we were before we existed, we shall never go out and deny ourselves. The masters say that we exist in two parts: an outer and an inner self. The action of the inner self is spiritual while that of the outer self is physical. With the inner self we seek God through a contemplative life, and with the outer self we seek him through an active life. Observe the following! I have sometimes said, and this is what I still affirm, that no external devotional practice leads to very much, for they serve only to tame nature. You should understand that all the external works which we may practise serve only to constrain nature and not to eradicate it. In order to eradicate nature it is spiritual works that we must perform. Now there are many people who rather than denying themselves actually maintain themselves in their own self-esteem. But truly, all these are deceived for this is contrary to human reason, contrary to the practice of graces and contrary to the testimony of the Holy Spirit. I will not say that those who hold external observance to be the best shall be damned, but only that they shall not come to God without great purification in Purgatory. For these people do not follow God if they do not abandon themselves; rather they follow the self-esteem in which they hold themselves. God is no more likely to be found in external observances than he is in sin. But these people, who practise many external devotions, have great status in the eyes of the world, which comes from their likeness to it. For those who understand only physical things, have a high regard for the kind of life which they can perceive with the senses. Thus one ass is adored by another!

Secondly, we should understand the function of the inner self, which is contemplation in knowledge and love. It is here that the beginning of a holy life lies. And with these activities the essence of the soul is described. Thus the masters say that every being exists on account of what it does. If we can only comprehend this essence in these two powers, then these are the noblest activities that exist in us. I have sometimes said that it is through virtue that we progress from vice to perfection. Now love is the form of all virtue, without which nothing can be a virtue. When we act virtuously, then this is the work of love and not our own work, for every work of virtue takes from love its power to bring us to God.[128] Thus St Denys says that it is the nature of love to transform us into that which is the object of our love.[129] Therefore we should live in such a way that the whole of our life is love. Then all virtues can be praised, whether external or internal. Thus David says: 'You should go from virtue to virtue, for the God of Gods shall be seen in Zion' (cf. Ps. 84:8). Seeing God is above the virtues. Just as I have said that virtue is the path from vice to perfection, in the same way the fruit of virtue – that is the goal to which virtue leads – shall not be grasped unless the soul is raised above the virtues. Know this: as long as we maintain ourselves with particularity of self in virtue, we shall neither taste nor possess the fruit of virtue, which is nothing other than gazing upon God in Zion. Seeing God is not in Jacob, who is the practice of virtue. But seeing God is in Zion. Zion is equivalent to a mirror and signifies a simple gazing upon the divine being in a naked vision. But be certain of this – no virtue can enter into this contemplation.

Now it might be asked whether we ought to abandon virtue itself. I say that we should not! We should practise virtue and not possess it. That is the perfection of virtue – to be free of virtue. Therefore Christ says: 'When you have done all that you can, you should say: we are useless servants' (Luke 17:10). Thus we should understand how the soul goes out of all her works.

But now we should address the question of how she is to lose her own being. Teachers maintain that everything God has made has been raised to such a state of nobility that nothing can fail to desire its own existence. But the soul must abandon her own being. This is where the death that is spiritual begins. If the soul is to undergo this death, then she must take leave of herself and all things, holding herself and all things to be as insignificant as they were before they existed. Christ says: 'Unless this mustard seed dies, it shall remain alone' (John 12:24). Death means the loss of life. Be sure therefore of this, that as long as we live and life lives in us, we shall know nothing of this death. St Paul says: 'It is not I who live' (Gal. 2:20). Some people understand this death as being dead to God, to oneself and to any creature. And this is true, since death is the loss of life. I shall put it even better and say: even if we are dead to all things, to God and creatures, if God can still find a space in the soul where he may live, then the soul is not yet dead nor has she yet gone out into the highest point of her created being. For to die, properly understood, is nothing other than the cessation of all that is. I do not mean that the being of the soul falls into nothingness as she was before she was created, rather we should understand this cessation to be the eradication of possessing and having. Here the soul forsakes all things, God and all creatures.

Of course, it sounds astonishing to say that the soul should forsake God, but I assert that it is more important for the soul to forsake God to attain perfection than it is for the soul to forsake creatures, or all will be lost. The soul must exist in a free nothingness. That we should forsake God is altogether what God intends, for as long as the soul has God, knows God and is aware of God, she is far from God. This then is God's desire – that God should reduce himself to nothing in the soul so that the soul may lose herself. For the fact that God is called God comes from creatures. When the soul was a creature, she had a God, and then as she lost her createdness, God remained for himself as he is. And this is the greatest honour that the soul can pay to God, to leave God to himself and to be free of him.

This is how we should understand the smallest death which the soul undergoes in order to become divine. Such people go virtually unknown, for as St Paul says: 'You are dead, and your life is hidden with Christ in God' (Col. 3:3).

Now you might ask whether such people only perform good works from within, and I say: Yes, they do! Just as Christ, who was the image of all perfection, was a light that shone spontaneously from within for all people, so too these people are turned outwards to all in divine life and in complete openness in a way that is beyond their own control. And so this is how we should understand the first kind of going-out, which is the going-out of the soul from the createdness of her own being in order to seek the kingdom of God.

Secondly, the soul should go out from the being that she has in her eternal image in God. The teachers say that the image of the soul is a divine idea. The divine idea takes personal form in the Son. Therefore the Son is the blueprint of all creatures and is an image of the Father, in which image the being of all creatures is suspended. Now as the soul loses her created being, she sees the light of the uncreated image, in which the soul finds her own uncreatedness, for all things are one in this image and in the nature of this image.

Now the soul should go out of this image, where she finds her being in the uncreatedness of the image, and this the soul must do with a divine death. The soul knows in herself that neither this image nor this being is what she seeks, for the soul knows in this being that she possesses both distinction and multiplicity in this image. For the very least thing that we understand concerning the Godhead is itself a form of multiplicity. The eternal being in which the soul finds herself is the property of the eternal image

Selected Writings

in multiplicity – since the Persons are distinct from one another – and so the soul breaks through her eternal image in order to penetrate to where God is rich in unicity. That is why one master says that the breakthrough of the soul is nobler than her flowing-out. Christ says: 'No one comes to the Father except through me' (John 14:6). Christ is the eternal image. Now the soul should not remain in him but rather must pass through him, as he himself says. This breaking-through is the second death of the soul, which is far greater than the first. St John speaks of it when he says: 'Blessed are the dead who die in the Lord' (Rev. 14:13), that is in God.

Now listen to this, which is a wonder beyond all wonders. How can there be a death in him who says of himself that he is life? Let us answer this question in the following way. Just as all creatures flowed forth in the generation of the Son, receiving both life and being, in the same way all things take on their living form within the Son. If then the soul is to enter in again, she must leave the Son behind. The masters say that where the Son turns back upon the unity of the natures, there he is neither a Person nor a particular nature, and thus the Son loses himself. I say this of the soul too, that when she breaks through and loses herself in her eternal image, then this is the death that the soul dies in God. St Denys says that if God does not exist for the spirit, then neither does the eternal image, which is its origin. In this image the soul possesses the quality of identity, since the Son is identical with the Father. But where they are one, they are not identical, since identity requires distinction. And so I say that if the soul is to enter the divine unity, then she must leave behind the identity she has in the eternal image. This is why Denys says that the spirit's greatest delight is in the nothingness of its image. A pagan master says: the nothingness of God fills all things while his somethingness is nowhere. And so the soul cannot find God's somethingness unless first she is reduced to nothingness wherever she may be, whether created or uncreated, as has been said of the eternal image. This is the second death and the second going-out, when the soul goes out from the being she has in her eternal image in order to seek the kingdom of God. Therefore a master says: whoever wishes to come to God should take nothing with them.

The third kind of being from which the soul must go out is the divine, outflowing nature that is active in the Father, for some masters teach that the Father possesses knowledge in an anticipation of the out-flowing before giving birth to the Word. But all masters are agreed that God the Father comprehends his essence where he is the origin of the eternal Word and of all creatures. The masters make a distinction between being and essence.[130] Where being is active being in the Father, it is also essence. Therefore the distinction is a logical one. And therefore where God is active, all creatures peer out from him in search of possibility. But we do not understand this to be divine union at the highest level, and so the soul should not remain here.

Now know this: the soul must die to all the divine activity which we attribute to the divine nature, if she is to enter the divine essentiality where God is free of all his work. For the highest image in the soul sees the essence of the Godhead without means where it is free and empty of all forms of work. Therefore this highest image should guide the soul but it should die with her.

Now note this: the Godhead hovers in itself and is all things to itself. Therefore God and his divinity are above everything that the creature as creature has comprehended or ever shall comprehend. St Paul says that God dwells in an unapproachable light (1 Tim. 6:16). Now when the soul has gone out from her created being and from the uncreated being in which she finds herself in the eternal image, and has entered the divine essence where she cannot comprehend the kingdom of God and where she knows that no creature can enter the kingdom of God, then the soul discovers herself,[131] goes her own way and never seeks God; and thus she dies her highest death. In this death the soul loses all her desire, all images, all understanding and form and is stripped of all her being. And be sure of this, by the living God: just as a dead person, a corpse, cannot move themselves, neither can a soul who has experienced this spiritual death present an image or a particular manner of being to anyone else, since this spirit is dead and is buried in the Godhead, for the Godhead lives as no one other than itself.

O noble soul, consider your nobility! For until you have entirely abandoned yourself and have cast yourself into the fathomless ocean of the Godhead, you cannot know this divine death. The wise man says: the Lord possessed me at the beginning of his way. God possesses all things in the way of his divinity, not in that of the soul, for no creature has ever found God nor shall any creature as creature ever come near him.

Now as the soul loses herself in all ways, as we have said here, she finds that she is herself that same thing which she has sought without success. Then the soul finds herself in the highest image in which God is essentially present with all his divinity since he is his own kingdom. Here the soul knows her own beauty. Then the soul should go out in order that she might enter herself and know that she and God are a single blessedness and a single kingdom which she has found without trying. As the prophet said: 'I poured forth my soul into myself'. This is how we should understand the line: 'If you do not know yourself, most beautiful among women, then you must go out' (cf. S. of S. 1:8). Therefore the soul should go out, as we have said here, in order that she should enter into the knowledge of herself, and then, without even trying, she shall find the kingdom of God. This is what St Paul says: 'I have unworthily considered the sufferings of the present time and not the future glory which shall be revealed to us' (Rom. 8:18).

Now pay careful attention to this! I have occasionally said, as I do again now, that I already have all that I ever shall possess in eternity, since God, with all his blessedness and all his divinity, delights in the highest image and this is concealed in the soul. Therefore the prophet says: 'Truly, Lord, you are a hidden God'. This treasure is the kingdom of God which has been covered up by time, multiplicity, the soul's own activity and createdness. Therefore the more the soul departs from all this multiplicity, the more the kingdom of God is uncovered in her. This can only happen through grace and not by the soul's own powers. The soul can discover the kingdom only with the help of the grace which inheres naturally within the highest image. Here the soul is God, savouring and delighting in all things as God. And here the soul receives nothing from God nor from creatures, since she it is who contains herself and receives all things from herself. Here the soul and the Godhead are one, and here the soul has discovered that she herself is the kingdom of God.

Now someone may ask what is the best exercise we can do to help the soul to attain this. The answer to this is that the soul must remain in death and must not flinch from death. St Paul says: 'Christ was obedient to the Father unto death on the Cross, therefore he raised him up and gave him a name which is above all other names' (Phil. 2:8–9). Now I say the same of the soul: if she remains obedient to God in death, then he shall raise her up and give her a new name which is above all other names. Just as the Godhead is unnamed and without name, so too the soul is as nameless as God for she is the same as he is. Therefore Christ says: 'I shall no longer call you servant but rather my friend, for all that my Father has told me I have told you' (John 15:15). A friend is another self, says a pagan philosopher. God became another self in order that I might become another him. Augustine says that God became man in order that man might become God.[132] In God the soul receives new life. Here the soul rises from the dead into the life of the Godhead, and here God pours into her all his divine wealth and she receives her new name which is above all other names. This is what St John means when he says: 'We have emerged from death into life when we love' (cf. 1 John 4:7). This then is how we should understand Christ's words: 'Seek first the kingdom of God and his justice' (Luke 12:31).

Now note how 'all things shall be thrown at us' (cf. John 15:21). We should understand this in two ways. The first is that what is perfection in all things is to be found in the first kingdom which is in God.[133] The second is that perfection is to be maintained in all our works. Therefore we should perform all our works from the basis of God's kingdom. Be sure of this, that if someone acts in such a way that their actions reduce other people, then they are not acting on the basis of God's kingdom. And when works are performed purely from our human nature, they are troubled and agitated, but when we act within God's kingdom, we are at peace in all that we do. Holy Scripture says: 'God saw everything that he had made, and behold it was very good' (Gen. 1:31). This is what I say of the soul too, that when she looks at all her works as they are in the kingdom of God, then they are all perfect, for there all works are equal. There the least of my works is the greatest and the greatest is the least. But if it is the case that our works are rooted in ourselves, then they are not perfect, for works in themselves are multiple and bring us into multiplicity, which is why we are often troubled in what we do. That is why Christ said: 'Martha, you are concerned about many things; only one is necessary' (Luke 10:41–42).

Be sure of this: in order to be perfect it is necessary for us to raise ourselves up in our works so that all we do is a single work. This must happen in the kingdom of God, where we are God. There all things obey us in a divine manner, and there we are lord of all that we do. I tell you truly: all that we do outside the kingdom of God is dead, but if we act within God's kingdom, then our works shall live. Therefore the prophet said that God no more loves his works than he is troubled and changed by them. The same is true of the soul when she acts from the basis of God's kingdom. And so whether such people act or refrain from acting, they will remain the same, for their works are neither given them nor taken from them. This is how we should understand the phrase: 'all things shall be thrown at us'.

These words are spoken only to those who can receive them with their lives or with the powers of their heart.

That this may be revealed to us, so help us God. Amen.

Selected Latin Sermons

SERMON I (LW XXIV, 2)

Domus mea domus orationis est (Luke 19:46)

'My house is a house of prayer.'

Put the words in the following order: the house of prayer is my house. 'House' means freedom from passions. First note how far passion ranks below the soul according to its nature, as has been said in the previous sermon on 'Be merciful' (Luke 6:36), and thus how shameful it is to be in its power. Secondly, note the stillness of the soul. The reason for this is that the Word in which and through which and through whose descent into the soul the Father acts, is 'without sound', according to Augustine,[1] 'while everything preserved a deep silence', that is all that possesses being, life and knowledge (Wisd. 18:14–15). Therefore no hammer could be heard when the temple was being built (1 Kgs. 6:7).

'Of prayer'. Observe that when we listen or read, God speaks to us. But when we pray, we speak to God. Note that in the opinion of the theologians the lower angels speak to the higher but do not illumine them. But when we look carefully, everyone who speaks is above those who listen in this respect and comes first. We can see therefore how far the soul must be raised up and exalted if she is to speak to God. Explain how this exaltation can only be achieved through humility. For in the projection of a sphere on to a flat surface, the pole and the central point coincide. Say how we should pray like the apostle 'in spirit and mind' (1 Cor. 14:15) in such a way that you cast yourself down, together with all the failings of the present world, at the feet of God and, secondly, that you offer yourself with all the merits and light of the Mother of God and all the saints and, thirdly, that you present yourself to God in the Word itself, in that purity, for only there are all things pleasing: 'in you I am well pleased' (Luke 3:22).

Take note of this: every departure from God means dissimilarity and thus conflict and impurity. See John 4:24: 'In the spirit', meaning 'in the Holy Spirit' and 'in truth', meaning 'we should pray' in the Son. 'For even the father seeks such people'. Note that it says 'seeks'. Whatever is sought is something higher, at least in principle. The soul must strip herself of all things therefore so that, made bare, she can seek God as he is bare in himself and not anything which is in him.

The second principal point to be noted is that according to John Damascene prayer is 'the ascent of the intellect to God'.[2] Therefore the intellect does not touch God unless it first rises up. Rising up means advancing to a higher state. Accordingly, the intellect must transcend not only the dimension of the imagination but also that of the intellect. Further, since the intellect refers everything to being, it must also transcend being. For being is not the cause of being, just as fire is not the cause of fire, but that is rather something far higher, to which it must ascend.

Moreover, the intellect receives God in the clothing of truth, and thus it must rise higher. Therefore it is said 'to God'. But then the soul must also transcend God himself, in so far as he is concealed by this name, or by any name.

Thirdly, since the intellect, as its very name suggests, proceeds from externality to interiority, unlike the will, and in accordance with its nature abstracts from all that comes to it from outside itself, therefore its ascent is its entrance into the primal root of the purity of all beings, which is in the Word. Observe therefore: 'ascent of the intellect'. In the Book of Wisdom (1:5) it is said that 'the Holy Spirit withdraws from all reflections that occur without the aid of the intellect'. Reflection means movement and running from one point to the next. Further, reflection without the intellect is imagination and is bound to corporal conditions, such as images and the like. 'Ascent of the intellect', for God properly dwells in the substance of the soul. But this is higher than the intellect. The greatest thing of all is to be capable of knowing God and of receiving him: 'Israel, how great is the house of God' (Baruch 3:24).

'My house'. Note first that the house of God is the essence of the soul into which only God, in his naked being, can descend. Discuss the point here that he descends into the soul when the powers of the mind have first been purged of sense impressions. Avicenna has a different understanding of this, which you should discuss.

Secondly, note that it is the higher reason that is the house of God. That is why the 'buyers and sellers' are ejected from it (Matt. 21:12). In the first place, because the work of virtue and the work of love are not a matter of profit. Secondly, because peace and silence reign where the Father speaks the Word 'soundlessly'. Temporal things, which are linked to movement, belong to the lower reason.

Note thirdly that the intellect grasps God more fully and in a truer and nobler manner than the whole of the natural world, and yet every creature lives and remains in being because it grasps something of him. It is precisely for this reason that every creature seeks to become like him. Show that this is particularly true of the heavens.[3]

Fourthly, note that according to Plato the soul is immortal since she can know Wisdom.[4] How much more shall she be immortal if she can know God! Therefore every cognitive faculty from the family of the intellect is beyond suffering and is accordingly from and in itself immortal.

SERMON 2 (LW XXIX)

The Thirteenth Sunday after Trinity. On the Epistle Gal. 3:16–22.

Deus unus est

'God is one'.[5]

'God'. Anselm says: God is that being than which nothing better can be thought.[6] In the eleventh chapter of the first book of *On Christian Doctrine* Augustine says: 'we think of the highest God as that in comparison with which there is nothing better or higher'.[7] Later he adds: 'we will find no one who holds God to be a being in comparison with which there can be anything better'.[8] In the fifth book of *On Contemplation* Bernard asks: 'What is God? That being in comparison with which nothing better can be conceived',[9] and Seneca in the prologue to his *Questions on Natural Science* asks: 'What is God? All that you see and all that you cannot see. Thus the greatness attributed to him is such that nothing greater can be conceived.'[10]

God is infinite in his simplicity and simple in his infinity. Therefore he is everywhere and is everywhere complete. He is everywhere on account of his infinity, and is everywhere complete on account of his simplicity. Only God flows into all things, their very essences. Nothing else flows into something else. God is in the innermost part of each and every thing, only in its innermost part, and he alone is *one*.

It should be noted that every creature in God loves the One and loves God for the sake of the One and loves God because he is the One. In the first place, because all that is loves likeness to God and seeks it out. But likeness is a certain kind of unity or the unity of certain things.[11]

Secondly, in the One there is never any suffering, pain or grief, not even proneness to suffering or mortality.

Thirdly, all things are contained in the One, by virtue of the fact that it is one, for all multiplicity is one and is one thing and is in and through the One.

And fourthly, we would not love power, wisdom, goodness as such, not even being, if these were not one with us and we with them.

Fifthly, they who truly love can love only one thing. Accordingly, the phrase 'God is one' is followed by: 'you should love the Lord your God with all your heart' (Deut. 6:5). And, without doubt, no one who loves desires that the object of their love should be anything but one.

In the sixth place, lovers wish to be united with the beloved. This is impossible if the latter is not one. Furthermore, God unites things with himself only because he is one and only in so far as he is one. Indeed, he must unite all things, uniting them with and in himself on the grounds that he is himself one.

In the seventh place, the One is indistinct from all things. Therefore all things and the fullness of being are in the One by virtue of its indistinction and unity.

In the eighth place, note that the One in its most proper sense refers to perfection and to the whole, for which reason, again, it lacks nothing.

In the ninth place, note that the One, according to its own essence, refers to being itself or to essence – that is to a single essence. For even essence is always one, so that union and uniting are appropriate to it on the grounds of its unity.

Further, it should be noted that someone who truly loves God as the One and for the sake of the One and of oneness, is not at all concerned with his omnipotence or wisdom, for these things are multiple and refer to multiplicity. They are not even concerned with his goodness in general, since this refers to externality, to what is in things, and since goodness is a form of adhering, as we read in the Psalm: 'For me it is good to cleave to God' (Ps. 73:28).

In the tenth place, note that the One is higher, prior and simpler than goodness itself, that it is closer to being itself and to God or rather, according to its name, is one being with being.

In the eleventh place, God is overflowingly rich because he is one. He is the first and the highest because he is one. Therefore the One descends into everything and into each single thing, yet remaining the One that unites what is distinct. That is why six is not twice three but six times one.

'Hear, O Israel, your God is one God' (Deut. 6:4). Note that unity or oneness appears to be the distinguishing characteristic only of the intellect, since it is evident with regard to material things that they are both one and not one in that they possess dimensionality or are at least compounded of matter and form. Non-material or spiritual entities, on the other hand, are not one either because essence and being are not identical in them or perhaps even more because thought and being are not identical in them. They are compounded of being and essence or of being and thought. See the explanation of the final proposition in *The Book of Causes*. Therefore it is well said: 'Your God is one God', the God of Israel, the God who sees, the God of those who see, which means to say the God who understands and who can be grasped only by the intellect, and who is in himself all intellect.

'God is one'. It should be noted that this can be understood in two different ways. Firstly as: God, the One, is. He possesses being precisely because he is one, which means that he is his own being, that he is pure being, and that he is the being of all things. Secondly in this way: Your God is one God, meaning that nothing else is truly one, since nothing created is pure being or is in itself wholly intellect. If it were, it would no longer be capable of being created. Moreover, I ask with respect to every thing whether or not it has intellect or thought in it. If not, then it is clear that this, which lacks intellect, is not God or the First Cause of all things which have so evidently been created to a particular end. But if there is intellect in it, then I ask whether there is being in it as well as thought. If not, then I instantly know that it is a simple One, and moreover that it cannot be created, but is the First Cause and so on, and is thus God. But if it possesses any being which is distinct from its thought, then it is compounded and is not simply one. It is evident therefore that God alone truly is and that he is intellect or thought and that he is thought alone to which no other being is added. Therefore only God calls things into being through the intellect for only in him are intellect and being identical. Further, it is clear that nothing besides him can be pure thought, but rather possesses a being which is distinct from thought. Otherwise such a thing would not be a creature, since thought cannot be created and since being is 'the first of all created things'.[12]

On the basis of what has been said, observe that all that is a consequence of the One, or of oneness, such as identity, likeness, image, relation and the like, are properly to be found only in God or in divinity. Accordingly, Augustine says in the fifty-third chapter of *On True Religion*: 'but true identity or likeness and true, primal unity are not seen with physical eyes or with the aid of another sense but are seen by the intellect'.[13]

The reason for this is firstly that identity and likeness and so forth are consequent upon oneness and this, as we have said, is a property peculiar to God.

Secondly, all these signify unity in multiplicity. But this can never occur anywhere but in the intellect and even here it is more thought than existent. Therefore where being is not thought, there can never be identity. But only in God are being and thought identical.

Thirdly, two entities which are similar or identical cannot be identity itself or similarity itself, and so on with the other qualities.

Fourthly, nowhere in the world can there be two wholly

identical objects, nor indeed two that are alike in all respects. For then they would no longer be two objects nor would they be capable of comparison with each other.

Fifthly, outside the intellect we only ever find diversity, distinction and the like: 'But you are always the same' (Ps. 102:27). Identity is therefore oneness.

From what has been said we can see how it is that 'whoever cleaves to God is one spirit with him' (1 Cor. 6:17). The intellect is properly of God, and God is one. Something possesses God, the One and oneness with God therefore to the extent that it possesses intellect or the intellectual. For the one God is intellect, and intellect is the one God. Therefore God is never and nowhere God except in intellect. Augustine says in the fifteenth chapter of the tenth book of his *Confessions*: 'where I found truth, there I found my God, who is truth itself'.[14] To rise up to the intellect, subordinating ourselves to it, is to be united with God. To be united, to be one, is to be one with God. For God is one God, and all being besides or outside intellect is a creature, or is subject to creation, and is something other than God, is not God. For in God there is no other.

Act and potency are the ontological divisions in all created existence. But being is the first reality, and thus the first division. But in intellect, in God, there is no division. Thus Scripture always urges us to abandon the world, to abandon ourselves, to forget our house and the house of our birth, our land and our relations, in order that we may grow to be a great people in which all peoples are blessed (cf. Gen. 12:1–3). This is brought about most excellently in the domain of the intellect where, in so far as they are intellect and nothing else, all things are without doubt in all things.

SERMON 3 (XL, 3)

Quid vobis videtur de Christo? Cuius filius est? (Matt. 22:42)

'What do you think of Christ? Whose son is he?'
Christ, anointed with grace, whose son is he? The answer is: 'David's son'. But Peter says: 'the son of the living God' (Matt. 16:16). Whose son therefore is the soul that has been anointed with grace? Certainly David's son, either according to the promise – 'one of the sons of your body I shall set upon the throne' (Ps. 132:11) and similar passages – or according to the meaning of the name. David means 'lovely to look upon' (cf. 1 Sam. 17:42) or 'with a strong hand'. Treat this theme. Secondly, the grace-filled soul is 'the son of the living God'.

Take note: everything active has an effect which is as similar to itself as possible. Indeed, it actually works another self so that the birth of a female is against the intention of the one who reproduces.[15] And if there were neither matter, nor time, nor space, then what works and what is wrought, what produces and what is produced would be one and the same. See therefore how great is the likeness between the soul and God, and how great her sonship in God when she is raised above time. Discuss all this and point to the example of the soul's faculties in which the cognitive image of the object is produced, or indeed to the production of an echo.

We find a reference to this in the first part of the text: 'you should love the Lord your God' (Deut. 6:5). It is well said: 'from the whole of your heart'. The heart is the principle of temporal and corporal life. God should be loved from out of the heart, which means from outside and above all that is temporal and corporal, but in the 'whole of the soul', which means in the innermost part of the whole soul. Alternatively 'in the whole soul' can mean: with respect to all the faculties of the soul which are linked to a physical organ, not only in so far as they are directed outwards towards bodies and actions but also in so far as they are directed within, towards the substance and being of the soul from which they emerged. Therefore there follows: 'in the whole mind'. The image of God is in the mind.[16] Further, the mind is of an intellectual nature and is above time. But it is said: 'in the mind' and not 'from the mind'. This is because the soul must be altogether firm and enclosed so that the image of God can be produced in her like a mountain which produces an echo, so that she is not only a daughter but is herself fertile and attains a yet greater likeness to God.

SERMON 4 (LW XLVII, 2)

Hoc oro, ut caritas vestra magis ac magis abundet (Phil. 1)

'I pray that your love shall overflow more and more.'
Note concerning prayer that there are nine things that we should bear in mind with respect to the words of prayer.[17] Firstly, they have God as their object and receive their character from him. Secondly, they have been given us by God through Holy Scripture which was inspired by the Holy Spirit, and thus something divine has been stamped upon them. Thirdly, they express something of God and commend it to us, namely his mercy, his justice and so forth, his paternal nature and his love. Fourthly, the name of God is often uttered in prayer, which is sweet on the lips of those who love and is potent for those who are in need. Fifthly, prayer is a conversation with God, and lovers take great delight in converse that is intimate and secret. In the sixth place, the

words of prayer often bring us to see our personal failings, as well as those of human nature, so that we are humbled in ourselves. In the seventh place, the vanity, falsity and inconstancy of the world are frequently considered and recalled, which creates in us a disdain for the world. In the eighth place, the misery of the damned or of sinners is sometimes brought to mind. In the ninth place, the blessedness of the saints is often evoked, thus awakening our desire.

ABBREVIATIONS

DP   Quint, J., *Meister Eckhart: deutsche Predigten und Traktate* (Munich, 1963).

DW   German Works. *Meister Eckhart: die deutschen und lateinischen Werke* (Stuttgart and Berlin, Kohlhammer Verlag, 1936–).

J   Jostes, F. (ed.), *Meister Eckhart und seine Jünger: ungedruckte zur Geschichte der deutschen Mystik* (Freiburg, Switzerland, 1895; repr. De Gruyter, 1972).

LW   Latin works. *Meister Eckhart: die deutschen und lateinischen Werke* (Stuttgart and Berlin, Kohlhammer Verlag, 1936–).

PF   Pfeiffer, F. (ed.), *Meister Eckhart* (Deutsche Mystiker des Mittelalters Bd. 2) (Leipzig, 1857; repr. Scientia Verlag, Aalen, 1962).

PL   Migne, J. P. (ed.), *Patrologia Latina* (Paris, 1844–64).

W   Walshe, M. O'C., *Meister Eckhart: German Sermons and Treatises*, 3 vols. (London and Dulverton, Element Books, 1979, 1981 and 1985).

SELECT BIBLIOGRAPHY

This bibliography contains only the most important works on Eckhart. More complete bibliographies can be found in Degenhardt (1967), Schaller (1968 and 1969), O'Meara (1978), Fues (1981), Sturlese (1987) and Largier (1989).

Texts

Meister Eckhart: Die deutschen und lateinischen Werke, hrsg., im Auftrage der deutschen Forschungsgemeinschaft (Stuttgart and Berlin, Kohlhammer Verlag, 1936–).

Jostes, F. (ed.), *Meister Eckhart und seine Jünger: ungedruckte zur Geschichte der deutschen Mystik* (Freiburg, Switzerland, 1895; repr. De Gruyter, 1972).

Pfeiffer, F. (ed.), *Meister Eckhart* (Deutsche Mystiker des Mittelalters Bd. 2) (Leipzig, 1857; repr. Scientia Verlag, Aalen, 1962).

Historical Documents

Daniels, A. (ed.), 'Eine lateinische Rechtfertigungsschrift des Meister Eckharts' in *Beiträge zur Geschichte der Philosophie des Mittelalters* 23, 5 (Münster, 1923).

Kaepelli, Th. (ed.), 'Kurze Mitteilungen über mittelalterliche Dominikanerschriftsteller' in *Archivum fratrum Praedicatorum* 10 (1940), pp. 293–4.

Kaepelli, Th. (ed.), 'Praedicator monoculus. Sermons parisiens de la fin du XIIIe siècle' in *Archivum fratrum Praedicatorum* 27 (1957), pp. 120–67.

Kaepelli, Th. (ed.), 'Eine Kölner Handschrift mit lateinischen Eckhart-Exzerpten' in *Archivum fratrum Praedicatorum* 31 (1961), pp. 204–12.

Laurent, M. H., 'Autour du procès de Maître Eckhart: Les documents des Archives Vaticanes' in *Divus Thomas* ser. III, 13 (1936), pp. 331–48, 430–47.

Pelster, F. (ed.), 'Ein Gutachten aus dem Eckehart-Prozess in Avignon' in *Beiträge zur Geschichte der Philosophie des Mittelalters*, suppl. vol. III, 2 (Münster, 1935), pp. 1099–1124 (Festschrift for M. Grabmann, vol. 2).

Théry, G. (ed.), 'Edition critique des pièces relatives au procès d'Eckhart continues dans le manuscrit 33b de la bibliothèque de Soest' in *Archives d'histoire doctrinale et littéraire du moyen âge* 1 (1926), pp. 129–268.

English Translations

Blakney, R. B., *Meister Eckhart* (New York, Harper & Row, 1941).

Clark, J. M., *Meister Eckhart: an Introduction to the Study of his Works with an Anthology of his Sermons* (Edinburgh, Nelson, 1957).

Clark, J. M., and Skinner, J. V., *Treatises and Sermons of Meister Eckhart* (New York, Harper & Row, 1958).

Colledge, E., and McGinn, B., *Meister Eckhart: the Essential Sermons, Commentaries, Treatises and Defence* (New York, Paulist Press, 1981).

Davies, O., *The Rhineland Mystics: an anthology* (London, SPCK, 1989; New York, Crossroad, 1990).

Evans, C. de B., *Meister Eckhart by Franz Pfeiffer*, 2 vols. (London, 1924 and 1931).

Fleming, U., *Meister Eckhart: the Man from whom God nothing hid* (London, Fount, 1988) (based on C. de B. Evans's translation).

Fox, M., *Breakthrough: Meister Eckhart's Creation Spirituality in New Translation* (New York, Image Books, 1980).

Maurer, A., *Master Eckhart: Parisian Questions and Prologues* (Toronto, Pontifical Institute of Medieval Studies, 1974).

McGinn, B., with Tobin, F., and Borgstadt, E., *Meister Eckhart: Teacher and Preacher* (Classics of Western Spirituality, London, SPCK; New York, Paulist Press, 1986).

Walshe, M. O'C., *Meister Eckhart: German Sermons and Treatises*, 3 vols. (London and Dulverton, Element Books, 1979, 1981 and 1985).

The most authoritative translation of the German sermons and treatises is that by M. O'C. Walshe, while A. Maurer and B. McGinn provide good translations of the Latin prologues, Parisian questions and biblical commentaries.

Secondary Literature

BOOKS

Albert, K., *Meister Eckharts These vom Sein: Untersuchungen zur Metaphysik des Opus Tripartitum* (Saarbrücken, 1976).

Breton, S., *Deux mystiques de l'excès* (Paris, 1985).

Brunner, F., *Maître Eckhart* (Paris, 1969).

Caputo, J., *The Mystical Element in Heidegger's Thought* (Ohio, 1978).

Cognet, L., *Introduction aux mystiques rhéno-flamands* (Paris, 1968).

Davies, O., *God Within: The Mystical Tradition of Northern Europe* (London, Darton, Longman and Todd; New York, Paulist Press, 1988).

Davies, O., *Meister Eckhart: Mystical Theologian* (London, SPCK, 1991).

Degenhardt, I., *Studien zum Wandel des Eckhartbildes* (Leiden, 1967).

Fischer, H., *Meister Eckhart* (Freiburg and Munich, Verlag Karl Alber, 1974).

Flasch, K. (ed.), *Von Meister Dietrich zu Meister Eckhart* (Hamburg, 1984).

Forman, R. K. C., *Meister Eckhart: Mystic as Theologian* (Massachusetts, Dorset, Element Books, 1991).

Fues, W. M., *Mystik als Erkenntnis? Kritische Studien zur Meister-Eckhart-Forschung* (Bonn, 1981) (with thematic bibliography).

Haas, A. M., *Sermo mysticus: Studien zu Theologie und Sprache der deutschen Mystik* (Freiburg, Switzerland, 1979).

Haas, A. M., and Stirnimann, H., *Das 'Einig Ein'* (Freiburg, Switzerland, 1980).

Haas, A. M., *Geistliches Mittelalter* (Freiburg, Switzerland, 1984).

Haas, A. M., *Gott leiden, Gott lieben* (Frankfurt am Main, Insel Verlag, 1989a).

Haas, A. M., *Deum mistice videre ... in caligine coincidencie: Zum Verhältnis Nikolaus' von Kues zur Mystik* (Basel and Frankfurt am Main, 1989b).

Kelley, C. F., *Meister Eckhart on Divine Knowledge* (New Haven, Yale University Press, 1977).

Koch, J., *Kleine Schriften* I (Rome, 1973).

La mystique rhénane: colloque de Strasbourg (Paris, 1963).

Langer, O., *Mystische Erfahrung und spirituelle Theologie* (Munich, 1987).

Largier, N., *Bibliographie zu Meister Eckhart* (Freiburg, Switzerland, 1989).

Libera, A. de, *Le problème de l'être chez Maître Eckhart: logique et métaphysique de l'analogie* (Geneva–Lausanne–Neuchâtel, 1980).

Libera, A. de, *Introduction à la mystique rhénane* (Paris, O.E.I.L., 1984).

Lossky, V., *Théologie négative et connaissance de Dieu chez Maître Eckhart* (Paris, 1960).

McDonnell, E., *The Beguines and Beghards in Medieval Culture* (New York, 1969).

Mieth, D., *Die Einheit von Vita activa und Vita contemplativa in den deutschen Predigten und Traktaten Meister Eckharts und bei Johannes Tauler* (Regensburg, 1969).

Mojsisch, B., *Meister Eckhart. Analogie, Univozität und Einheit* (Hamburg, 1983).

Quint, J., *Die Überlieferung der deutschen Predigten Meister Eckharts* (Bonn, 1932).

Ruh, K. (ed.), *Altdeutsche und altniederländische Mystik* (Darmstadt, 1964).

Ruh, K., *Meister Eckhart: Theologe, Prediger, Mystiker* (Munich, 1985 (1989²)).

Schürmann, R., *Meister Eckhart: Mystic and Philosopher* (Bloomington and London, 1978).

Seppanen, L., *Meister Eckeharts Konzeption der Sprachbedeutung* (Tübingen, 1985).

Smith, C., *Meister Eckhart: The Way of Paradox* (London, Darton, Longman and Todd, 1988).

Soudek, E., *Meister Eckhart* (Stuttgart, Metzler, 1973).

Tobin, P., *Meister Eckhart: Thought and Language* (Philadelphia, University of Pennsylvania Press, 1986).

Trusen, W., *Der Prozess gegen Meister Eckhart* (Paderborn, Schöningh, 1988).

Tugwell, S., *Albert and Thomas: Selected Writings* (New York, Paulist Press, 1988).

Woods, R., *Eckhart's Way* (Delaware, Michael Glazier, 1986; London, Darton, Longman and Todd, 1987).

Zum Brunn, E., and Libera, A. de, *Métaphysique du verbe et théologie négative* (Paris, 1984).

ARTICLES

Albrecht, E., 'Zur Herkunft Meister Eckharts' in *Amtsblatt der Evangelisch-Lutherischen Kirche in Thüringen* Jg. 31, nr. 3, 10 (February 1978).

Brunner, F., 'L'analogie chez Maître Eckhart' in *Freiburger Zeitschrift für Philosophie und Theologie* 16 (1969), pp. 333–49.

Colledge, E., and Marler, J. C., '"Poverty of the will": Ruusbroec, Eckhart and "The Mirror of Simple Souls"' in Mommaers, P., and de Paepe, N. (eds.), *Jan van Russbroec: the sources, content and sequels of his mysticism* (Louvain, 1984), pp. 14–47.

Davies, O., 'Why were Meister Eckhart's propositions condemned?' in *New Blackfriars* 71 (October 1990), pp. 433–45.

Davies, O., 'Hildegard of Bingen, Mechthild of Magdeburg and the young Meister Eckhart' in *Mediävistik* 4 (1991).

Flasch, K., 'Die Intention Meister Eckharts' in Röttges, Scheer and Simon (eds.), *Festschrift für Bruno Liebrucks* (Meisenheim, Glan, 1974), pp. 292–318.

Flasch, K., 'Kennt die mittelalterliche Philosophie die konstitutive Funktion des menschlichen Denkens?' in *Kant-Studien* 63 (1972), pp. 182–206.

Haas, A. M., 'Die Problematik von Sprache und Erfahrung in der deutschen Mystik' in *Grundfragen der Mystik* (Einsiedeln, 1974), pp. 73–104.

Haas, A. M., 'Schools of Late Medieval Mysticism' in Raitt, J. (ed.), *Christian Spirituality: High Middle Ages and Reformation* (London, Routledge, 1987), pp. 140–75.

Löser, F., 'Als ich mê gesprochen hân' in *Zeitschrift für deutsches Altertum und deutsche Literatur* 115 (1986), pp. 206–27.

McGinn, B., 'Meister Eckhart's condemnation reconsidered' in *The Thomist* 44 (1980), pp. 390–414.

McGinn, B., 'Meister Eckhart on God as Absolute Unity', in O'Meara, D. (ed.), *Neoplatonism and Christian Thought* (Albany, State University of New York Press, 1982), pp. 128–39.

O'Meara, Th. F. *et al.*, 'An Eckhart Bibliography' in *The Thomist* 42 (1978), pp. 313–36.

Quint, J., 'Die Sprache Meister Eckharts als Ausdruck seiner mystischen Geisteswelt' in *Deutsche Vierteljahrsschrift für Literaturwissenschaft und Geistesgeschichte* 6 (1928), pp. 671–701.

Schaller, T., 'Die Meister-Eckhart Forschung von der Jahrhundertwende bis zur Gegenwart' in *Freiburger Zeitschrift für Philosophie und Theologie* 15 (1968), pp. 262–316, 403–26.

Schaller, T., 'Zur Eckhart-Deutung der letzten 30 Jahre' in *Freiburger Zeitschrift für Philosophie und Theologie* 16 (1969), pp. 22–39.

Steer, G., 'Germanistische Scholastikforschung: ein Bericht' in *Theologie und Philosophie* 45 (1970), pp. 204–26; 46 (1971), pp. 195–222; 48 (1973), pp. 65–106.

Steer, G., 'Der Prozess Meister Eckharts und die Folgen' in *Literaturwissenschaftliches Jahrbuch* 27 (1986), pp. 47–64.

Steer, G., 'Meister Eckhart – Predigten in Handschriften des 14. Jahrhunderts' in Honemann, V., and Palmer, N. (eds.), *Deutsche Handschriften 1100–1400, Oxforder Colloquium 1985* (Tübingen, 1988), pp. 399–407.

Stötzel, G., 'Zum Nominalstil Meister Eckharts' in *Wirkendes Wort* 16 (1966), pp. 289–309.

Sturlese, L., 'Recenti studi su Eckhart' in *Giornale critico della filosofia italiana* an. LXVI, fasc. II (Florence, 1987), pp. 368–77.

Sturlese, L., 'Mystik und Philosophie in der Bildlehre Meister Eckharts' in *Festschrift W. Haug und B. Wachinger*, vol. 1 (Tübingen, 1992, pp. 349–61.

A REGISTER OF THE GERMAN SERMONS

W	DW	DP	PF	B	FOX	EV	CS	CL	SCH	OD
1		57	1	1						
2		58	2	2						24
3			3	3						
4		59	4	4	17					25
5	65		5							
6	1	1	6	13	32			i		12
7	76	35	7		23				p. 131	
8	2	2	8	24	20			ii	p. 3	13
9	86	28	9		34	1,2				21
10	25	38	10	17	16	2,11		iii		
11	26	49	11						p. 55	
12	27	50	12		22					
13a	5a							xxii		19
13b	5b	6	13	5	14					
14a	16a									20
14b	16b		14					iv		
15		44	15							
16	29	29	74	21	25					
17	28	31	81	20						3
18	30	43	66		2		p. 58		p. 181	4
19	71	37	19						p. 122	
20	44		20							
21	17		21					v		
22	53		22		1					5
23	47		23	7						
24a	13							xxiii		
24b	13a		24							
25	3		25	9				vi		

W	DW	DP	PF	B	FOX	EV	CS	CL	SCH	OD
24b	13a		24							
25	3		25	9				vi		
26	**57**					**2,45**				
27	34		27							
28	78		28							
29	**38**		**29**			**1,29 & 2,27**				**2**
30	45		30							
31	**37**		**31**							
32a	20a		32					vii		
32b	**20b**									
33		35	33							
34	55		34							
35	**19**		35					viii		
36	18		36					ix		
37			37							
38	36a		38							
39	36b									
40	4	4	40	19	29			x		
41	**70**	**53**	**41**							
42	69	40	42	15				xi		23
43	41	46	43			2,12				9
44	58									
45	**60**	**45**	**45**		**27**					**6**
46	54b		46							
47	46		47							
48	31	47								
49	77									
50	14							xxv		
51	15				11			xxi		
52	**32**	**30**		**14**						
53	22	23	88					xviii		
54	23									
55	62	48	55							
56		26	56	27	3			xii		27
57	12	13	96					xx		16

W	DW	DP	PF	B	FOX	EV	CS	CL	SCH	OD
58	26	27	58			2,13				
59	39	25	59		33		p. 53			10
60	48	34	60							7
61			61							
62	82	54	62							
63	40		63							11
64	81		64		26					
65	6	7	65	18				xiii		
66	10	11	83					xvi		15
67	9	10	84					xvii		
68	11	12	90	12				xix		
69	68	36	69	6	9					
70	67				28					
71	59									
72	7	8	72		31			xiv		
73	73	33	73							
74	74		86							
75			75							
76	61					2,50				
77	63									
78	64					2,1				
79	43	52	79							
80	42	39	80	7	8					18
81	33					2,38				1
82	8	9	82	16	4				xv	14
83	51	24	102	11						
84	84					2,42				
85	85				19	2,43				26
86	56					2,32				
87	52	32	87	28	15				p. 214	22
88	75		85		5					
89	49		89		24	2,14				
90			103							
91	79	41	91	10	10					

W	DW	DP	PF	B	FOX	EV	CS	CL	SCH	OD
92	24		94		6					
93	50		95							8
94	**80**	*55*	97							
95	72	*56*	98							
96	83	42	99		12					28
97	21	22	100		13			xxi		17

The above register is adapted from that provided by Richard Woods in his *Eckhart's Way*, with the additional denotation by bold face of all those sermons in English translation which are contained in the *Paradisus animae* collection. The German sermons included in the two volumes edited by B. McGinn (translated by E. Colledge and F. Tobin respectively) follow the DW numbering. The present selection is recorded under the abbreviation OD.

NOTES

Introduction

1. See my *Meister Eckhart: Mystical Theologian* (SPCK, 1991), pp. 22–95, for details of Eckhart's life and background.

2. These two sermons are included in the *Paradisus animae intelligentis* collection, which originates from Erfurt and may contain sermons which Eckhart delivered during the early years of his career.

3. I first argued the following in 'Why were Meister Eckhart's propositions condemned?' in *New Blackfriars* 71 (October 1990) and presented the same case in *Meister Eckhart: Mystical Theologian* (SPCK, 1991), pp. 31–45.

4. Both *De intellectu et intelligibili* and *De visione beatifica* are to be found in Dietrich von Freiberg, *Opera omnia*, Vol. I, ed. B. Mojsisch (Hamburg, 1977).

5. Although at one point he does in fact echo Proclus's view that in speaking of the One, we are actually speaking of our idea of the One and not the One at all (see Sermon 28).

6. Karl Albert, *Meister Eckharts These vom Sein: Untersuchungen zur Metaphysik des Opus Tripartitum* (Saarbrücken, 1976), p. 152.

7. Foreword to V. Lossky, *Théologie négative et connaissance de Dieu chez Maître Eckhart* (Paris, 1960).

8. For references to the Latin works and further discussion on this point, see my *God Within* (Darton, Longman and Todd, 1988) p. 45.

9. *Defence*, IX, 38. A. Daniels (ed.), 'Eine lateinische Rechtfertigungsschrift des Meister Eckharts', in *Beiträge zur Geschichte der Philosophie des Mittelalters* (Münster, 1923), 23,5.

10. See the *Commentary on Exodus*, 112–18.

The Talks of Instruction

1. As mentioned in the Note on the Selection and Translation (p. xl), the term *werk* has different nuances in Eckhart's writings. Sometimes it

means specific devotional practices, as in the present passage, but sometimes it means actions we carry out in the world. In this second sense *werk* recalls the verb *werken* ('to work', 'to do' or even 'to be active') and it stands in contrast to *sîn*, or 'being'.

2. The phrase 'way of devotion' here translates Eckhart's *wîse* ('way') which is his shorthand for a particular devotional practice or practices. Eckhart is concerned to challenge a mentality which places too much stress on an external asceticism rather than the internal life of the spirit. See Introduction, p xxxi.

3. Augustine, *Confessions*, X, ch. 26, n. 37 [D W V].

4. Here I understand the word *ungelâzen* to have essentially the same meaning as *abegescheiden*, although neither term has yet developed its full metaphysical weight at this early stage in Eckhart's writing.

5. The saint in question might be Gregory the Great (*Homilies on the Gospels*, I, hom. 5, n. 2), Augustine (*Commentary on the Psalms*, (103, sermon 3, n. 16) or Jerome (*On Matthew*, 19, 27) [D W V].

6. An alternative reading of this is 'and withdrawing from externality to a place of solitude'. This is the way Clark translates *von ûzwendicheit* (Clark and Skinner, p. 70), though Quint (D W V, p. 324) disagrees.

7. This word translates *eigenschaft*, which in Eckhart means both 'selfhood' and the possession of 'individual properties or characteristics'.

8. Or possibly 'from the influence of the heavenly bodies'; see Quint's note on this (D W V, pp. 330f.).

9. Walshe reads 'for a better one of love' here (W III, p. 24); I am following Quint at this point.

10. *Jâ, ie mêr wir eigen sîn, ie minner eigen.* The meaning of this compact sentence is not entirely clear, and I am following Quint in his reading of it.

11. *On Free Will*, 3, 9 [D W V].

12. The original text wrongly attributes this quotation to St Paul.

13. The German verb I have rendered as 'sharing' here (and below) is *sich erbilden*, which escapes exact translation. It carries a greater ontological weight than 'sharing' and suggests a personal transformation, a 'self-forming' into the life and work of Jesus. The underlying notion is one of 'participation', in its mystical sense.

14. Walshe omits this sentence.

15. Here I am borrowing Walshe's felicitous opposition between 'feast' and 'fast' (W III, p. 38).

16. Walshe reads *sunderlîche* as meaning 'especially' (W III, p. 41). I agree with Quint, however, that its meaning is *für sich getrennt* or 'separately' (DW V, p. 526).

17. Eckhart's meaning is that perfect faith is unchanging and is independent of the world and our experience of it. Thus, being always *glîch* ('equal', 'the same'), it allows us to accept all things equally, both the good and the bad, which is the sign for Eckhart of true detachment. The 'external' criteria are those of the world (rather than those of true, inner, essential and invisible being), and they are thus fluctuating and suspect.

18. Cf. Augustine, *Commentary on the Psalms*, 35.

19. Some, though not all, of the manuscripts include the following passage at this point: 'For the just person, whose will is wholly good, no time can be too short. For whenever the will is such that it wills all that it can – not just now but, should that person live for a thousand years, then they would wish to do all that they could – such a will achieves as much as could be achieved in a thousand years through works: in God's eyes it has all been done.' This seems to represent a hiatus with its abrupt reference to time, and I cannot agree with Quint that it is 'wholly meaningful' in its position at the end of Chapter 21, given the 'loose sequence of ideas in the Talks of Instruction' (DW V, p. 330). I have chosen to omit it from the text therefore, following the practice of a number of earlier translators, and would surmise that its original position must have been in Chapter 10 of the work.

20. Cf. Thomas Aquinas, *Summa theologica*, I, q. 1, a. 1 and 2.

21. Cf. Pseudo-Denys, *The Mystical Theology*, ch. 1, para. 1.

22. I am following Walshe (p. 54) rather than Quint (p. 372) by supplying a suppressed *mir* to the phrase *Nie enwart nihtes sô eigen*.

23. This reference must be to Diogenes, the founder of the Cynic sect.

The Book of Divine Consolation

1. This is a summary of Eckhart's system of analogy in particular as he develops it in the opening sections of his *Commentary on John*, where the

inner-Trinitarian distinction between the Father and the Son serves also to distinguish the created from the uncreated order. See Introduction, pp. xxii–xxvi.

2. *Commentary on the Psalms*, 36, Sermon 1, n. 3 [DW V].

3. I am following Walshe in moving between the personal and impersonal possessive adjective with 'the just'. The German form, which is untranslatable, is that of a singular personal substantival adjective (*den gerehten*), which Eckhart sometimes uses to mean an individual who is just and sometimes to mean the justice that exists in an individual in such a way as to make them just.

4. Literally, 'impressing it upon themselves and themselves upon it'.

5. Augustine, *Confessions*, X, ch. 41, n. 66 [DW V].

6. Cf. Augustine, Sermon 105, n. 3, 4 and Sermon 53, 6, 6 [DW V].

7. Cf. Aristotle, *Physics*, IV, ch. 1, 208a, 27ff. [DW V].

8. Augustine, *On the Quantity of the Soul*, ch. 5, n. 9 [DW V].

9. Seneca, *Natural Questions*, III, para. 12 [DW V].

10. Seneca, *Letter to Lucilius*, 107, 11 (inaccurately quoted by Augustine in *The City of God*, V, ch. 8 [DW V].

11. Cf. Thomas Aquinas, *Summa theologica*, I q. 12, a. 9 [DW V].

12. Eckhart's point is that we should have a 'God's eye' view of our own sin. He is anxious that we should not dwell on what has been done but should rather become united with God in such a way that we are no longer capable of willing what is contrary to his will. Underlying this passage is also the idea that sin or evil is essentially nothingness, and so through becoming united with God and his goodness, all evil necessarily drops away.

13. Eckhart is advocating the value of renunciation when we suffer a loss or a lack. This, he says, is founded upon our acceptance that God does not will us to have the thing concerned. This acceptance is in turn founded upon a conforming of our will to his, and thus a union with him, which is far more enriching than what we lack could ever be.

14. Cf. Augustine, *On the Trinity*, b. 8, ch. 3, n. 4 [DW V].

15. *Commentary on the Psalms*, 30, Sermon 3, n. 11 [DW V].

16. Cf. Aristotle, *On the Soul*, II, t. 71 [DW V].

17. 'Likeness' (in the sense of 'identity') translates the German *glîchnisse*, which is itself a rendering of the Latin *aequalitas*, which is the quality

that describes the relationship between the Father and the Son. It is therefore the principle of 'being the same as'. It is of great importance in Eckhart's mystical theology in that it is in so far as we are the same as God that we are united with him.

18. Eckhart is of course using a medieval scheme of the universe here according to which the earth is surrounded by rings of fire. See note 7 above.

19. 'Mode of being' (literally, 'way' or *wîse*) always refers to specific mode of being in Eckhart, that is to particular and local existence as distinct from universal, undifferentiated and divine existence.

20. Untypically, Walshe mistranslates *enfangen wird der sun in uns* (DW V, p. 41, 12) as 'the spirit is begotten in us' (W III, p. 85) rather than 'the Son'. It is through the birth of the Son in us that we become the 'sons of God' who are the theme of this passage.

21. In this difficult passage, Eckhart brings a number of metaphysical themes together. He applies to a theology of works his own metaphysics of being, whereby the 'inner work' is the superior, invisible essence and the 'outer work' is the visible, differentiated and inferior form. He speaks then of the integration of the human person into the Trinity through adoptive Sonship, as we ascend away from the domain of the individual instance (the 'outer work') to the inner and unified realm of essence (the 'inner work'). Finally, he invokes the concept of the One as the original unity of the Trinity. Although Eckhart here identifies the One with the Father, elsewhere he can speak of the One as being prior to the Father.

22. This may indeed be the influential *Glossa ordinaria*, as Walshe suggests (W I, p. 103, n. 45), but the principle expressed here is one which is fundamental to patristic and medieval exegesis.

23. Eckhart continually stresses that God creates the world from eternity. God himself, being eternal, acts outside time and his acts cannot therefore be thought of as temporal. But in his defence Eckhart is careful to point out that he does not believe in the eternal existence of the world, which would contradict the Christian teaching on 'creation from nothing'. His inquisitors failed to understand the subtlety of this point.

24. See below, pp. 97–108.

25. The German verb *ûfheben* means both 'to take up' and 'to cancel or remove'.

26. Eckhart is playing here on the theme of oneness: our sonship is to be united (one) with the Son who is himself united (one) with God, whose highest property is transcendent oneness or unicity.

27. *Lives of the Fathers*, I, ch. 9 [DW V].

28. Augustine, Letter 138, ch. 3, n. 12 [DW V].

29. Cf. Augustine, Sermon 105, n. 3, 4 [DW V].

30. The source for this quotation is unclear, but compare Augustine's *Confessions*, XIII, ch. 8 [DW V].

31. Bernard of Clairvaux, *On the Psalms*, sermon 17, n. 4 [DW V].

32. See note 7 above.

33. Cf. Jerome, Letter 120, ch. 10 [DW V].

34. *Lives of the Fathers*, III [DW V].

35. Cf. *Platonis Timaeus interprete Chalcidio*, ed. J. Wrobel (Leipzig, 1876), p. 210, 26ff. [DW V].

36. Here Eckhart is speaking from experience; we can imagine too that he frequently kept the company of merchants when, as Provincial of the Dominican province of Saxonia, he himself constantly journeyed across Europe.

37. This is one of the earliest indications of accusations levelled against the orthodoxy of Eckhart's teaching. The fact that he goes on to quote Augustine (whose orthodoxy is beyond question) on the eternal character of God's *act* of creation may mean that Eckhart is seeking to defend himself against the charge that he has taught the eternal existence of the consequence of that act, namely the world. The Augustine reference is to his *Confessions*, I, ch. 6, n. 10 [DW V].

38. *Confessions*, X, ch. 23, n. 34 [DW V].

39. *Confessions*, XI, ch. 8, n. 10, and XI, ch. 11, n. 13 [DW V].

40. *Letters*, 71, 24 [DW V].

On the Noble Man

1. Isaac Israeli, *The Book of Definitions* [DW V].

2. Eckhart follows medieval patriarchal tradition when he describes the higher mental powers as the 'man' (= 'male') in the soul. It is this linkage of masculinity with the higher powers of the soul which makes it particularly difficult to translate this text according to the requirements of inclusive language.

3. Cicero, *Tusculan Questions*, III, ch. 1, n. 2; Seneca, *Letters*, 73, 16 [DW V].

4. Origen, *Sermons on Genesis*, 13, n. 4 [DW V].

5. Augustine, *On True Religion*, ch. 26, n. 49 [DW V].

6. See note 4 above.

7. *On the Trinity*, XII, ch. 7, n. 10 [DW V].

8. There is a play on words here, for the German *ein* is both the indefinite article ('a', as in 'a dog') and the word for 'one'.

9. Macrobius, *The Dream of Scipio*, I, ch. 6, nn. 7–10 [DW V].

10. See note 8 above.

11. Augustine, *Literal Commentary on Genesis*, IV, ch. 23, n. 40. The section concerning morning and evening knowledge is reproduced by Henry Suso in his *Little Book of Truth*, ed. Bihlmeyer, pp. 346f. [DW V].

12. For example, Thomas Aquinas, *Summa contra Gentiles*, I, c. 71 [DW V].

13. This passage on blessedness is again substantially taken over by Henry Suso in his *Little Book of Truth*, ed. Bihlmeyer, p. 346, 8–16 [DW V].

14. In order to make his point, Eckhart is in fact inverting his usual position here by prioritizing the individual instance of 'being white' above the universal principle of 'whiteness' itself.

Selected German Sermons

1. The volitional, rational and irascible parts of the human person belong to scholastic anthropology. According to Eckhart, the action of grace produces in these the 'divine' (or 'theological', as they are more generally known) virtues, which is to say faith, hope and love.

2. Eckhart may owe this parallel to the work of Hildegard of Bingen, who made an explicit link between the action of divine grace as the animating force within nature and the sanctifying action of grace which enlivens the human soul. See Davies, *Meister Eckhart: Mystical Theologian*, pp. 51–9, for a discussion of Eckhart and Hildegard.

3. Quint suggests the *Tractatus de statu virtutum, pars tertia: De timore et charitate*, n. 37, PL 184, 810 by Pseudo-Bernard as a possible source [DW II].

4. Augustine, *Commentary on the Psalms*, 72, n. 16 [DW II].

5. There is an untranslatable word-play in the German here between *rîche* ('rich'), *rîche* ('kingdom') and *rîchtuom* ('wealth').

6. Cf. Thomas Aquinas, *Summa theologica*, I, q. 50, a. 3, ad 1.

7. Cf. Thomas Aquinas, *Summa theologica*, I, q. 50, a. 4, ad 4.

8. Cf. Isidore of Seville, *Etymologies*, ch. 5, n. 10 [DW II].

9. That is to say, a daughter. It was assumed in medieval culture that procreation occurred through the father with no direct contribution by the mother, who served merely as a vessel for the father's seed. It was also believed that the male was the norm, and hence the birth of a female child was the result of some kind of malfunction.

10. *On the Epistle of John to the Parthians*, tr. 2, n. 14 [DW II].

11. Here Eckhart begins a passage which is an interpretation of the opening lines of the prayer of the rosary: 'Hail Mary (*Ave* Maria) [full of grace], the Lord is with you'. Elsewhere he derives *ave* from *sine vae*, meaning 'without pain'.

12. Walshe has 'God be with you' at this point, which deviates from the traditional form of the prayer of the rosary.

13. It is unclear which book Eckhart is referring to here.

14. See note 6 above.

15. Eckhart is perhaps following Cassiodorus in referring to Plato as 'a great priest' [DW II].

16. Eckhart is referring to the doctrine of exemplarism here, whereby the 'ideas' of creatures are first created within the Word and are therefore divine and eternal. Material creation occurs at a later point but is based upon these concepts.

17. This is Eckhart's alternative rendering of *fiat voluntas tua*.

18. Augustine, *Confessions*, IV, ch. 12, n. 18 [DW II].

19. Cf. Augustine, Sermon 117, ch. 5, n. 7 [DW II].

20. Walshe changes Quint's 'physical creatures' here to Pfeiffer's 'physical things' (W I, p. 180, n. 1). I agree with Quint's reading in that Eckhart's point is to make a distinction between *rational* creatures, which is to say human kind who possess the spark of the soul or intellect, and non-rational creatures, both animate and inanimate, which do not. Since it is the spark/intellect which alone is the site of God's reproductive birth, Eckhart wishes to make a rational/non-rational distinction rather than an animate/inanimate one.

21. *Natural Questions*, I, *praef.* 5 [D W II].

22. Chrysostom, *Incomplete Commentary on Matthew*, sermon XIV [D W II].

23. Pseudo-Denys, *Divine Names*, V, 2 [D W II].

24. Here Eckhart is following a neoplatonic metaphysics according to which the being of the spiritual is prior to or 'higher' than the physical and can be said to contain it. This is a hierarchical system based upon degrees of emanation from an ultimate source.

25. Augustine, *Confessions*, X, ch. 26, n. 37 [D W II].

26. *Celestial Hierarchy*, ch. 3, para. 2 [D W II].

27. Perhaps Thomas Aquinas, *Summa theologica*, I, II, q. 29, a. 1 [D W II], although the general principle that like attracts like was a universally held tenet of medieval philosophy.

28. Moses Maimonides, *Guide for the Perplexed*, II, ch. 27; Aristotle, *On Heaven and Earth, passim* [D W II].

29. Augustine, *Confessions*, XII, ch. 9, n. 9 [D W II].

30. The language of this section with its trinitarian imagery of 'flowing' and interpenetration seems remarkably close to Mechthild von Magdeburg's *The Flowing Light of the Godhead*, which text Eckhart must surely have known (see Davies, *Meister Eckhart: Mystical Theologian*, pp. 59–65).

31. The two saints concerned are the martyrs Cosmas and Damian, whose feast day fell on 27 September (now 26 September). They are remembered as doctors who were renowned for healing people at no cost, which well accords with Eckhart's theme in this sermon of acting without premeditated reasons.

32. See Jerome, *On the Book of Jeremiah*, 6, for this quotation [D W II].

33. The possible meaning of this difficult sentence is that if we have entirely become love, and are assumed into God, then the forms of intersubjective knowing break down. Walshe suggests: 'One who is thus *in* love and is all love, will think God loves him alone, and he knows of none who loved, or was loved by any but Him alone' (W II, p. 100).

34. The Aristotelian term 'accidence' is used here in opposition to 'essence' or 'being'.

35. These texts are provided in Pfeiffer and are the texts for the feast of St Vitalis.

36. Cf. Thomas Aquinas, *Summa theologica*, I, q. 30, a. 3 ad 2 [D W II]. The point is that the Trinity embodies the principle of multiplicity but not

number, since that would mean that the three Persons are distinct beings.

37. This passage is a key to understanding Eckhart's rhetorical technique, which always concentrates upon our likeness to God and not our difference from him.

38. Augustine, *On the Epistle of John to the Parthians*, tr. 2, n. 14 [DW II].

39. Literally, 'God does not seek his own'.

40. Quint points out that the word *understât*, which means 'to stand under', is an exact equivalent of the Latin *substare*, which means 'to be substantial' (DW I, pp. 14f.). Eckhart is playing with paradoxical metaphysical concepts in order to convey the transformation of a soul in union with God which passes from (its own) somethingness to nothingness to (God's) somethingness again.

41. Walshe points out both that there is no mention of a virgin in the Latin text and that the German word *enpfangen* means 'to conceive' as well as 'to receive' (W I, pp. 77f.).

42. That is, 'before I emerged into existence from the mind of God'.

43. This is the will, while the former is the intellect, which, together with the will, forms the basis of medieval psychology.

44. Walshe notes that according to the Basel print of Tauler's works this is a sermon for the feast of SS. John and Paul on 26 June [W II, p. 247].

45. Aristotle, *On Generation and Corruption*, A, ch. 6 [DW I].

46. Another of Eckhart's sermons (Latin sermon XLVII, n. 486) reveals that the reference is to Gregory's gloss on Exodus 33 [DW I].

47. Cf. Albert the Great, *On Generation and Corruption*, I, tr. 1, ch. 25 [DW I].

48. Thomas Aquinas, *Summa theologica*, I, q. 4, a. 2, ad 3 [DW I].

49. Or, alternatively, 'all creatures are a single being'. If the latter is intended (as Quint and Walshe suppose), then the meaning is that being is univocal: it is a unified property which is common to all existents. But it seems that Eckhart intends no more here than to remind us that the *being* of creatures serves to align them with God.

50. Cf. *The Book of Causes*, prop. 3. In order to understand the preceding passage it is worth considering the scholastic philosophy of forms, which maintained a distinction between 'being' as such, which might be the potential being of creatures in the mind of God or the actual being of creatures, and 'living', which is brought about by the activation of the

being of one creature by another. 'Being' therefore is always the gift of God, while 'living' (that is 'activated being') is caused by the action of one creature on another.

51. That is, of God, according to Quint [DW I]. Alternatively, this phrase might mean that being is the first creature.

52. Walshe translates this wrongly as 'So far as our life is one being ...' (W II, p. 245).

53. Augustine, *Literal Commentary on Genesis*, I. 4, ch. 23, n. 40; ch. 24, n. 41, and Thomas Aquinas, *Summa theologica*, I, q. 58, a. 6, ad 2 [DW I].

54. Elsewhere Eckhart refers this same point to Aristotle's *On the Soul*, I [DW I].

55. Thomas Aquinas, *Summa theologica*, I, q. 77, a. 8 [DW I].

56. This text is taken from the old Dominican Missal for the Feast of St Germanus, who is probably the 'holy confessor' to which Eckhart refers in the following line [DW I].

57. As Quint points out, Eckhart translates the Latin *inventus* (meaning 'found') as 'found within' in order that it should suit what he has to say [DW I].

58. The more likely source for this quotation is not *Commentary on the Psalms*, 74, n. 9, as Théry asserts (followed by Quint and Walshe), but *Confessions*, III, ch. 3, n. 6.

59. This passage reflects Augustinian epistemology, whereby human cognition depends upon the reception of a divine light of truth. Quint refers to a number of parallel passages in Thomas Aquinas, namely *Summa theologica*, I, q. 77, a. 8, and I, II, q. 67, a. 1, ad 3 [DW I].

60. Aristotle, *Metaphysics*, I, 1 (W II, p. 147).

61. Augustine, *On the Gospel of John*, tr. 13, n. 3 [DW I].

62. This is broadly the teaching of Peter Lombard, *Sentences*, I, d. 17 [DW I].

63. Since God is one, we too must be one where we are conformed to his nature. Preference and distinction, however, belong to the world of multiplicity and are therefore opposed to God. This is the central principle of Eckhart's ethical thinking.

64. The word *glich* actually means both 'equal' and 'alike'. For an understanding of the following passage it is important to note that 'likeness' for Eckhart is 'oneness', which is the specific quality of God and of all things as they exist in God.

65. There is perhaps an echo here of Eckhart's reverie upon the moment of creation which we find in his *Commentary on Exodus*, n. 16: 'It shows also a kind of self-reflection of being upon itself, a dwelling or settling within itself; it shows even a rising up, or self-generation – being seething within itself, flooding and simmering in and upon itself...' (L W II, 21f.).

66. Quint rightly suggests that this word must be 'is' [DW I].

67. Cf. Boethius, *The Consolation of Philosophy*, III, 9 [DW I].

68. What seems to underlie this statement is the general Dominican position that love cannot unite to the extent that knowledge can. See Thomas Aquinas, *Summa theologica*, I, 2, q. 3, a. 4.

69. Here Eckhart is equating the Father with oneness; elsewhere he includes the Father with the other divine Persons as being contrary to oneness.

70. The phrase 'negation of negation' also occurs in Thomas Aquinas, *Quodlibet*, X, q. 1, a. 1, ad 3 [DW I], but it originates in William of Moerbeke's Latin translation of Proclus's commentary on the Parmenides.

71. I have followed Walshe in placing this line here rather than in the following paragraph.

72. Thomas Aquinas, *Summa theologica*, I, q. 112, a. 1, c [DW I].

73. ibid., I, q. 54, a. 5, c [DW I].

74. Clark suggests that Aristotle's *Metaphysics*, XI, 7, may underlie this statement.

75. Cf. Aristotle, *On the Soul*, III, ch. 8, 431 b [DW I].

76. Quint points out that the first 'power' in this sentence is desire, while 'the other power in the soul' refers back to the transcendent 'something', which is the soul's 'spark' [DW II].

77. That is to say, closer to her original source in God.

78. 'Being' here signifies limited and temporal existence.

79. Walshe unaccountably renders this as 'What is it that God "tells" us?'.

80. The mark of spiritual progress for Eckhart is the lessening of the sense of individual self as we grow into universal human nature, in which there can be no distinctions and no self-interest. Jesus Christ assumed universal human nature, and thus to make universal human nature our own is to become united with Christ. See also note 63 above.

81. *On the Epistle of John*, tr. II, n. 14 [DW I].

82. Quint suggests that the text is corrupt here, and I am following Walshe's translation (W I, p. III).

83. The conclusion seems to be missing from this particular sermon, since it does not end with the usual formula.

84. See the remarks on this sermon in the Introduction, p. xxvi.

85. In his defence Eckhart distances himself from the line 'I myself am this image' on the grounds that no creature can be this image (A. Daniels, 'Eine lateinische Rechtfertigungsschrift des Meister Eckhart' in *Beiträge zur Geschichte der Philosophie des Mittelalters* (Münster, 1923), p. 18. This apparent inconsistency only serves to underline the rhetorical character of much in the German sermons.

86. In the old Dominican missal this is the text for the feast of the Assumption. It is reasonable to suppose that this is a relatively late sermon, dating from Eckhart's last years in Strasburg or Cologne, since it contains both a reference to an individual who is accused of heresy (who may well be Eckhart himself) and numerous strictures against precisely those pantheistic and immoral ways of misinterpreting Eckhart's teachings which formed a central part of the accusations against Eckhart himself.

87. It is customary in patristic literature to use the Martha–Mary story to exemplify the priority of the contemplative life (Mary) over the active one (Martha). Eckhart is consciously inverting this structure in order to state his belief in the ultimate unity of being and ethics.

88. Walshe renders *nâch den nidern sinnen* as 'in their inner senses', rather than 'lower senses'. But 'inner' always signifies the 'higher' or 'more essential' in Eckhart, and he is clearly referring here to the bodily senses.

89. The meaning here appears to be that the value of experience is greater even than that of internal revelation. In the eternal light we see all things as one, while at the level of creation (life) distinctions are visible.

90. Quint notes that he cannot find any trace of this quotation in Isidore [DW III].

91. The words *sorge* and *sorcsam* sustain meanings that are not easily reproduced in English (e.g. 'care', 'concern', 'oppression' or even 'prudence'). Eckhart is evidently seeking to interpret Christ's remark to

Martha in a positive sense, as meaning that she is intellectually detached and circumspect.

92. Walshe wisely suggests that the passage omitted at this point is corrupt.

93. An account of this legend is given in the *Legenda aurea* by Eckhart's fellow Dominican, Jacobus a Voragine [DW III].

94. Since the manuscript tradition does not support the possibility of the transposition of the names of Mary and Martha at this point, the likely meaning is that Martha too once sat at the feet of Christ just as Mary now does. See Quint [DW III, pp. 502–3, n. 50].

95. There is something defensive in the rhetorical *élan* of this sermon which supports the opinion of Edmund Colledge that it may have been delivered during the process against Eckhart at a point when the Meister felt that he was unlikely to win the day. It is certainly one of the most rhetorical of any of Eckhart's surviving sermons. The key to its imagery is Eckhart's belief that we should progress from the first level of our existence as ordinary, contingent beings in time and space to the second, more essential level of our existence, which is that which we enjoy from eternity, in the mind of God.

96. Albert the Great, *Commentary on Matthew*, V, 3 [DW II].

97. Walshe renders this difficult phrase: 'But when I left my free will behind ...' (W II, p. 271), but it seems to me Eckhart's meaning is that God's free will (through which the Creation came about) was my free will since, prior to the Creation, I was in God and was one with God.

98. Eckhart is distinguishing here between God in himself and the 'God' who exists as a name and concept in the minds of his creatures. Eckhart is constantly concerned that we should abandon our restricting ideas about God and come to perceive him in his true transcendence.

99. Literally, 'that the accidental in him was perfected into essence'.

100. It seems to me that Quint is wrong to insert the epithet 'eternal' before 'birth' at this point and that Eckhart is specifically referring to 'birth in time' (DW II, p. 730).

101. The key to this difficult passage is that Eckhart is enjoining his listeners to conceive of an absolute unity with God by reflecting back to a point before their own creation as creatures separate from God. In such a unity, God's knowledge becomes their knowledge and God's action their action. Again, this is a rhetorical device pursued for spiritual effect.

102. This reading is for the third Sunday after Easter.

103. Aristotle, *On the Soul*, B, 7, 419a. But elsewhere Eckhart refers the first quotation to Democritus [DW III].

104. Boethius, *The Consolation of Philosophy*, I, 7 [DW III].

105. The following lines suggest that Eckhart is talking here about the identity between the Son, who is the 'image' of God in the Trinity, and the intellect, which is the 'image' of God in the human soul.

106. The word 'vestige' translates *fouzstapfe* (literally, 'footprint'). Eckhart must be referring here to Bonaventure's understanding of the created order as the *vestigia* of God (Latin: 'footprints' or 'vestiges'; e.g. *The Journey of the Mind into God*, I, 11; II, 7).

107. This story is told of Archimedes (DP, pp. 526f.).

108. This is reminiscent of Gregory of Nyssa's understanding of *epektasis* (as infinite progression into God) which he discusses in particular in his *Life of Moses*.

109. This sermon was probably preached on the 24th Sunday after Trinity [DW III].

110. Cf. Augustine, *Literal Commentary on Genesis*, VII, ch. 21 [DW III].

111. God cannot unite himself with the soul where she is different from him but only where she is his equal, that is where she already exists within him.

112. Cf. Augustine, *Commentary on the Psalms*, 69, n. 6 [DW III].

113. By arguing that we 'spiritualize' objects through allowing them to penetrate our consciousness, Eckhart appears to be anticipating the redemptive view of consciousness that we find in a modern poet such as Rainer Maria Rilke.

114. *Ratio* is a term from medieval philosophy which in this case means the intelligible reality of a thing.

115. According to the old Dominican missal, this text belongs to the 19th Sunday after Trinity [DW III].

116. Proclus, *The Book of Causes*, prop. 6 [DW III].

117. Actually Pseudo-Denys, *Mystical Theology*, ch. 1, para. 1 [DW III].

118. Augustine, sermon 117, ch. 3, n. 5 [DW III].

119. Eckhart actually uses the term *geistlich* here, which refers to *geist* or 'spirit' in the sense of 'mind'.

120. This final phrase might also read 'from nothing into nothing', which Walshe prefers, but see also Sermon 12, particularly p. 156.

121. The second part of this line seems obscure. I have inserted the subject 'Word' in order to convey the sense of a reciprocal gazing which seems to be indicated by the following section.

122. This sentence must refer to the paradigm of divine immanence and transcendence which characterizes the status of the created world and which Eckhart explores more generally in his theory of analogy.

123. Cf. Pseudo-Denys, *Celestial Hierarchy*, III, 2.

124. *Eia, in gezogenheit bechenne di cher dein selbs* ... (J, p. 49, l. 24f.).

125. I have not translated the first half of this sermon which is in the main a technical discussion of trinitarian theology.

126. This appears to echo the line from the twenty-seventh sermon by Leo the Great which reads, 'Awake, O man, and recognize the dignity of your nature. Remember that you were made in the image of God' (PL 54, 220).

127. That is in the Son, or Second Person of the Trinity.

128. There must be a pun here on the Latin *virtus*, which means both 'virtue' and 'power' ('efficacy').

129. Eckhart usually quotes Augustine on this point. See note 10 above.

130. See Thomas Aquinas, *Summa theologica*, I, q. 3, a. 4.

131. Literally, 'perceives herself'. In this passage Eckhart is postulating the absolute identity of the soul with God at a point in the future.

132. For example, Sermon 342 (PL 39, 1534).

133. This refers back to an earlier distinction (J, p. 85) between the first kingdom of God which is in God's unity, and the second kingdom which is in the soul.

Selected Latin Sermons

1. Cf. *Commentary on the Psalms*, 103, Sermon 4, n. 9 [LW IV].

2. *On the Orthodox Faith*, III, ch. 24 [LW IV].

3. Koch suggests that the reference here is to the outer ring of the heavens which, according to medieval cosmology, makes a complete circle every twenty-four hours and hence imitates God in its desire to be everywhere present at the same time [LW IV].

4. Cf. Augustine, *On the Immortality of the Soul*, ch. 1, n. 1 [LW IV].

5. English translations of this sermon can be found in Clark and Skinner,

Meister Eckhart: Selected Treatises and Sermons, pp. 208–12, and McGinn, *Meister Eckhart: Teacher and Preacher*, pp. 223–7.

6. This is the so-called ontological argument for the existence of God which Anselm gives in the *Proslogion*, ch. 2.

7. Actually ch. 7, n. 7 [LW IV].

8. ibid. [LW IV].

9. Ch. 7, n. 15 [LW IV].

10. I, praef. 13 [LW IV].

11. Cf. Aristotle, *Metaphysics*, V, t. 20, which Thomas Aquinas quotes in *Summa theologica*, I, q. 93, a. 9 [LW IV].

12. *The Book of Causes*, prop. 4.

13. Actually ch. 30, n. 55 [LW IV].

14. Ch. 24. n. 35 [LW IV].

15. According to medieval biology, the male is the reproductive agent.

16. Augustine, *On the Trinity*, XIV, ch. 8, n. 11 [LW IV].

17. Here Eckhart is thinking of the formal prayers of the Church.

READ MORE IN PENGUIN

In every corner of the world, on every subject under the sun, Penguin represents quality and variety – the very best in publishing today.

For complete information about books available from Penguin – including Puffins, Penguin Classics and Arkana – and how to order them, write to us at the appropriate address below. Please note that for copyright reasons the selection of books varies from country to country.

In the United Kingdom: Please write to *Dept. EP, Penguin Books Ltd, Bath Road, Harmondsworth, West Drayton, Middlesex UB7 ODA*

In the United States: Please write to *Consumer Sales, Penguin Putnam Inc., P.O. Box 999, Dept. 17109, Bergenfield, New Jersey 07621-0120.* VISA and MasterCard holders call 1-800-253-6476 to order Penguin titles

In Canada: Please write to *Penguin Books Canada Ltd, 10 Alcorn Avenue, Suite 300, Toronto, Ontario M4V 3B2*

In Australia: Please write to *Penguin Books Australia Ltd, P.O. Box 257, Ringwood, Victoria 3134*

In New Zealand: Please write to *Penguin Books (NZ) Ltd, Private Bag 102902, North Shore Mail Centre, Auckland 10*

In India: Please write to *Penguin Books India Pvt Ltd, 210 Chiranjiv Tower, 43 Nehru Place, New Delhi 110 019*

In the Netherlands: Please write to *Penguin Books Netherlands bv, Postbus 3507, NL-1001 AH Amsterdam*

In Germany: Please write to *Penguin Books Deutschland GmbH, Metzlerstrasse 26, 60594 Frankfurt am Main*

In Spain: Please write to *Penguin Books S. A., Bravo Murillo 19, 1° B, 28015 Madrid*

In Italy: Please write to *Penguin Italia s.r.l., Via Benedetto Croce 2, 20094 Corsico, Milano*

In France: Please write to *Penguin France, Le Carré Wilson, 62 rue Benjamin Baillaud, 31500 Toulouse*

In Japan: Please write to *Penguin Books Japan Ltd, Kaneko Building, 2-3-25 Koraku, Bunkyo-Ku, Tokyo 112*

In South Africa: Please write to *Penguin Books South Africa (Pty) Ltd, Private Bag X14, Parkview, 2122 Johannesburg*

READ MORE IN PENGUIN

A CHOICE OF CLASSICS

Adomnan of Iona	**Life of St Columba**
St Anselm	**The Prayers and Meditations**
St Augustine	**Confessions**
	The City of God
Bede	**Ecclesiastical History of the English People**
Geoffrey Chaucer	**The Canterbury Tales**
	Love Visions
	Troilus and Criseyde
Marie de France	**The Lais of Marie de France**
Jean Froissart	**The Chronicles**
Geoffrey of Monmouth	**The History of the Kings of Britain**
Gerald of Wales	**History and Topography of Ireland**
	The Journey through Wales and **The Description of Wales**
Gregory of Tours	**The History of the Franks**
Robert Henryson	**The Testament of Cresseid and Other Poems**
Walter Hilton	**The Ladder of Perfection**
St Ignatius	**Personal Writings**
Julian of Norwich	**Revelations of Divine Love**
Thomas à Kempis	**The Imitation of Christ**
William Langland	**Piers the Ploughman**
Sir John Mandeville	**The Travels of Sir John Mandeville**
Marguerite de Navarre	**The Heptameron**
Christine de Pisan	**The Treasure of the City of Ladies**
Chrétien de Troyes	**Arthurian Romances**
Marco Polo	**The Travels**
Richard Rolle	**The Fire of Love**
François Villon	**Selected Poems**